2018 SQA Past Papers with Answers

Higher
ENGLISH

2016, 2017 & 2018 Exams

HODDER GIBSON
AN HACHETTE UK COMPANY

Hodder Gibson is grateful to the copyright holders, as credited on the final page of the Answer section, for permission to use their material. Every effort has been made to trace the copyright holders and to obtain their permission for the use of copyright material. Hodder Gibson will be happy to receive information allowing us to rectify any error or omission in future editions.

Hachette UK's policy is to use papers that are natural, renewable and recyclable products and made from wood grown in sustainable forests. The logging and manufacturing processes are expected to conform to the environmental regulations of the country of origin.

Orders: please contact Bookpoint Ltd, 130 Park Drive, Milton Park, Abingdon, Oxon OX14 4SE. Telephone: (44) 01235 827827. Fax: (44) 01235 400454. Lines are open 9.00–5.00, Monday to Saturday, with a 24-hour message answering service. Visit our website at www.hoddereducation.co.uk. Hodder Gibson can also be contacted directly at hoddergibson@hodder.co.uk

This collection first published in 2018 by
Hodder Gibson, an imprint of Hodder Education,
An Hachette UK Company
211 St Vincent Street
Glasgow G2 5QY

Typeset by Aptara, Inc.

Printed in the UK

A catalogue record for this title is available from the British Library

ISBN: 978-1-5104-5555-9

2 1

2019 2018

Introduction

Higher English

The course

The Higher English course aims to enable you to develop the ability to:

- read, write, talk and listen in detailed and complex contexts, as appropriate to purpose and audience
- understand, analyse and evaluate detailed and complex texts, including Scottish texts, in the contexts of literature, language and the media
- create and produce written texts and spoken language, as appropriate to purpose, audience and context, through the application of knowledge and understanding of detailed and complex language

The basics

The grade you finally get for Higher English depends on three things:

- The "Performance–Spoken Language" component which is assessed in your school or college; this doesn't count towards your final grade, but you must have achieved the minimum requirements in it in order to get a final graded award.
- Your Portfolio of Writing – this is submitted in April for marking by SQA and counts for 30% of your final grade.
- The two exams you sit in May – that's what this book is all about.

The exams

Reading for Understanding, Analysis and Evaluation

- exam time: 1 hour 30 minutes
- total marks: 30
- weighting in final grade: 30%
- what you have to do: read two passages and answer questions about the ideas and use of language in one of them (25 marks), and then compare the ideas in both passages (5 marks)

Critical Reading

- exam time: 1 hour 30 minutes
- total marks: 40 (20 marks for each Section)
- weighting in final grade: 40%
- what you have to do: (Section 1) read an extract from one of the Scottish Texts which are set for Higher and answer questions about it; (Section 2) write an essay about a work of literature you have studied during your course.

1 Reading for Understanding, Analysis and Evaluation

Questions which ask for understanding (e.g. questions which say "Identify ... " or "Explain what ... " etc.)

- Keep your answers fairly short and pay attention to the number of marks available.
- Use your own words as far as possible. This means you mustn't just copy chunks from the passage – you have to show that you understand what it means by rephrasing it in your own words.

Questions about language features (e.g. questions which say "Analyse how ... ")

- This type of question will ask you to comment on features such as Word Choice, Imagery, Sentence Structure and Tone.
- You should pick out a relevant language feature and make a valid comment about its impact. Try to make your comments as specific as possible and avoid vague comments (such as "It is a good word to use because it gives me a clear picture of what the writer is saying"). Remember that you will get no marks just for picking out a word, image or feature of a sentence structure – it's the comment that counts.
- Some hints:
  - **Word choice:** Always try to pick a single word and then give its connotations, i.e. what it suggests.
  - **Sentence structure:** Don't just name the feature – try to explain what effect it achieves in that particular sentence.
  - **Imagery:** Try to explain what the image means literally and then go on to explain what the writer is trying to say by using that image.
  - **Tone:** This is always difficult – a good tip is to imagine the sentence or paragraph being read out loud and try to spot how the words or the structure give it a particular tone.

The last question

- Make sure you follow the instruction about whether you're looking for agreement or disagreement (or possibly both).
- When you start on Passage 2, you will have already answered several questions on Passage 1, so you should know its key ideas quite well. As you read Passage 2, try to spot important ideas in it which are similar or different (depending on the question).
- Stick to **key ideas** and don't include trivial ones; **three** relevant key ideas will usually be enough – your task is to decide what the most significant ones are.

2 Critical Reading

Section 1 – Scottish Text

The most important thing to remember here is that there are two very different types of question to be answered:

- Three or four questions (for a total of 10 marks) which focus entirely on the extract.
- One question (for 10 marks) which requires knowledge of the whole text (or of another poem or short story by the same writer).

The first type of question will typically ask you to use the same types of skills as you use in the RUAE paper, e.g. word choice, sentence structure, etc. As always, the golden rule is to do exactly as the question directs you, and to remember that (as in the RUAE paper) there are no marks just for picking out a word or a feature of sentence structure, so all the marks have to be earned by your comments.

The second type of question requires you to discuss common features (of theme and/or technique) in the extract and elsewhere in the writer's work. You can answer this question with a series of bullet points or by writing a mini-essay, so choose the approach you feel most comfortable with.

Finally, a bit of advice for the Scottish Text question: when you see the extract in the exam paper, don't get too confident just because you recognise it (you certainly should recognise it if you've studied properly!). And even if you've answered questions on it before, remember that the questions in the exam are likely to be different, so stay alert.

Section 2 – Critical Essay

A common mistake is to rely too heavily on ideas and whole paragraphs you have used in practice essays and try to use them for the question you have chosen in the exam. The trick is to come to the exam with lots of ideas and thoughts about at least one of the texts you have studied and use these to tackle the question you choose from the exam paper. You mustn't use the exam question as an excuse to trot out an answer you've prepared in advance.

Structure

Every good essay has a structure, but there is no "correct" structure, no magic formula that the examiners are looking for. It's **your** essay, so structure it the way **you** want. As long as you're answering the question all the way through, then you'll be fine.

Relevance

Be relevant to the question **all of the time** – not just in the first and last paragraphs.

Central concerns

Try to make sure your essay shows that you have thought about and understood the central concerns of the text, i.e. what it's "about" – the ideas and themes the writer is exploring in the text.

Quotation

In poetry and drama essays, you're expected to quote from the text, but never fall into the trap of learning a handful of quotations and forcing them all into the essay regardless of the question you're answering. In prose essays, quotation is much less important, and you can show your knowledge more effectively by referring in detail to what happens in key sections of the novel or the short story.

Techniques

You are expected to show understanding of how various literary techniques work within a text, but simply naming them will not get you marks, and structuring your essay around techniques rather than around relevant ideas in the text is not a good idea.

Good luck!

Remember that the rewards for passing Higher English are well worth it! Your pass will help you get the future you want for yourself. In the exam, be confident in your own ability. If you're not sure how to answer a question, trust your instincts and just give it a go anyway – keep calm and don't panic! GOOD LUCK!

Study Skills – what you need to know to pass exams!

General exam revision: 20 top tips

When preparing for exams, it is easy to feel unsure of where to start or how to revise. This guide to general exam revision provides a good starting place, and, as these are very general tips, they can be applied to all your exams.

1. Start revising in good time.

Don't leave revision until the last minute – this will make you panic and it will be difficult to learn. Make a revision timetable that counts down the weeks to go.

2. Work to a study plan.

Set up sessions of work spread through the weeks ahead. Make sure each session has a focus and a clear purpose. What will you study, when and why? Be realistic about what you can achieve in each session, and don't be afraid to adjust your plans as needed.

3. Make sure you know exactly when your exams are.

Get your exam dates from the SQA website and use the timetable builder tool to create your own exam schedule. You will also get a personalised timetable from your school, but this might not be until close to the exam period.

4. Make sure that you know the topics that make up each course.

Studying is easier if material is in manageable chunks – why not use the SQA topic headings or create your own from your class notes? Ask your teacher for help on this if you are not sure.

5. Break the chunks up into even smaller bits.

The small chunks should be easier to cope with. Remember that they fit together to make larger ideas. Even the process of chunking down will help!

6. Ask yourself these key questions for each course:

- Are all topics compulsory or are there choices?
- Which topics seem to come up time and time again?
- Which topics are your strongest and which are your weakest?

Use your answers to these questions to work out how much time you will need to spend revising each topic.

7. Make sure you know what to expect in the exam.

The subject-specific introduction to this book will help with this. Make sure you can answer these questions:

- How is the paper structured?
- How much time is there for each part of the exam?
- What types of question are involved? These will vary depending on the subject so read the subject-specific section carefully.

8. Past papers are a vital revision tool!

Use past papers to support your revision wherever possible. This book contains the answers and mark schemes too – refer to these carefully when checking your work. Using the mark scheme is useful; even if you don't manage to get all the marks available first time when you first practise, it helps you identify how to extend and develop your answers to get more marks next time – and of course, in the real exam.

9. Use study methods that work well for you.

People study and learn in different ways. Reading and looking at diagrams suits some students. Others prefer to listen and hear material – what about reading out loud or getting a friend or family member to do this for you? You could also record and play back material.

10. There are three tried and tested ways to make material stick in your long-term memory:

- Practising – e.g. rehearsal, repeating
- Organising – e.g. making drawings, lists, diagrams, tables, memory aids
- Elaborating – e.g. incorporating the material into a story or an imagined journey

11. Learn actively.

Most people prefer to learn actively – for example, making notes, highlighting, redrawing and redrafting, making up memory aids, or writing past paper answers. A good way to stay engaged and inspired is to mix and match these methods – find the combination that best suits you. This is likely to vary depending on the topic or subject.

12. Be an expert.

Be sure to have a few areas in which you feel you are an expert. This often works because at least some of them will come up, which can boost confidence.

13. Try some visual methods.

Use symbols, diagrams, charts, flashcards, post-it notes etc. Don't forget – the brain takes in chunked images more easily than loads of text.

14. Remember – practice makes perfect.

Work on difficult areas again and again. Look and read – then test yourself. You cannot do this too much.

15. Try past papers against the clock.

Practise writing answers in a set time. This is a good habit from the start but is especially important when you get closer to exam time.

16. Collaborate with friends.

Test each other and talk about the material – this can really help. Two brains are better than one! It is amazing how talking about a problem can help you solve it.

17. Know your weaknesses.

Ask your teacher for help to identify what you don't know. Try to do this as early as possible. If you are having trouble, it is probably with a difficult topic, so your teacher will already be aware of this – most students will find it tough.

18. Have your materials organised and ready.

Know what is needed for each exam:

- Do you need a calculator or a ruler?
- Should you have pencils as well as pens?
- Will you need water or paper tissues?

19. Make full use of school resources.

Find out what support is on offer:

- Are there study classes available?
- When is the library open?
- When is the best time to ask for extra help?
- Can you borrow textbooks, study guides, past papers, etc.?
- Is school open for Easter revision?

20. Keep fit and healthy!

Try to stick to a routine as much as possible, including with sleep. If you are tired, sluggish or dehydrated, it is difficult to see how concentration is even possible. Combine study with relaxation, drink plenty of water, eat sensibly, and get fresh air and exercise – all these things will help more than you could imagine. Good luck!

HIGHER

2016

National Qualifications 2016

X724/76/11

English
Reading for Understanding,
Analysis and Evaluation — Text

THURSDAY, 5 MAY

9:00 AM – 10:30 AM

Total marks — 30

Read the passages carefully and then attempt ALL questions, which are printed on a separate sheet.

The following two passages consider whether or not 16-year-olds should be allowed to vote.

Passage 1

Read the passage below and then attempt questions 1 to 7.

In the first passage, Catherine Bennett puts forward the case for allowing 16-year-olds to vote.

Rude, impulsive, sulky . . . still, let our 16-year-olds vote.

There are hugely important questions to address before 16-year-olds can be invited into the complicated UK electoral process. Are they sufficiently mature? Can they tell one party from another? Are they too preoccupied by a combination of exams and hectic social lives to be bothered? Even worrying about their appearance has been cited as a reason why under-18s might
5 struggle to give adequate thought to the political and economic issues facing Britain today.

There was a long period, between being sixteen myself and then, decades later, getting to know some present-day teenagers, including the one in my own house, when I would have agreed with champions of the status quo. I presumed — without knowing any — that these 16-year-olds were as clueless as my younger self, but with an increased obsession with their peer group, a result of
10 unpatrolled access to social media, greater affluence, and being subject to a constant barrage of entertainment.

If these factors were not enough to guarantee extreme teen disengagement with the political process, scientists have supplied biological reasons to question the efficiency of teenagers' smartphone-fixated brains. The last time there was a significant move to reduce the voting age,
15 the biologist Richard Dawkins set out the potential risks posed by the undeveloped teenage brain to our current epistocracy. An epistocracy — as of course all older voters will know — is government by wise people, that is, those with fully developed grey matter. In the article, Dawkins cited evidence from neuroscientists that "the brain undergoes major reconstruction from the onset of puberty which continues until 20 or beyond". Crucial, if I understand them
20 correctly, is the importance of this continuing development to the frontal lobes. This is the area at the front of the brain which "enables us to think in the abstract, weigh moral dilemmas and control our impulses". It was not even clear, the author said, that teenagers are developed enough to "be making life-changing decisions for themselves".

If we simply accept this argument, what does it mean in practice? It means that a grown-up who
25 believes in wizardry or unicorns or vampires can become a Member of Parliament, but a school pupil the age of, say, Malala Yousafzai, has yet to acquire the intellectual credentials to vote. Malala had been the victim of a terrorist attack in Pakistan as a result of her blog advocating education for girls, had recovered and continued to campaign tirelessly for equal educational opportunities for all children. This led to her becoming, in 2014, at the age of seventeen, the
30 youngest recipient of the Nobel Peace Prize.

Of course, it would be naïve to suggest that all teenagers can be as accomplished as Malala. However, there is, in fact, considerable evidence that the "unfinished" brain can be pretty good at sport, music, creating computer software and raising thousands of pounds for charity. True, 16-year-olds can be rude, sulky, reckless and unreliable. But the adult world is scarcely exempt ·
35 from these characteristics. Perhaps — as politicians must hope — most teenagers know too little about politics to make self-congratulatory comparisons between themselves and the at times limited brain power on show during parliamentary debates. The evidence of their own eyes confirms that, when considering normal behaviour, 16-year-olds barely compete in terms of incivility, tantrums, profanity, impulsivity, prejudice, time-wasting and an unedifying
40 dependency on tabloid websites, when compared to millions of fully enfranchised grown-ups. If law-makers ever think of restricting voting by the inadequately brained, illiterate, non-taxpaying or ignorant, the consequences for some adults would be chilling.

Indeed, recent research suggests that those who have been emphasising the negative effects of
social media and modern technology on the developing brain may have got it all wrong. Sixteen
45   and seventeen-year-olds are part of the iGeneration, the first generation who have grown up
with the digital innovations of the 21st century. They are flexible enough mentally to develop
their political worldview from the wide range of sources to be found on the Internet, too media
aware to be taken in by spin doctors and manipulative politicians.

Our teenagers do have their flaws. No, they don't always evince much money sense, although
50   they do, as consumers, pay sales tax. Yes, if voting booths were bedrooms they would probably
leave wet towels all over them. But having now witnessed some of the more loveable teenage
qualities — idealism, energy, a sense of injustice, open-mindedness — these seem to be exactly
the ones of which modern politics is starved. Even a limited turnout by young voters, minus all
the ones who are supposedly too apathetic or too busy insulting police officers or attending
55   Ibiza-themed foam parties, might inject some life into the next election.

Naturally, engaged teenagers would want answers on stuff that directly affects them such as
unpaid internships, exams, student debt, the minimum wage, benefits and perhaps any military
engagements in which they might be invited to serve. However, it might lead to a fresh look at
policies that affect future generations, by voters who will actually be around to experience the
60   consequences. If voting has to be rationed, maybe it should be elderly citizens — who may not
see the impact of, say, political inaction on climate change or carelessness about fuel
sustainability — who should give way to 16-year-olds.

We could compromise: make it seventeen. Then 16-year-olds would only have a year to wait —
after they have already married, donated an organ, bought fireworks, and signed up to fight for
65   their country — before they would be allowed to choose, alone in an exposed voting booth,
between competing political visions. Judging by the current resistance of adults who believe
they know so much better, you'd think we were doing our young people a great big favour.

Passage 2

**Read the passage below and attempt question 8. While reading, you may wish to make notes
on the main ideas and/or highlight key points in the passage.**

*In the second passage, Julia Hartley-Brewer puts forward her arguments for not allowing 16-year-
olds to vote.*

Letting 16-year-olds vote would be a disaster.

I have decided that it is only right and fair that my 8-year-old daughter should be allowed to
vote. She knows her politics and can name the party leaders on sight, which is more than can be
said for a large proportion of voters — and she pays tax. Every time she saves up her pocket
money to buy a new toy or game, it comes with a price tag that includes a hefty 20 per cent of
5   VAT. On all these grounds, she has just as much of a claim to have her say about Britain's future
as do the   16 and 17-year-olds of this country. And yet no one is demanding that she is given
the vote because, well, she's an 8-year-old. She's a child; she doesn't have the intellectual and
emotional development of an adult so she doesn't get to have the rights of adults.

So why is it that so many people — including prominent politicians — believe that we should be
10   giving 16 and 17-year-olds the right to vote? The call for the voting age to be lowered to sixteen
is as absurd an idea as you'll hear.

Yes, 16 and 17-year-olds were allowed to vote in the Scottish referendum. And what did they achieve? The turn-out for that tiny age group was a lot higher than among most other younger voters (largely, it is thought, because they were encouraged to turn out to vote by their parents)

15 but it did not enthuse the 18 to 20 age bracket, which as per usual largely didn't bother at all. Wouldn't our democracy be better served if we spent more time, effort and resources on engaging the people who already have the right to vote, rather than just adding on a few million voters who will never vote again after their first trip to the polling station?

Ah, but that's not the point, the protagonists claim. We should allow 16 and 17-year-olds to vote

20 because they are legally allowed to do other, far more important, life-changing or life-risking things than put a cross on a ballot paper, so why not let them vote as well? And that would be a really good argument, if it were true. Because, in actual fact, we don't allow our 16 and 17-year-olds to do very much. They can't legally drink alcohol or smoke, for starters. We don't trust them to be sensible with a pint of lager so why trust them with a stubby pencil in a polling

25 booth?

Okay, but they can get a job and pay income tax and that's not fair if they don't have a say in the government that sets those taxes, right? But income tax isn't the only tax we pay so why should that be the crucial decider? We all pay VAT on many of the goods we purchase from a very young age so, on that argument, my 8-year-old should be eligible to vote too.

30 Allowing 16 and 17-year-olds to vote would be a disaster. Voting is, after all, not a privilege like receiving pocket money or being permitted to stay out past your usual curfew on a Saturday night. It's a right. And a hard-won right at that.

When politicians say they want 16 and 17-year-olds to vote, what they really mean is that they want 16 and 17-year-olds to vote for them. This is not about empowering young people or

35 shifting the focus of debate to issues more relevant to 16 and 17-year-olds. Mainstream politics will continue to focus on issues important to adults, such as the economy and the state of the health service. It is simply calculated electioneering on the part of cynical politicians to retain power.

Don't believe the nonsense being spouted in the name of democracy. There is absolutely nothing wrong with making people wait until they are eighteen to vote.

[END OF TEXT]

National Qualifications 2016

X724/76/21

**English
Reading for Understanding,
Analysis and Evaluation — Questions**

THURSDAY, 5 MAY

9:00 AM – 10:30 AM

Total marks — 30

Attempt ALL questions.

Write your answers clearly in the answer booklet provided. In the answer booklet, you must clearly identify the question number you are attempting.

Use **blue** or **black** ink.

Before leaving the examination room you must give your answer booklet to the Invigilator; if you do not, you may lose all the marks for this paper.

MARKS

Attempt ALL questions
Total marks — 30

1. Read lines 1—5.

    Analyse **two** ways in which the writer attempts to engage the reader's interest in the opening paragraph.

2

2. Read lines 6—23.

    (a) By referring to **either** the writer's viewpoint **or** to scientific research, explain why some people think teenagers should not be allowed to vote. Use your own words as far as possible in your answer.

2

    (b) By referring to **at least two** examples, analyse how language is used to suggest that young people are not capable of voting.

4

3. Read lines 24—30.

    Explain how the writer uses the example of Malala Yousafzai to develop her argument.

2

4. Read lines 31—42.

    By referring to both word choice **and** sentence structure, analyse how the writer creates a negative impression of adults.

4

5. Read lines 43—48.

    Explain why those who emphasise "the negative effects of social media and modern technology . . . may have got it all wrong". Use your own words in your answer.

3

6. Read lines 49—55.

    By referring to **at least two** examples, analyse how the writer uses language to emphasise the positive contribution which teenage voters could make.

4

7. Read lines 56—67.

    By referring to both tone **and** use of contrast, analyse how the writer emphasises her support of teenagers being allowed to vote.

4

Question on both passages

8. Look at both passages.

    The writers disagree about whether or not 16 and 17-year-olds should be allowed to vote.

    Identify **three** key areas on which they disagree. You should support the points by referring to important ideas in both passages.

    You may answer this question in continuous prose or in a series of developed bullet points.

5

[END OF QUESTION PAPER]

National Qualifications 2016

X724/76/12

English
Critical Reading

THURSDAY, 5 MAY

10:50 AM – 12:20 PM

Total marks — 40

SECTION 1 — Scottish Text — 20 marks

Read an extract from a Scottish text you have previously studied and attempt the questions.

Choose ONE text from either

Part A — Drama   Pages 2–7
or
Part B — Prose   Pages 8–17
or
Part C — Poetry   Pages 18–28

Attempt ALL the questions for your chosen text.

SECTION 2 — Critical Essay — 20 marks

Attempt ONE question from the following genres — Drama, Prose Fiction, Prose Non-Fiction, Poetry, Film and Television Drama, or Language.

Your answer must be on a different genre from that chosen in Section 1.

You should spend approximately 45 minutes on each Section.

Write your answers clearly in the answer booklet provided. In the answer booklet you must clearly identify the question number you are attempting.

Use **blue** or **black** ink.

Before leaving the examination room you must give your answer booklet to the Invigilator; if you do not, you may lose all the marks for this paper.

SECTION 1 — SCOTTISH TEXT — 20 marks

Choose ONE text from Drama, Prose or Poetry.

Read the text extract carefully and then attempt ALL the questions for your chosen text.

You should spend about 45 minutes on this Section.

PART A — SCOTTISH TEXT — DRAMA

Text 1 — Drama

If you choose this text you may not attempt a question on Drama in Section 2.

Read the extract below and then attempt the following questions.

The Slab Boys by John Byrne

In this extract, from Act 2 of the play, Jack Hogg is looking for Phil, who has received a phone call.

	JACK:	I'm looking for your chum.
	SPANKY:	What're you wanting him for?
	JACK:	There's a phone call in Mr Barton's office . . . sounded rather urgent. Girl said it was the hospital.
5	SPANKY:	That's all right, I'll take it.
	JACK:	No, no . . . she was most insistent she speak to McCann himself . . .
	SPANKY:	I'll take it, I said . . .
	JACK:	No, I don't think . . .
	SPANKY:	I'm authorised! (*Exits.*)
10	JACK:	Hey . . . (*Exits.*)
		(*Pause. Enter* SADIE.)
	SADIE:	Too bloody soft, that's my trouble . . . He's not getting off with it, this time. Fifteen shillings? Not on your nelly . . . (*Sits down. Eases shoes off.*) Oooooooohhhhh . . . I should trade these in for a set of casters . . .
15		(*Enter* LUCILLE. *Crosses to sink.*)
		Any Epsom salts, hen?
	LUCILLE:	Waaahh! God, it's you! What're you playing at, Sadie?
	SADIE:	Have you seen that shy boy McCann on your travels?
	LUCILLE:	Shy?
20	SADIE:	Aye . . . fifteen bob shy. He still owes us for that dance ticket he got.
	LUCILLE:	Not again? When're you going to wise up? You'll just need to wait and grab him at the Town Hall . . .
	SADIE:	Oh, no . . . I'll not be seeing any Town Hall the night, sweetheart. If I thought these had to burl me round a dance floor . . . (*Cradles feet.*)

MARKS

25 LUCILLE: Are you not going? Aw, Sadie, it was a right scream last year.

SADIE: I know, flower . . .

LUCILLE: That man of yours was a howl.

SADIE: Aye . . . hysterical. Who else would sprint the length of the hall with a pint of Younger's in their fist and try leapfrogging over the top of Miss Walkinshaw
30 with that beehive hairdo of hers . . . eh? Only that stupid scunner I've got . . .

LUCILLE: How long was he off his work with the leg?

SADIE: Too long, sweetheart. He had my heart roasted, so he did. Sitting there with the bloody leg up on the fender shouting at me to put his line on at the bookie's for him. "See that?" I says. "If you're not up and back at your work
35 tomorrow I'll draw this across your back!" I had the poker in my hand . . . and I would've done it and all. Had me up to high doh. Couldn't get the stookie down the dungarees quick enough. Men? I wouldn't waste my time, hen.

LUCILLE: Come off it, Sadie . . .

SADIE: I'd to take the first one that came along. I'd've been better off with a lucky bag.

40 LUCILLE: They're not all like that, for God's sake.

SADIE: You'll learn, flower . . . you're young yet. You can afford to sift through the dross . . . till you come to the real rubbish at the bottom.

LUCILLE: Not this cookie. Lucille Bentley . . . Woman of the World . . . Fling Out Your Men!

45 SADIE: Wait till you get to my age and all you've got to show's bad feet and a display cabinet . . .

LUCILLE: Who wants to get to your age?

Questions

1. Look at lines 1—10.

   Explain how dialogue and/or stage directions are used to convey Spanky's attitude to Jack.   **2**

2. Look at lines 12—31.

   By referring to at least **two** examples in these lines, analyse how humour is created.   **4**

3. Look at lines 32—47.

   By referring to at least **two** examples, analyse how language is used to convey the different attitudes of Sadie and Lucille towards men.   **4**

4. By referring to this extract and to elsewhere in the play, discuss the role played by women.   **10**

OR

Text 2 — Drama

If you choose this text you may not attempt a question on Drama in Section 2.

Read the passage below and then attempt the following questions.

The Cheviot, the Stag and the Black, Black Oil by John McGrath

In this extract, Patrick Sellar is standing trial for murder.

MC:	Of all the many evictors, Mr Patrick Sellar was the only one who did not escape the full majesty of the law. He was charged with the murder of three people and numerous crimes at — Inverness High Court.
	The Company become a murmuring JURY.
5	*Enter the* JUDGE. *They stand, then sit silently.*
	Enter PATRICK SELLAR.
SELLAR:	Re the charge of culpable homicide, my Lord — can you believe, my good sir, that I, a person not yet cognosed or escaped from a madhouse, should deliberately, in open day, by means of an officer who has a wife and family, burn a house with a woman in it? Or that the officer should do so, instead of ejecting the tenant? The said tenant and woman being persons of whom we have no felonious intent, no malice, no ill-will.
10	
JUDGE:	Therefore, I would ask you (the jury) to ignore all the charges except two. One of these concerns the destruction of barns. In this case, Mr Sellar has ignored a custom of the country, although he has not infringed the laws of Scotland. And the second case concerns the burning of the house of Chisholm. And here we are reminded of the contradictory nature of the testimony. Now if the jury are at all at a loss on this part of the case, I would ask them to take into consideration the character of the accused, for this is always of value in balancing contradictory testimony. For here there is, in the first place, real evidence as regards Mr Sellar's conduct towards the sick — which in all cases has been proved to be most humane. And secondly, there are the letters of Sir George Abercrombie, Mr Fenton and Mr Brodie — which, although not evidence, must have some weight with the jury. And there are the testimonies of Mr Gilzean, and Sir Archibald Dunbar — (*Sees him in the audience, waves.*) — hello, Archie. All of them testifying to Mr Sellar's humanity of disposition. How say you?
15	
20	
25	
JURY:	Oh, not guilty, no, no, no, etc.
JUDGE:	My opinion completely concurs with that of the jury.
30	JURY *applaud* PATRICK SELLAR.
SELLAR:	Every reformer of mankind has been abused by the established errors, frauds and quackery. But where the reformers have been right at bottom, they have, by patience, and by their unabating zeal and enthusiasm, got forward, in spite of every opposition. And so, I trust, will Lord and Lady Stafford, in their generous exertions to better the people in this country.
35	

MARKS

More applause. Distant humming of "Land of Hope and Glory".

SELLAR: *(pointing to the mountains, from behind which a giant statue slowly emerges — eventually dwarfing the entire hall.)*

40

In lasting memorial of George Granville, Duke of Sutherland, Marquess of Stafford, K.G., an upright and patriotic nobleman, a judicious, kind and liberal landlord; who identified the improvement of his vast estates with the prosperity of all who cultivated them; a public yet unostentatious benefactor, who, while he provided useful employment for the active labourer, opened wide his hands to the distresses of the widow, the sick and the traveller: a

45

mourning and grateful tenantry, uniting with the inhabitants of the neighbourhood, erected *this pillar* . . .

Questions

5. Look at lines 7—12.

    Identify **one** tone used by Sellar in these lines and analyse how language is used to create this tone.

    2

6. Look at lines 13—27.

    By referring to at least **two** examples, analyse how the language of the speech suggests the Judge's bias in favour of Sellar.

    4

7. Look at lines 31—46.

    By referring to at least **two** examples, analyse how Sellar attempts to present "the reformers" and/or the Duke of Sutherland in a positive light.

    4

8. Discuss how McGrath presents authority in this scene and elsewhere in the play.

    10

[Turn over

OR

Text 3 — Drama

If you choose this text you may not attempt a question on Drama in Section 2.

Read the extract below and then attempt the following questions.

Men Should Weep **by Ena Lamont Stewart**

In this extract from Act 1, scene 1, John comes in to find Maggie talking to her sister, Lily.

John comes in carrying books under his arm. He is a big, handsome man. He puts down his books, gives Maggie a pat: they exchange warm smiles. He goes to sink and has a glass of water.

	Maggie:	Ye dry, John? I'll pit the kettle on. I've jist minded I promised yer auld lady a
5		cup in her bed.
	John:	She a right?
	Maggie:	Oh aye. Jist as usual . . . greetin an eatin.
	John:	(*turning to Lily with as much of a smile as he can muster*) An how's Lil?
	Lily:	I wish you'd leave aff cryin me Lil. Ma name's Lily.
10	John:	An it couldna suit ye better.
	Lily:	Whit d'ye mean by that, eh?
	Maggie:	Don't you two stert up! I've had enough the day. (*To Lily*) He didna mean onythin.
	Lily:	Well if he didna mean onythin he shouldna say onythin!
15	John:	Goad help us!
	Lily:	(*to Maggie*) Whit aboot yon ironin?
	Maggie:	Och, never heed. I'm that tired it wad kill me tae watch ye.
	Lily:	It'll be steamie day again afore ye've got that lot done.
	Maggie:	Well, I canna help it.
20	John:	Yous women! Ye've nae system!
	Lily:	Oh, I suppose if *you* was a wumman you'd hae everythin jist perfect! The weans a washed and pit tae bed at six, an everythin a spick an span. Naethin tae dae till bedtime but twiddle yer thumbs. Huh!
	John:	I'd hae a system . . .
25	Lily and Maggie:	(*together*) He'd hae a system!
	John:	Aye, I'd hae a *system*. Ony man wull tell ye, ye can dae naethin properly wi'oot ye hae a *system*.
	Lily:	And ony wumman'll tell ye that there's nae system ever inventit that disnae go tae Hell when ye've a hoose-fu o weans and a done aul granny tae look efter.
30	Maggie:	Never heed him, Lily. Ye should see him tryin tae mak the breakfast on a Sunday; ye'd get yer kill! If he's fryin bacon, he's fryin bacon, see? He's no keepin an eye on the toast an on the kettle, an breakin the eggs intae the pan a at the same time.

MARKS

	John:	Well, it's no ma job. If it *wis* ma job . . .
35	Maggie:	We ken: ye'd hae a system.
	Lily:	Well, if you're sure there's naethin I can dae, Maggie, I'll awa.
	Maggie:	Och no, wait and hae a wee cup wi us.
	Lily:	Naw . . . I'll mak yin at hame and hae something tasty tae it. A rarebit, mebbe.
	John:	(*winking at Maggie*) Aye, you dae that Lily; nae use hintin for ony rarebits here.
40	Lily:	(*not having seen the wink*) I like that! Hint! The cheek! It was me brung yon tin o baked beans that's sittin up on your dresser this minute, John Morrison!
	Maggie:	Och, he's only pullin yer leg, Lily.
	Lily:	If that's a sense o humour I'm glad I hevna got one. Yous men! I wouldna see one o you in ma road.
45	John:	Oh ho! If a man jist crep ontae your horizon, ye'd be efter him like a cock at a grosset.
	Lily:	(*hauling on her coat*) I'm no stayin here tae be insultit. Ye can keep the beans, Maggie, but that's the last ye're getting frae me till ye learn some folks their manners. Aye. And ye can tell yon precious Alec o yours that the next time he maks enough at the dugs, tae get fleein drunk in the middle o Argyle Street, he can pay me back ma ten shillingy note.
50		
		She stamps out of the room, slamming the door
	Maggie:	Ye shouldna tease Lily, John. Yin o they days she'll tak the huff and no come back, and whaur'll I be then?

Questions

9. Look at lines 1—15.

   Analyse how dialogue and/or stage directions are used to convey John's relationship with Maggie, **and** John's relationship with Lily in these lines.   4

10. Look at lines 20—35.

    By referring to at least **two** examples, analyse how both Maggie and Lily try to undermine John's opinion that women have "nae system".   4

11. Look at lines 39—52.

    Explain any **two** reasons for Lily's negative feelings when she leaves.   2

12. By referring to this extract and to elsewhere in the play, discuss John's role within the family.   10

[Turn over

SECTION 1 — SCOTTISH TEXT — 20 marks

Choose ONE text from Drama, Prose or Poetry.

Read the text extract carefully and then attempt ALL the questions for your chosen text.

You should spend about 45 minutes on this Section.

PART B — SCOTTISH TEXT — PROSE

Text 1 — Prose

If you choose this text you may not attempt a question on Prose (Fiction or Non-Fiction) in Section 2.

Read the extract below and then attempt the following questions.

The Crater by Iain Crichton Smith

"All present and correct, sir," said Sergeant Smith.

"All right, let's go then," said Lieutenant Mackinnon.

Down the trench they went, teeth and eyes grinning, clattering over the duckboards with their Mills bombs and their bayonets and their guns. "What am I doing here?" thought
5   Robert, and "Who the hell is making that noise?" and "Is the damned wire cut or not?" and "We are like a bunch of actors," and "I'm leading these men, I'm an officer."

And he thought again, "I hope the guns have cut that barbed wire."

Then he and they inched across No Man's Land following the line of lime which had been laid to guide them. Up above were the stars and the air was cool on their faces. But there
10   were only a few stars, the night was mostly dark, and clouds covered the moon. Momentarily he had an idea of a huge mind breeding thought after thought, star after star, a mind which hid in daylight in modesty or hauteur but which at night worked out staggering problems, pouring its undifferentiated power over the earth.

On hands and knees he squirmed forward, the others behind him. This was his first raid
15   and he thought, "I am frightened." But it was different from being out in the open on a battlefield. It was an older fear, the fear of being buried in the earth, the fear of wandering through eternal passageways and meeting grey figures like weasels and fighting with them in the darkness. He tested the wire. Thank God it had been cut. And then he thought, "Will we need the ladders?" The sides of the trenches were so deep sometimes
20   that ladders were necessary to get out again. And as he crawled towards the German trenches he had a vision of Germans crawling beneath British trenches undermining them. A transparent imagined web hung below him in the darkness quivering with grey spiders.

He looked at his illuminated watch. The time was right. Then they were in the German trenches. The rest was a series of thrustings and flashes. Once he thought he saw or
25   imagined he saw from outside a dugout a man sitting inside reading a book. It was like looking through a train window into a house before the house disappears. There were Mills bombs, hackings of bayonets, scurryings and breathings as of rats.

A white face towered above him, his pistol exploded and the face disappeared. There was a terrible stink all around him, and the flowing of blood. Then there was a long silence.
30 Back. They must get back. He passed the order along. And then they wriggled back again avoiding the craters which lay around them, created by shells, and which were full of slimy water. If they fell into one of these they would be drowned. As he looked, shells began to fall into them sending up huge spouts of water. Over the parapet. They were over the parapet. Crouched they had run and scrambled and were over. Two of them were
35 carrying a third. They stumbled down the trench. There were more wounded than he had thought. Wright . . . one arm seemed to have been shot off. Sergeant Smith was bending over him. "You'll get sent home all right," he was saying. Some of the men were tugging at their equipment and talking feverishly. Young Ellis was lying down, blood pouring from his mouth. Harris said, "Morrison's in the crater."

40 He and Sergeant Smith looked at each other. They were both thinking the same: there is no point, he's had it. They could see each other's eyes glaring whitely through the black, but could not tell the expressions on the faces. The shells were still falling, drumming and shaking the earth. All these craters out there, these dead moons.

Questions

13. Look at lines 1—13.

    Analyse how language is used to convey Robert's state of mind.   2

14. Look at lines 14—22.

    By referring to at least **two** examples, analyse how language is used to create a sense of threat.   4

15. Look at lines 23—43.

    By referring to at least **two** examples, analyse how language is used to highlight the tense nature of the soldiers' situation.   4

16. By referring to this and to at least one other short story by Iain Crichton Smith, discuss the impact of extreme situations on his characters.   10

[Turn over

OR

Text 2 — Prose

If you choose this text you may not attempt a question on Prose (Fiction or Non-Fiction) in Section 2.

Read the extract below and then attempt the following questions.

The Whaler's Return by George Mackay Brown

He put his head through the door and saw a few farmers sitting round the fire drinking. The barmaid was standing at a mirror twisting her yellow hair at the back of her head. At last she got a fine burnished knot on it and drove a pin through to hold it in place.

Flaws hadn't seen a woman for six months. He went in and asked for a mug of ale.

5   "We only sell whisky here," said the girl, "threepence a glass."

"A glass of whisky then," said Flaws.

He thought it might be the last chance he would ever have to speak to a pretty girl. Peterina was good and hard-working, but rather ugly.

Flaws stood at the bar and drank his whisky. The four farmers sat round the fire saying
10   little. It was Wednesday in Hamnavoe, the day they drove in their beasts to sell at the mart.

"Do you do much trade in the White Horse?" said Flaws to the barmaid.

"We welcome only the better sort of person here," said the girl, "the quiet country men, not the ruffians and tramps from the herring boats and the whalers. And of course the office workers too, and business people. We're always very busy in the evening after the
15   shops and offices close. No fighting scum from the boats ever cross the threshold of the White Horse." Out of her pretty mouth she spat on the stone floor.

Flaws was glad he was wearing his decent suit of broadcloth, the one his old mother always packed in mothballs at the bottom of his chest for departures and home-comings.

He ordered two glasses of whisky, one for the barmaid. She smiled at him sweetly. They
20   touched rims till the glasses made a small music and the whisky trembled into yellow circles. Flaws was transported. He longed to touch her burnished head. Given time, solitude, and another dram or two, he could well imagine himself kissing her across the bar.

"I haven't seen you in the White Horse before," said the barmaid. "What is your occupation,
25   sir?"

"God forgive me for telling a lie," said Flaws to himself. Then he squared his shoulders and said, "I only visit the islands now and then. I'm a commercial traveller. I travel for earthenware and china."

The barmaid glittered at him with eyes, teeth, hair, rings.

30   The door opened and Small the lawyer's clerk tiptoed in, his drunken nose (Flaws thought) redder than ever. He went up to the bar slowly, eyeing Flaws the way a hunter eyes his quarry. "If it isn't Flaws!" he cried at last. "If it isn't my old friend! And did you catch many whales at Greenland, eh? I can smell the blubber and the oil with you. I warrant you have a fine pile of sovereigns in your pocket. You're the first seaman ever to get into the White
35   Horse."

Flaws could have killed the little drunken clerk at that moment. The barmaid was suddenly looking at him with eyes as cold as stones.

MARKS

Flaws hoisted his box on his shoulder and made for the door without a word. His pocket was heavy with more silver and copper; he had broken another sovereign in the White
40 Horse. He stood, hot with shame and resentment, on the road outside.

"A commercial traveller!" cried Small the lawyer's clerk at the bar. Suddenly the interior of the White Horse was loud with merriment, the deep bass laughter of the farmers mingling with the falsetto mirth of the lawyer's clerk and the merry tinkle of the barmaid.

Flaws walked on towards Birsay, red in the face.

Questions

17. Look at lines 1—16.

By referring to at least **two** examples, analyse how language is used to create a striking impression of the barmaid.   4

18. Look at lines 17—29. `

By referring to at least **two** examples, analyse how language is used to indicate the significance of this moment for Flaws.   4

19. "He stood, hot with shame and resentment . . ." (line 40)

From your reading of the whole extract, explain why Flaws felt "shame" and "resentment" at this point.   2

20. By referring to this extract and to at least one other short story, discuss the use of literal and metaphorical journeys in Mackay Brown's stories.   10

[Turn over

OR

Text 3 — Prose

If you choose this text you may not attempt a question on Prose (Fiction or Non-Fiction) in Section 2.

Read the extract below and then attempt the following questions.

The Trick Is To Keep Breathing by Janice Galloway

In this extract, Joy describes her home and the early days of her relationship with Michael.

The cottage was tiny but cheap. There was a bus stop right outside the door and people with no sense used to look in while they were waiting for the bus, as though I was TV. But it also meant travel: buses stopping and starting right outside my door for whenever I needed to go somewhere. It made me feel free. I papered every wall myself and built shelves, wired my own plugs and painted the place fresh. A kind of damp smell hung on in the kitchen but it was my own place, my home now. Paul helped move my things. The parting wasn't bitter. We wanted to be civilised and polite. Unexplained bouts of weeping disturbed the quiet some evenings but I figured they were good signs. Everybody needs to cry now and then. I was there less than six months when Michael phoned his two word call.

10   *She knows.*

He moved in the same night with three carrier bags. There was nowhere else for him to go. He missed the kids but we were OK. Some nights we'd stay awake right through on the pleasure of holding the other warm body in the dark we never expected would be there. We got up red-eyed for work to go to the same place in the same car, came home together at night. When we washed the dishes, we'd watch our reflections in the night-blacked window, kissing.

One night, he got out of bed and didn't come back for a while. It was 2am. I got uneasy about it. I found him in the kitchenette, right at the back of the cottage, turning lilac in the cold. He was kneeling on the concrete looking at something. I kneeled down too and tried to see what it was. There was a mushroom growing out of the skirting. **LOOK** he said, **LOOK**. We didn't know what to think. I poked it with a fork and it broke off. We went back to bed and tried to forget about it.

We were in the kitchen cooking: I was throwing spaghetti onto the roughcast to see if it was ready while he was stirring sauce. The spaghetti landed awkwardly and I saw another mushroom right next to where it had settled on the wall. **LOOK** I said and we both looked again. This one was more securely attached. It didn't break first time so Michael got a knife and cut it away from the side of the window. It left a little pink trail like anaemic blood where it had been growing. After a month there were little shoots all along the hallway. Mould drew lines round the tops of walls and baby mushrooms appeared overnight. I wouldn't let him touch them because I thought they were dangerous or something. I didn't know where they were coming from and preferred just to let them alone in case. In case. Maybe I thought they would go away if we pretended hard enough. Every so often, I would find him in the hall or the kitchen, peering down and scratching with a penknife, then trying to hide it when he saw me coming. I would hear him in the bathroom, running the taps and washing his hands. He got a book from the library and read up about mushrooms.

MARKS

Dry rot, he said, matter-of-factly.

Dry rot. He gave me the book so I could read about it too. It was more sinister than the name. The house was being eaten from the inside by this thing. The spores could pass through concrete and plaster and multiply by the thousand thousand as we slept. They
40 could take over the whole structure if they wanted. I lay awake at night wondering what was going on out there in the hall while we were in our beds. The estimates for fixing it were unbelievable. I started having trouble sleeping. I avoided looking at the walls or skirting during the day.

Meantime Michael's council application paid off. The place was too big but he took it. It
45 was cheerful, bright, full of windows. Yellow walls and white woodwork. It was important he had his own place so he needn't feel dependent. Besides I didn't want anyone staying with me out of necessity. People gave us bits of things to fill it with. We shipped in the clothes from the cottage during the night, away from the silent spores, the creeping red clouds.

Questions

21. Look at lines 1—9.

By referring to at least examples, analyse how the writer's use of language conveys Joy's attempts to be optimistic about her new life.   3

22. Look at lines 17—35.

By referring to at least examples, analyse how the writer's use of language conveys Joy's growing sense of anxiety.   3

23. Look at lines 36—49.

Analyse how the writer's use of language highlights the contrast between the cottage and Michael's council house. You should refer to both sides of the contrast in your answer.   4

24. By referring to this extract, and to elsewhere in the novel, discuss how Galloway conveys the impact of Joy's relationship with Michael.   10

[Turn over

OR

Text 4 — Prose

If you choose this text you may not attempt a question on Prose (Fiction or Non-Fiction) in Section 2.

Read the extract below and then attempt the following questions.

Sunset Song by Lewis Grassic Gibbon

In this extract, which is from Part III (Seed-Time), Chris's father has just died.

And out she went, though it wasn't near kye-time yet, and wandered away over the fields; it was a cold and louring day, the sound of the sea came plain to her, as though heard in a shell, Kinraddie wilted under the greyness. In the ley field Old Bob stood with his tail to the wind, his hair ruffled up by the wind, his head bent away from the smore of it. He heard
5   her pass and gave a bit neigh, but he didn't try to follow her, poor brute, he'd soon be over old for work. The wet fields squelched below her feet, oozing up their smell of red clay from under the sodden grasses, and up in the hills she saw the trail of the mist, great sailing shapes of it, going south on the wind into Forfar, past Laurencekirk they would sail, down the wide Howe with its sheltered glens and its late, drenched harvests, past Brechin
10   smoking against its hill, with its ancient tower that the Pictish folk had reared, out of the Mearns, sailing and passing, sailing and passing, she minded Greek words of forgotten lessons, Παντα ρεί, *Nothing endures*. And then a queer thought came to her there in the drookèd fields, that nothing endured at all, nothing but the land she passed across, tossed and turned and perpetually changed below the hands of the crofter folk since the oldest of
15   them had set the Standing Stones by the loch of Blawearie and climbed there on their holy days and saw their terraced crops ride brave in the wind and sun. Sea and sky and the folk who wrote and fought and were learnéd, teaching and saying and praying, they lasted but as a breath, a mist of fog in the hills, but the land was forever, it moved and changed below you, but was forever, you were close to it and it to you, not at a bleak remove it held
20   you and hurted you. And she had thought to leave it all!

She walked weeping then, stricken and frightened because of that knowledge that had come on her, she could never leave it, this life of toiling days and the needs of beasts and the smoke of wood fires and the air that stung your throat so acrid, Autumn and Spring, she was bound and held as though they had prisoned her here. And her fine bit plannings!
25   — they'd been just the dreamings of a child over toys it lacked, toys that would never content it when it heard the smore of a storm or the cry of sheep on the moors or smelt the pringling smell of a new-ploughed park under the drive of a coulter. She could no more teach a school than fly, night and day she'd want to be back, for all the fine clothes and gear she might get and hold, the books and the light and learning.

30   The kye were in sight then, they stood in the lithe of the freestone dyke that ebbed and flowed over the shoulder of the long ley field, and they hugged to it close from the drive of the wind, not heeding her as she came among them, the smell of their bodies foul in her face — foul and known and enduring as the land itself. Oh, she hated and loved in a breath! Even her love might hardly endure, but beside it the hate was no more than the
35   whimpering and fear of a child that cowered from the wind in the lithe of its mother's skirts.

MARKS

And again that night she hardly slept, thinking and thinking till her head ached, the house quiet enough now without fairlies treading the stairs, she felt cool and calm, if only she could sleep. But by morning she knew she couldn't go on with Uncle and Auntie beside her,
40 they smothered her over with their years and their canny supposings. Quick after breakfast she dressed and came down and Auntie cried out, real sharplike, *Mighty be here, Chris, where are you going?* as though she owned Blawearie stick and stone, hoof and hide. And Chris looked at her coolly, *I'm away to Stonehaven to see Mr Semple, can I bring you anything?* Uncle Tam rose up from the table then, goggling, with his medals clinking, *Away*
45 *to Stonehive? What are you jaunting there for? I'll transact any business you have.* Their faces reddened up with rage, she saw plain as daylight how near it lay, dependence on them, she felt herself go white as she looked at them.

Questions

25. Look at lines 1—20.

   By referring to at least **two** examples, analyse how the writer creates a sense of Chris's physical surroundings **and/or** her awareness of Scotland's past.   4

26. Look at lines 21—36.

   By referring to at least **two** examples, analyse how the writer reveals Chris's feelings about staying on the land **and/or** her previous plans to leave.   4

27. Look at lines 37—47.

   Analyse how dialogue is used to convey the attitude of at least **one** of the characters.   2

28. By referring to this extract and to elsewhere in the novel, discuss how Grassic Gibbon develops the idea that *"Nothing endures"*.   10

[Turn over

OR

Text 5 — Prose

If you choose this text you may not attempt a question on Prose (Fiction or Non-Fiction) in Section 2.

Read the extract below and then attempt the following questions.

The Cone-Gatherers by Robin Jenkins

In this extract, Roderick is on his way to visit the cone-gatherers in their hut.

By the time the hut came in sight he was exhausted, in body and spirit; sweat of exertion and of fear drenched him. Near some yew trees whose branches reached the ground, forming dark caverns, he halted, to look into his bag to make sure that the cake, the symbol of reconciliation, had not been made to vanish by the evil presences he had just
5 defied. Reassured, he stood breathing in the woodsmoke drifting up so peacefully out of the rusted chimney.

If his senses had not been so preternaturally alert, and if from the dirty hut had not irradiated a light illuminating every leaf on all the trees about it, he would never have noticed the lurker under the cypress, entangled in the thin green bony arms that curled
10 out like an octopus's. No sunshine struck there, and even the luminance from the hut seemed to fail. At first he could not tell who it was, although he was sure it was not one of the cone-gatherers. He felt cold, and frightened, and sick at heart. Here at the very hut was the most evil presence of all, and it was visible.

When he realised that the motionless figure under the cypress was Duror, he crept in
15 dismay into a cave of yew. It was his first retreat, and it was cowardly. Yet he could not force himself to complete the pilgrimage and knock on the door. Duror was a barrier he could not pass.

As he crouched in the earthy darkness like an animal, he wondered what Duror's purpose could be in lurking there. The gamekeeper hated the men in the hut and wished to have
20 them expelled from the wood. Was he now spying on them in the hope that he would find them engaged in some wrong-doing, such as working today, which was Sunday? By their agreement with his mother they were not to work on Sundays. But Duror himself shot deer on Sundays; he did not often go to church, and when he did he sat with his arms folded and a smile of misery on his lips. Why then did he hate the cone-gatherers and wish to
25 drive them away? Was it because they represented goodness, and himself evil? Coached by his grandfather, Roderick knew that the struggle between good and evil never rested: in the world, and in every human being, it went on. The war was an enormous example. Good did not always win. So many times had Christian been overcome and humiliated; so long had Sir Galahad searched and suffered. In the end, aye, in the bitter end, the old judge
30 had said, with a chuckle, good would remain alone in the field, victorious.

The minutes passed. Nothing had changed. The blue smoke still rose from the chimney. Duror had not moved. In his den of yew Roderick grew cramped; and in an even darker, narrower den of disillusionment his mind whimpered.

Half an hour, at insect's pace, crept by. Only a leaf or two had fallen from a tree, as a
35 breeze stirred. Far away, over the loch, a gull had screamed.

MARKS

40   Had Duror gone mad? Was this the change his mother had asked Mrs. Morton about? Again Roderick recalled the scene at the deer drive with Duror embracing as if in love the screaming deer and hacking at its throat with a knife. Mrs. Morton, who was Duror's friend, had talked about the perils of the wood; she had mentioned the cone-gatherers, but perhaps in her heart she had been meaning Duror. If he was mad, then, was he now waiting with a gun to commit murder?

45   Peeping through the yew needles, Roderick saw in imagination the door of the hut open, and the cone-gatherers come out, the tall one who slightly limped and always frowned, and the small one who stooped and smiled. Then in the cypress the gun cracked, and the two men lay dead on the grass.

Questions

29.   Look at lines 1—13.

By referring to at least **two** examples, analyse how the writer uses language effectively to create a sinister atmosphere.   4

30.   Look at lines 18—45.

By referring to at least **two** examples, analyse how Roderick is presented as a mature character despite his youth.   4

31.   Duror is important in this extract, although he actually does very little. With reference to the extract as a whole, explain why he is important.   2

32.   With reference to this extract, and to elsewhere in the novel, discuss how the writer develops the theme of conflict between good and evil.   10

[Turn over

SECTION 1 — SCOTTISH TEXT — 20 marks

Choose ONE text from Drama, Prose or Poetry.

Read the text extract carefully and then attempt ALL the questions for your chosen text.

You should spend about 45 minutes on this Section.

PART C — SCOTTISH TEXT — POETRY

Text 1 — Poetry

If you choose this text you may not attempt a question on Poetry in Section 2.

Read the poem below and then attempt the following questions.

A Poet's Welcome to His Love-Begotten Daughter; The First Instance that entitled him to the Venerable Appellation of Father **by Robert Burns**

> Thou's welcome, wean, mishanter fa' me,
> If thought of thee, or of thy mammy,
> Shall ever daunton me or awe me,
>   My sweet wee lady!
> 5   Or if I blush when thou shalt ca' me
>   Ti-ta or daddy.
>
> Tho' now they ca' me fornicator,
> An' tease my name in kintry clatter,
> The mair they talk, I'm kent the better,
> 10   E'en let them clash;
> An auld wife's tongue's a feckless matter
>   To gie ane fash.
>
> Welcome! my bonnie, sweet, wee dochter,
> Tho' ye come here a wee unsought for,
> 15 And tho' your comin' I hae fought for,
>   Baith kirk and queir;
> Yet, by my faith, ye're no unwrought for
>   That I shall swear!
>
> Sweet fruit o' monie a merry dint,
> 20 My funny toil is now a' tint,
> Sin' thou came to the warl' asklent,
>   Which fools may scoff at;
> In my last plack thy part's be in 't
>   The better ha'f o't.
>
> 25 Tho' I should be the waur bestead,
> Thou's be as braw and bienly clad,
> And thy young years as nicely bred
>   Wi' education,
> As onie brat o' wedlock's bed,
> 30   In a' thy station.

MARKS

Wee image o' my bonnie Betty,
I, fatherly, will kiss and daut thee,
As dear, an' near my heart I set thee
        Wi' as guid will
35 As a' the priests had seen me get thee
        That's out o' hell.

Lord grant that thou may ay inherit
Thy mither's person, grace an' merit,
An' thy poor, worthless daddy's spirit,
40   Without his failins,
'Twill please me mair to see thee heir it,
        Than stockit mailens.

For if thou be what I wad hae thee,
And tak the counsel I shall gie thee,
45 I'll never rue my trouble wi' thee,
        The cost nor shame o't,
But be a loving father to thee,
        And brag the name o't.

Questions

33. Look at lines 1—6.

    Analyse how the speaker conveys his feelings about his newly born child.   2

34. Look at lines 7—18.

    By referring to at least **two** examples, analyse how the poet's language makes clear the speaker's response to his critics.   4

35. Look at lines 25—48.

    By referring to at least **two** examples, analyse how the poet's language effectively reveals aspects of the speaker's personality.   4

36. Discuss Burns' treatment of the religious **and/or** moral concerns of his time in this, and at least one other, poem.   10

[Turn over

OR

Text 2 — Poetry

If you choose this text you may not attempt a question on Poetry in Section 2.

Read the extract below and then attempt the following questions.

Mrs Midas **by Carol Ann Duffy**

It was late September. I'd just poured a glass of wine, begun
to unwind, while the vegetables cooked. The kitchen
filled with the smell of itself, relaxed, its steamy breath
gently blanching the windows. So I opened one,
5   then with my fingers wiped the other's glass like a brow.
He was standing under the pear tree snapping a twig.

Now the garden was long and the visibility poor, the way
the dark of the ground seems to drink the light of the sky,
but that twig in his hand was gold. And then he plucked
10 a pear from a branch — we grew Fondante d'Automne —
and it sat in his palm like a light bulb. On.
I thought to myself, Is he putting fairy lights in the tree?

He came into the house. The doorknobs gleamed.
He drew the blinds. You know the mind; I thought of
15 the Field of the Cloth of Gold and of Miss Macready.
He sat in that chair like a king on a burnished throne.
The look on his face was strange, wild, vain. I said,
What in the name of God is going on? He started to laugh.

I served up the meal. For starters, corn on the cob.
20 Within seconds he was spitting out the teeth of the rich.
He toyed with his spoon, then mine, then with the knives, the forks.
He asked where was the wine. I poured with shaking hand,
a fragrant, bone-dry white from Italy, then watched
as he picked up the glass, goblet, golden chalice, drank.

25 It was then that I started to scream. He sank to his knees.
After we had both calmed down, I finished the wine
on my own, hearing him out. I made him sit
on the other side of the room and keep his hands to himself.
I locked the cat in the cellar. I moved the phone.
30 The toilet I didn't mind. I couldn't believe my ears:

how he'd had a wish. Look, we all have wishes; granted.
But who has wishes granted? Him. Do you know about gold?
It feeds no one; aurum, soft, untarnishable; slakes
no thirst. He tried to light a cigarette; I gazed, entranced,
35 as the blue flame played on its luteous stem. At least,
I said, you'll be able to give up smoking for good.

MARKS

Questions

37. Look at lines 1–12.

By referring to at least **two** examples, analyse how the poet's language conveys the contrast in atmosphere between stanza 1 and stanza 2.   4

38. Look at lines 13–24.

Analyse how the poet's language in these lines creates an unsettling mood.   2

39. Look at lines 25–36.

By referring to at least **two** examples, analyse how the poet's language presents the character of Mrs Midas.   4

40. By referring closely to this poem, and to at least one other poem by Duffy, discuss how the poet explores the attempts of characters to cope with life-changing situations.   10

[Turn over

OR

Text 3 — Poetry

If you choose this text you may not attempt a question on Poetry in Section 2.

Read the extract below and then attempt the following questions.

The Bargain by Liz Lochhead

The river in January is fast and high.
You and I
are off to the Barrows.
Gathering police-horses twitch and fret
5   at the Tron end of London Road and Gallowgate.
The early kick-off we forgot
has us, three thirty, rubbing the wrong way
against all the ugly losers
getting ready to let fly
10   where the two rivers meet.

January, and we're
looking back, looking forward,
don't know which way

but the boy
15   with three beautiful Bakelite
Bush radios for sale in Meadow's Minimarket is
buttonpopping stationhopping he
doesn't miss a beat   sings along   it's easy
to every changing tune

20   Yes today we're in love aren't we?
with the whole splintering city
its big quick river   wintry bridges
its brazen black Victorian heart.
So what if every other tenement
25   wears its hearth on its gable end?
All I want
is my glad eye to catch
a glint in your flinty Northern face again
just once. Oh I know it's cold
30   and coming down
and no we never lingered long among
the Shipbank traders.
Paddy's Market   underneath the arches
stank too much today
35   the usual wetdog reek rising
from piles of old damp clothes.

MARKS

Questions

41. Look at lines 1—13.

    By referring to at least **two** examples, analyse how the language in these lines introduces the deterioration of the speaker's relationship.

    4

42. Look at lines 14—19.

    Analyse how the poet's language creates a change of mood.

    2

43. Look at lines 20—36.

    By referring to at least **two** examples, analyse how the poet uses setting to reflect the current state of the speaker's relationship.

    4

44. By referring to this poem, and at least one other poem by Lochhead, discuss how she explores the theme of difficult relationships.

    10

[Turn over

OR

Text 4 — Poetry

If you choose this text you may not attempt a question on Poetry in Section 2.

Read the poem below and then attempt the following questions.

Memorial by Norman MacCaig

Everywhere she dies. Everywhere I go she dies.
No sunrise, no city square, no lurking beautiful mountain
but has her death in it.
The silence of her dying sounds through
5　the carousel of language, it's a web
on which laughter stitches itself. How can my hand
clasp another's when between them
is that thick death, that intolerable distance?

She grieves for my grief. Dying, she tells me
10　that bird dives from the sun, that fish
leaps into it. No crocus is carved more gently
than the way her dying
shapes my mind. — But I hear, too,
the other words,
15　black words that make the sound
of soundlessness, that name the nowhere
she is continuously going into.

Ever since she died
she can't stop dying. She makes me
20　her elegy. I am a walking masterpiece,
a true fiction
of the ugliness of death.
I am her sad music.

MARKS

Questions

45. Look at lines 1—8.

    By referring to at least **two** examples, analyse how the language emphasises the devastating impact of the loved one's death on the speaker's life.

    3

46. Look at lines 9—17.

    By referring to at least **two** examples, analyse how the language conveys the close bond between the loved one and the speaker.

    4

47. Look at lines 18—23.

    By referring to at least **two** examples, analyse how the language emphasises the fact that the subject's death remains ever present in the speaker's mind.

    3

48. Discuss how reaction to suffering is explored in this, and at least one other, poem by MacCaig.

    10

[Turn over

OR

Text 5 — Poetry

If you choose this text you may not attempt a question on Poetry in Section 2.

Read the poem below and then attempt the following questions.

Shores **by Sorley MacLean**

If we were in Talisker on the shore
where the great white mouth
opens between two hard jaws,
Rubha nan Clach and the Bioda Ruadh,
5   I would stand beside the sea
renewing love in my spirit
while the ocean was filling
Talisker bay forever:
I would stand on the bareness of the shore
10 until Prishal bowed his stallion head.

And if we were together
on Calgary shore in Mull,
between Scotland and Tiree,
between the world and eternity,
15 I would stay there till doom
measuring sand, grain by grain,
and in Uist, on the shore of Homhsta
in presence of that wide solitude,
I would wait there forever
20 for the sea draining drop by drop.

And if I were on the shore of Moidart
with you, for whom my care is new,
I would put up in a synthesis of love for you
The ocean and the sand, drop and grain.
25 And if we were on Mol Stenscholl Staffin
when the unhappy surging sea dragged
the boulders and threw them over us,
I would build the rampart wall
against an alien eternity grinding (its teeth).

MARKS

Questions

49. Look at lines 1—14.

By referring to at least **two** examples, analyse how language is used to convey the powerful impact of the landscape on the speaker.

4

50. Look at lines 15—24.

By referring to at least **two** examples, analyse how language is used effectively to convey the intensity of the speaker's love.

4

51. Look at lines 25—29.

By referring to ideas **and/or** language, evaluate the effectiveness of these lines as a conclusion to the poem.

2

52. Referring closely to this and to at least one other poem, discuss how MacLean explores the impact of time on human experience.

10

[Turn over

MARKS

OR

Text 6 — Poetry

If you choose this text you may not attempt a question on Poetry in Section 2.

Read the poem below and then attempt the following questions.

The Thread by Don Paterson

Jamie made his landing in the world
so hard he ploughed straight back into the earth.
They caught him by the thread of his one breath
and pulled him up. They don't know how it held.
5 And so today I thank what higher will
brought us to here, to you and me and Russ,
the great twin-engined swaying wingspan of us
roaring down the back of Kirrie Hill

and your two-year-old lungs somehow out-revving
10 every engine in the universe.
All that trouble just to turn up dead
was all I thought that long week. Now the thread
is holding all of us: look at our tiny house,
son, the white dot of your mother waving.

Questions

53. Look at lines 1—4.

    By referring to at least **two** examples, analyse how the poet's use of language suggests the difficulties surrounding Jamie's birth.   4

54. Look at lines 5—10.

    Analyse how the poet's use of language conveys the present circumstances of the family.   2

55. Look at lines 11—14.

    By referring to at least **two** examples, evaluate the effectiveness of these lines as a conclusion to the poem.   4

56. Discuss how the poet explores the fragility of human life in this, and at least one other, poem.   10

[END OF SECTION 1]

SECTION 2 — CRITICAL ESSAY — 20 marks

Attempt ONE question from the following genres — Drama, Prose Fiction, Prose Non-fiction, Poetry, Film and Television Drama, or Language.

Your answer must be on a different genre from that chosen in Section 1.

You should spend approximately 45 minutes on this Section.

PART A — DRAMA

> *Answers to questions on Drama should refer to the text and to such relevant features as characterisation, key scene(s), structure, climax, theme, plot, conflict, setting . . .*

1. Choose a play in which a central character is in conflict with **or** rejects another character.

    Briefly explain the circumstances of the conflict or rejection and go on to discuss the consequences of this conflict or rejection for the play as a whole.

2. Choose a play in which the historical **and/or** geographical **and/or** social setting is important to your understanding of the play.

    Explain how the dramatist presents the setting and discuss why it is important to your understanding of the play as a whole.

3. Choose a play which has an effective opening scene **or** concluding scene.

    By briefly referring to details of the scene, explain how the dramatist made it effective and discuss how it contributes to your appreciation of the text as a whole.

[Turn over

PART B — PROSE FICTION

> *Answers to questions on Prose Fiction should refer to the text and to such relevant features as characterisation, setting, language, key incident(s), climax, turning point, plot, structure, narrative technique, theme, ideas, description . . .*

4. Choose a novel **or** short story in which there is a central character to whom you react with mixed feelings.

    With reference to appropriate techniques, briefly explain why you react to the character in this way and discuss how this reaction adds to your understanding of the text as a whole.

5. Choose a novel **or** short story that deals with a theme of moral **or** social significance.

    With reference to appropriate techniques, explain how the writer develops this theme and discuss why its development adds to your appreciation of the text as a whole.

6. Choose a novel **or** short story in which the choice of setting is central to your appreciation of the text.

    Briefly explain how the writer effectively creates setting and, with reference to appropriate techniques, discuss how the writer's presentation of the setting is central to your appreciation of the text as a whole.

PART C — PROSE NON-FICTION

> *Answers to questions on Prose Non-Fiction should refer to the text and to such relevant features as ideas, use of evidence, stance, style, selection of material, narrative voice . . .*
>
> *Non-fiction texts can include travel writing, journalism, autobiography, biography, essays . . .*

7. Choose a non-fiction text in which the writer engages your interest in a place **or** culture.

    Discuss, with reference to appropriate techniques, how the writer successfully engages your interest in this place or culture.

8. Choose a non-fiction text in which the writer describes a traumatic **or** rewarding experience.

    Discuss, with reference to appropriate techniques, how the writer conveys the traumatic or rewarding nature of the experience.

9. Choose a non-fiction text in which the writer attempts to influence the reader's opinion on a person **or** an issue.

    Discuss, with reference to appropriate techniques, how the writer attempts to influence the reader's opinion on the person or the issue.

PART D — POETRY

> *Answers to questions on Poetry should refer to the text and to such relevant features as word choice, tone, imagery, structure, content, rhythm, rhyme, theme, sounds, ideas . . .*

10. Choose a poem in which the poet creates a vivid sense of a particular time or a particular place. *The lake Isle of Innessfree.*
    The second Coming.
    Discuss how the poet's vivid depiction of time or place adds to your appreciation of the central concern(s) of the poem.

    Sailing to Byzantium,

11. Choose a poem with a moral or social or political theme. *the second Coming*

    Discuss, with reference to appropriate techniques, how the poet's presentation of the theme deepens your understanding of the poem as a whole.

12. Choose a poem in which the poet effectively creates a character or persona.

    Discuss, with reference to appropriate techniques, how the poet's effective creation of the character or persona enhances your appreciation of the poem as a whole.

[Turn over for next question

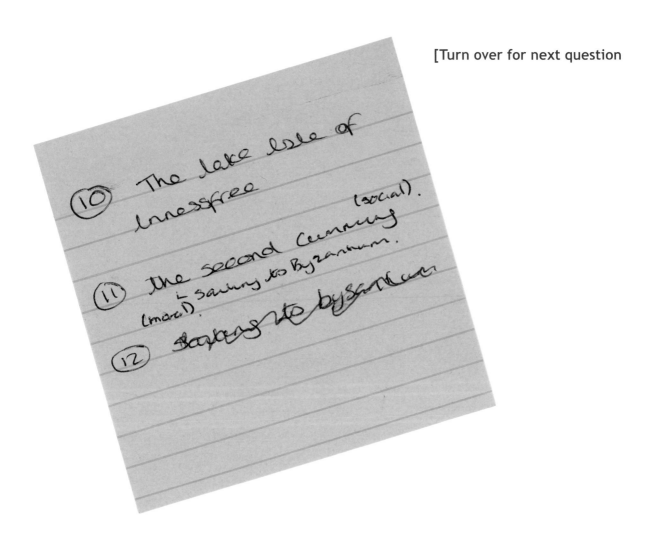

PART E — FILM AND TELEVISION DRAMA

> *Answers to questions on Film and Television Drama* should refer to the text and to such relevant features as use of camera, key sequence, characterisation, mise-en-scène, editing, music/sound, special effects, plot, dialogue . . .*

13. Choose a film **or** television drama in which there is a particularly tense or dramatic sequence.

    Explain how the film or programme makers use media techniques to achieve this effect.

14. Choose a film **or** television drama which concerns an individual **or** a group of characters facing a significant challenge.

    Explain how the film or programme makers use media techniques to convey the significance of this challenge.

15. Choose a film **or** television drama which is targeted at a specific audience.

    Explain how the film or programme makers use media techniques to target this audience.

* "television drama" includes a single play, a series or a serial.

PART F — LANGUAGE

> *Answers to questions on Language should refer to the text and to such relevant features as register, accent, dialect, slang, jargon, vocabulary, tone, abbreviation . . .*

16. Choose a particular area of language associated with mass communication, eg advertising, broadcasting, technology.

    Identify specific examples and discuss to what extent they are effective.

17. Choose language used in a specific work setting such as hospital, courtroom, garage, school, parliament . . .

    Identify specific examples of the language used and evaluate their effectiveness within the work setting.

18. Choose the language associated with pressure groups (multi-cultural organisations, environmental agencies, faith groups, campaigners for equality . . .)

    By referring to specific examples, discuss what makes the language of one such group successful in achieving its purpose to persuade.

[END OF SECTION 2]

[END OF QUESTION PAPER]

National Qualifications 2017

X724/76/11

English
Reading for Understanding, Analysis and Evaluation — Text

THURSDAY, 11 MAY

9:00 AM – 10:30 AM

Total marks — 30

Read the passages carefully and then attempt ALL questions, which are printed on a separate sheet.

This Question Paper replaces the original SQA 2017 Past Paper, which cannot be reproduced for copyright reasons. As such, it should be stressed that it is not an official SQA-verified section, although every care has been taken by the Publishers to ensure that it offers appropriate practice material for Higher English.

The following two passages focus on video games.

Passage 1

Read the passage below and then attempt questions 1 to 5.

In the first passage, Steven Johnson, writing in The Times newspaper, considers whether video games are as bad for young people as is often claimed.

Reading books enriches the mind; playing video games deadens it — you can't get much more conventional than the conventional wisdom that kids today would be better off spending more time reading books, and less time zoning out in front of their video games.

5   For the record, I think that the virtues of reading books are great. We should all encourage our kids to read more. But even the most avid reader is inevitably going to spend his or her time with other media — games, television, movies, the internet. Yet the question is whether these other forms of culture have intellectual virtues in their own right — different from, but comparable to, reading. Where most critics allege a dumbing down, I see a progressive story: popular culture steadily, but almost imperceptibly, making our brains sharper as we soak in
10   entertainment usually dismissed as so much lowbrow fluff. I hope to persuade you that increasingly the non-literary popular culture is honing different mental skills that are just as important as the ones exercised by reading books.

The most powerful example of this trend is found in the world of video games. And the first and last thing that should be said about the experience of playing today's video games, the thing
15   you almost never hear, is that games are fiendishly, sometimes maddeningly, hard. The dirty little secret of gaming is how much time you spend not having fun. You may be frustrated; you may be confused or disorientated; you may be stuck. But when you put the game down and move back into the real world, you may find yourself mentally working through the problem you have been wrestling with, as though you were worrying a loose tooth.

20   So why does anyone bother playing these things? And why does a seven-year-old soak up, for instance, the intricacies of industrial economics in the game form of SimCity 2000, when the same subject would send him screaming for the exits in a classroom? To date, there has been little direct research into the question of how games get children to learn without realising that they are learning. But I believe a strong case can be made that the power of games to captivate
25   largely involves their ability to tap into the brain's natural reward circuitry. If you create a system in which rewards are both clearly defined and achieved by exploring an environment, you will find human brains drawn to those systems, even if they are made up of virtual characters and simulated sidewalks. In the game world, reward is everywhere. The gaming universe is literally teeming with objects that deliver very clearly articulated rewards: more life, access to
30   new levels, new equipment, new spells. Most of the crucial work in game design focuses on keeping players notified of potential rewards available to them, and how much these rewards are currently needed. Most games offer a fictional world where rewards are larger, and more vivid, and more clearly defined than life.

35 You may just want to win the game, of course, or perhaps you want to see the game's narrative completed, or in the initial stages of play, you may just be dazzled by the game's graphics. But most of the time, when you're hooked on a game, what draws you in is an elemental form of desire: the desire to see the Next Thing. After all, with the occasional exception, the actual content of the game is often childish or gratuitously menacing. Much of the role play inside the gaming world alternates between drive-by shooting and princess-rescuing. It is not the

40 subject matter that attracts; it is the reward system that draws those players in, and keeps their famously short attention spans locked on the screen.

Playing down the content of video games shouldn't be seen as a cop-out. We ignore the content of many other activities that are widely considered to be good for the brain. No one complains about the simplistic, militaristic plot of chess games. We teach algebra to children

45 knowing full well that the day they leave the classroom 99 per cent of those kids will never again directly employ their algebraic skills. Learning algebra isn't about acquiring a specific tool; it's about building up a mental muscle that will come in handy elsewhere.

So it is with games. It's not what you're thinking about when you're playing a game, it's the way you're thinking that matters. Novels may activate our imagination and may conjure up powerful

50 emotions, but games force you to analyse, to choose, to prioritise, to decide. From the outside, the primary activity of a gamer looks like a fury of clicking and shooting. But if you peer inside the gamer's mind, the primary activity turns out to be another creature altogether: making decisions, some of them snap judgements, some of them long-term strategies.

Adapted from an article in The Times newspaper, May 2005

Passage 2

Read the passage below and attempt question 6. While reading, you may wish to make notes on the main ideas and/or highlight key points in the passage.

In the second passage, the politician and journalist Boris Johnson, writing on his own website, takes a different view about video games.

It's the snarl that gives the game away. It's the sobbing and the shrieking and the horrible pleading — that's how you know your children are undergoing a sudden narcotic withdrawal. As the strobing colours die away and the screen goes black, you listen to the wail of protest from the offspring and you know that you have just turned off their drug, and you know that they are,

5 to a greater or lesser extent, addicts.

Millions of seven-to-fifteen-year olds are hooked, especially boys, and it is time someone had the guts to stand up, cross the room and just say no to Nintendo. It is time to garrotte the Game Boy and paralyse the PlayStation, and it is about time, as a society, that we admitted the catastrophic effect these blasted gizmos are having on the literacy and the prospects of young

10 males.

We demand that teachers provide our children with reading skills; we expect the schools to fill them with a love of books; and yet at home we let them slump in front of the consoles. We get on with our hedonistic 21st-century lives while in some other room the nippers are bleeping and zapping in speechless rapture, their passive faces washed in explosions and gore. They sit for so

15 long that their souls seem to have been sucked down the cathode ray tube.

They become like blinking lizards, motionless, absorbed, only the twitching of their hands showing that they are still conscious. These machines teach them nothing. They stimulate no ratiocination, discovery or feat of memory — though some of them may cunningly pretend to be educational. I have just watched an eleven-year-old play a game that looked fairly historical, on
20 the packet. Your average guilt-ridden parent might assume that it taught the child something about the Vikings and medieval siege warfare. Phooey! The red soldiers robotically slaughtered the white soldiers, and then they did it again, that was it. Everything was programmed, spoon-fed, immediate — and endlessly showering the player with undeserved praise, richly congratulating him for his bogus massacres.

25 The more addictive these games are to the male mind, the more difficult it is to persuade boys to read books. It's not that these young people lack the brains; the raw circuitry is better than ever. It's the software that's the problem. They have not been properly programmed, because they have not read enough. The only way to learn to write is to be forced time and again to articulate your own thoughts in your own words, and you haven't a hope of doing this if you haven't read enough
30 to absorb the basic elements of vocabulary, grammar, rhythm, style and structure; and young males in particular won't read enough if we continually capitulate and let them fritter their lives away in front of these drivelling machines.

So I say now: go to where your children are sitting in auto-lobotomy in front of the console. Summon up all your strength, all your courage. Steel yourself for the screams and yank out that
35 plug. And if they still kick up a fuss, then get out the sledgehammer and strike a blow for literacy.

Adapted from an article published on Boris Johnson's website in June 2006

[END OF QUESTION PAPER]

National
Qualifications
2017

X724/76/21

English
Reading for Understanding,
Analysis and Evaluation — Questions

THURSDAY, 11 MAY

9:00 AM – 10:30 AM

Total marks — 30

Attempt ALL questions.

Write your answers clearly in the answer booklet provided. In the answer booklet you must clearly identify the question number you are attempting.

Use **blue** or **black** ink.

Before leaving the examination room you must give your answer booklet to the Invigilator; if you do not, you may lose all the marks for this paper.

MARKS

Attempt ALL questions
Total marks — 30

1. Read lines 1—12.

   (a) Analyse how the writer's word choice in lines 1—3 emphasises the "conventional wisdom" that reading books is better than playing video games.   2

   (b) Explain in your own words "the question" the writer asks in line 6 about "other forms of culture".   2

   (c) **By referring to at least two features of language in lines 8—12** ("Where … books"), analyse how the writer emphasises the contrast between his positive view of "other forms of culture" and the negative view held by "most critics".   4

2. By referring to lines 13—19, analyse how the writer uses both sentence structure and imagery to convey the difficulty of playing video games   4

3. Read lines 20—33.

   Identify **three reasons** why "reward" is so important to the learning process involved in playing video games. Use your own words as far as possible.   3

4. Read lines 34—47.

   Identify **two** criticisms and **two** defences the writer makes of video games.   4

5. Read lines 48—54.

   (a) Explain in your own words the key distinction the writer makes between reading a novel and playing a video game.   2

   (b) Analyse how the writer's use of language in lines 50—54 ("From … strategies") conveys the contrast between what a gamer looks like from "the outside" and what is happening "inside the gamer's mind".   4

Question on both passages

6. Look at both passages.

   The writers disagree about video games.

   Identify three key areas on which they disagree.

   You should support the points by referring to important ideas in both passages.

   You may answer this question in continuous prose or in a series of developed bullet points.   5

[END OF QUESTION PAPER]

National
Qualifications
2017

X724/76/12

English
Critical Reading

THURSDAY, 11 MAY

10:50 AM — 12:20 PM

Total marks — 40

SECTION 1 — Scottish Text — 20 marks

Read an extract from a Scottish text you have previously studied and attempt the questions.

Choose ONE text from either

Part A — Drama   Pages 2–13
or
Part B — Prose   Pages 14–23
or
Part C — Poetry   Pages 24–35

Attempt ALL the questions for your chosen text.

SECTION 2 — Critical Essay — 20 marks

Attempt ONE question from the following genres — Drama, Prose Fiction, Prose Non-Fiction, Poetry, Film and Television Drama, or Language.

Your answer must be on a different genre from that chosen in Section 1.

You should spend approximately 45 minutes on each Section.

Write your answers clearly in the answer booklet provided. In the answer booklet, you must clearly identify the question number you are attempting.

Use **blue** or **black** ink.

Before leaving the examination room you must give your answer booklet to the Invigilator; if you do not, you may lose all the marks for this paper.

SECTION 1 — SCOTTISH TEXT — 20 marks

Choose ONE text from Drama, Prose or Poetry.

Read the text extract carefully and then attempt ALL the questions for your chosen text.

You should spend about 45 minutes on this Section.

PART A — SCOTTISH TEXT — DRAMA

Text 1 — Drama

If you choose this text you may not attempt a question on Drama in Section 2.

Read the extract below and then attempt the following questions.

The Slab Boys by John Byrne

In this extract, from Act 2 of the play, Spanky and Phil believe that Hector has just lost his job.

	SPANKY:	We'd like to present this little . . . er . . . this token of . . . er . . .
	HECTOR:	There was five of them . . . plus a squared-off fitch with my name on it . . .
	SPANKY:	Are you going to shut your face and listen, Shorty? Me and Phil's trying to make a presentation here.
5	PHIL:	It's a quid.
	SPANKY:	Shut up.
	HECTOR:	Sorry, what were you saying?
	SPANKY:	We know it's come as a bit of a surprise to you, Hector . . . you having to leave the Slab Room . . .
10	HECTOR:	It's a bombshell . . . no kidding . . .
	SPANKY:	(*to Phil*) Doesn't make it easy, does he? Er . . . so what me and Phil's done is . . . er . . . well, we put round the hat and . . . er . . .
	PHIL:	Carry on, you're doing fine.
	SPANKY:	It's not a lot, you understand . . .
15	PHIL:	It's a quid, son.
	SPANKY:	Shut up, will you!
	PHIL:	Give us it. (*Snatches 'presentation'.*) What Spanky was trying to say, Hector, is . . . er . . . och, here.
	SPANKY:	It's a quid.
20	*They clap.*	
	HECTOR:	What's this for?
	PHIL:	Not even a "Thank you, boys, I'm really touched." You are leaving the Slab Room, right?
	HECTOR:	Yeh, but . . .
25	SPANKY:	Then that'll tide you over . . . you and your maw . . .

PHIL: Till you get another job.

HECTOR: Eh?

SPANKY: He said, till you get another job.

HECTOR: Eh?

30 SPANKY *and* PHIL (*together*): Till you get another job!

HECTOR: I've already got another job.

PHIL: Christ, that was quick. Is there a mobile Broo outside?

HECTOR: That's what I was along seeing Willie about . . . my new job . . . I start on a desk
            on Monday.

35 SPANKY *and* PHIL (*together*): What????

HECTOR: I'm a Designer now. Seven quid a week back-dated a fortnight, rising in annual
            increments to twelve pounds fifteen and eleven after tax at the end of four
            years. God, I don't think I feel too well . . .

SPANKY: Me too . . .

40 HECTOR: It's the excitement.

        (*Enter* Alan.)

ALAN: Hey . . . guess what? Since two of you guys are vacating the Slab, Curry thought
            I should step in and fill the breach . . . how about that? Where are the gum
            crystals kept again? (*Hunts around.*) Oh . . . there was a phone call came
45   through to Willie's office . . . I said I'd pass the message on . . .

PHIL: Eh? Is my maw safe??

ALAN: You didn't get in.

PHIL: What?

ALAN: Exceptionally high number of applicants this year . . . something like that . . .

MARKS

Questions

1. Look at lines 1—20.

   By referring to **at least two** examples, analyse how dialogue is used to reveal the attitudes of the slab boys (Phil and Spanky) to Hector's situation at this point.   **3**

2. Look at lines 21—40.

   By referring to **at least two** examples, analyse how humour is used in relation to Hector's announcement.   **4**

3. Look at lines 42—49.

   By referring to **at least two** examples, analyse how language is used to convey Alan's character **and/or** attitudes.   **3**

4. By referring to this extract and to elsewhere in the play, discuss how Byrne develops the theme of opportunity.   **10**

[OPEN OUT FOR QUESTIONS]

DO NOT WRITE ON THIS PAGE

OR

Text 2 — Drama

If you choose this text you may not attempt a question on Drama in Section 2.

Read the extract below and then attempt the following questions.

The Cheviot, the Stag and the Black, Black Oil by John McGrath

This extract focuses on a shooting party in the Highlands.

Enter shooting party with large armoury. GHILLIE, LORD CRASK, *and* LADY PHOSPHATE OF RUNCORN.

LADY PH:	Her Royal Majesty the Queen is so right about the charm of this divine part of the world, what? Your estates, Lord Crask, abound in brown trout and grouse — what? —
LORD CRASK:	Has your Ladyship sampled the salmon?
LADY PH:	The rugged beauty hereabouts puts one in mind of the poetic fancies of dear Lord Tennyson — what?
LORD CRASK:	Lady Phosphate of Runcorn you are too kind.
LADY PH:	Oh listen for the vale profound is overflowing with the sound.

5

10

Blast of gunfire.

GHILLIE (*tries to stop them*): No no no no — the beaters are just having their tea.

LADY PH:	As one does. What?
LORD CRASK:	What?

Goes to fire; GHILLIE *restrains him.*

15

GHILLIE (*to audience*): That's nothing, you should see him when he's fishing.

LADY PH:	How far do your domains extend over this beauteous countryside, Lord Crask?
LORD CRASK:	I have about 120,000 acres down that way, but most of it's over that way.
LADY PH:	Oh Archie . . . Capital, capital, capital . . .
LORD CRASK:	Oh yes I've got bags of that too — 200,000 shares in Argentine Beef, half a million tied up in shipping, and a mile or two of docks in Wapping.
LADY PH:	Topping —
LORD CRASK:	No Wapping —
LADY PH:	What?

20

25

LORD CRASK goes to shoot — GHILLIE *restrains him.*

GHILLIE:	No no no no no.
LADY PH:	Your highland air is very bracing — I quite fancy a small port . . .
LORD CRASK:	Oh — how would you like Lochinver?
LADY PH:	No no no, I mean I'd like to wet my whistle —
LORD CRASK (*waving hand*): We've left a bush over there for that sort of thing . . .

30

GHILLIE *whistles up the beaters.*

GHILLIE: Any moment now sir . . .

LORD CRASK: Here come the grouse, Lady Phosphate —

35 LADY PH: What?

LORD CRASK: The grouse —

LADY PH: Oh, how lovely. (*She gets out a sten gun.*) I find it so moving that all over the north of North Britain, healthy, vigorous people are deriving so much innocent pleasure at so little cost to their fellow human beings.

40 *Barrage.* GHILLIE *aims* LORD CRASK's *gun up higher, struggles with him.* LADY PHOSPHATE *fires her sten from the hip. Bombs, shells, etc. Barrage ends.*

GHILLIE: Oh no — Thon was a nice wee boy.

Music — guitar and mandolin begins. LORD CRASK *and* LADY PHOSPHATE *sing a duet.*

BOTH: Oh it's awfully, frightfully, ni-i-ice,
45   Shooting stags, my dear, and grice —
              And there's nothing quite so righ-it-it
              As a fortnight catching trite:

              And if the locals should complain,
              Well we can clear them off again.

50 LADY PH: We'll clear the straths

LORD CRASK: We'll clear the paths

LADY PH: We'll clear the bens

LORD CRASK: We'll clear the glens

BOTH: We'll show them we're the ruling class.

MARKS

Questions

5. Look at lines 1—19.

   By referring to **at least two** examples, analyse how language is used to convey the characters of **both** Lady Phosphate and Lord Crask.   **4**

6. Look at lines 20—42.

   By referring to **at least two** examples, analyse how humour is used to reveal central concerns.   **4**

7. Look at lines 44—54.

   Explain how the singers' attitudes to **both** the local people and environment are made clear.   **2**

8. By referring to this extract and to elsewhere in the play, discuss how McGrath explores the effects of social class.   **10**

Page nine

[OPEN OUT FOR QUESTIONS]

DO NOT WRITE ON THIS PAGE

OR

Text 3 — Drama

If you choose this text you may not attempt a question on Drama in Section 2.

Read the extract below and then attempt the following questions.

Men Should Weep by Ena Lamont Stewart

In this extract from Act 2, scene 1, Granny is waiting to be collected by her daughter-in-law, Lizzie.

Mrs Harris opens the door to Lizzie, a hard-faced harridan about fifty

Lizzie: (*ignoring the others*) Well? Ye ready?

Mrs Bone: Ready? She's been sittin here waitin on ye for the last hauf-oor.

Lizzie: Got a yer claes packed? An yer pension book?

5 Granny: Aye, Lizzie; it's here.

Lizzie: See's a look at it. (*Granny starts to fumble with her bag. Mrs Bone goes to help her*) Hev they men no been for the bed yet?

Mrs Harris: If they'd hae been for the bed it wouldna be staunin up against yon wa, would it?

10 Lizzie: (*taking the pension book from Mrs Bone*) Here! Ye've drawn this week's. Ye got the money?

Granny: Naw, Lizzie . . . I gied it tae Maggie.

Lizzie: Well, it's no Maggie's, it's mines. If ye're comin tae bide wi me, ye're no comin tae bide *aff* me.

15 Granny: She got some things aff the grocer she'd tae pay for, an she wis needin a vest an socks for Bertie gaun up tae the hospital.

Lizzie: Oh? So Bertie gets new socks at ma expense, does he? And whit does she think you're gonna live on for the next week? Air?

Mrs Harris: Ach, leave the puir aul wife alane. Shairly ye can scrape up a bit tae eat for her;
20   it's no as if ye wis takin in a big hulkin brute o a man tae feed.

Lizzie: I'm no takin in naebody tae feed. Folks that canna pay for their meat'll find nae room in ma hoose.

Mrs Bone: Oo! An her yer puir dead husband's mither. Oo! I'm surprised at ye, Lizzie Morrison.

25 Mrs Harris: I thought you said you wis never surprised — at anythin human.

Mrs Bone: That's jist whit I said: *anythin human*.

They both stare hard at Lizzie, then shake their heads at each other

Lizzie: I've tae earn every penny that comes intae ma hoose.

Mrs Harris: Aye, we ken that. An you don't dae sae bad either, ye aul miser. Buyin up aul
30   claes for a copper or twa and sellin them at sixpence a week . . .

Mrs Bone: Or she'll loan ye the dough tae buy them outright — at fifty percent.

Mrs Harris: Aye, she's got a right kind heart, she wouldae see ye stuck; no if she could mak a guid thing oot o it.

35 Lizzie: Ye're jealous! Ye hevna the brains tae mak a bit yersels. But ye're no above tradin wi me when it suits ye. Aye, an gettin a bargain.

Mrs Harris
Mrs Bone: } (*together*) A bargain? Frae *you*?

They look at each other and shake their heads

Mrs Harris: I canna mind ony bargain.

Lizzie: Whit aboot yon veloory hat ye bought aff me?

40 Mrs Harris: Veloory hat? Veloory hat . . . ? Oh, ye mean yon scabby aul felt bunnet wi the moultin bird on tap? Oh aye, I mind! If yon wis veloory, I'm a wally dug.

Lizzie: It wis veloory. It belanged tae a lady in Kelvinside whaur I did a bit on a Saturday.

Mrs Bone: A bit whit? Pinchin?

45 Lizzie: Here! I could pit ye tae the Polis for that.

Mrs Harris: No roon aboot here ye couldnae. They a ken ye.

Granny: Oh, I'm nae wantin tae leave here! I wisht I could bide wi Maggie till I dee!

Lizzie: Bide then!

Granny: Ye ken I cannae bide. Alec and Isa's needin the room.

50 Mrs Harris: Some folks is right selfish. You've naebody but yersel tae think aboot, an ye'll no tak the aul wife aff Maggie's hauns wi'oot kickin up a fuss.

Lizzie sits down and loosens her coat

Mrs Bone: I thought you wis in a hurry tae get aff?

Lizzie: I'm sittin right here till Maggie comes hame wi whit's left o Granny's pension.

55 Mrs Bone: Huh! Whit a hope you've got. Whit d'ye think'll be left?

Lizzie: Aye . . . mebbe y're right . . . In that case, I'll jist hae tae tak whit she bought.

She gets up and goes to open food cupboard. Mrs Harris grabs her

Mrs Harris: Here! Mrs Bone and me's in chairge o this hoose till Lily comes; you keep yer dirty aul neb oot of the cupboards or we'll shout for the Polis.

MARKS

Questions

9. Look at lines 1–27.

    By referring to **at least two** examples, analyse how **both** stage directions and
    dialogue are used to create a clear impression of Lizzie in these lines.   4

10. Look at lines 28–46.

    By referring to **at least two** examples, analyse how language is used to convey the
    feelings of the neighbours (Mrs Harris and Mrs Bone) towards Lizzie.   4

11. Although Granny says very little in these lines, she is important in highlighting central
    concerns. By considering the extract as a whole, explain why she is important.   2

12. By referring to this extract and to elsewhere in the play, discuss how Lamont Stewart
    develops the theme of community.   10

[OPEN OUT FOR QUESTIONS]

DO NOT WRITE ON THIS PAGE

SECTION 1 — SCOTTISH TEXT — 20 marks

Choose ONE text from Drama, Prose or Poetry.

Read the text extract carefully and then attempt ALL the questions for your chosen text.

You should spend about 45 minutes on this Section.

PART B — SCOTTISH TEXT — PROSE

Text 1 — Prose

If you choose this text you may not attempt a question on Prose (Fiction or Non-Fiction) in Section 2.

Read the extract below and then attempt the following questions.

The Red Door by Iain Crichton Smith

As he stared at the door he felt strange flutterings within him. First of all the door had been painted very lovingly so that it shone with a deep inward shine such as one might find in pictures. And indeed it looked like a picture against the rest of the house which wasn't at all modern but on the contrary was old and intertwined with all sorts of rusty
5   pipes like snakes.

He went back from the door and looked at it from a distance as people in art galleries have to do when studying an oil painting. The more he regarded it the more he liked it. It certainly stood out against the drab landscape as if it were a work of art. On the other hand the more he looked at it the more it seemed to express something in himself which
10   had been deeply buried for years. After a while there was something boring about green and as for blue it wouldn't have suited the door at all. Blue would have been too blatant in a cold way. And anyway the sky was already blue.

But mixed with his satisfaction he felt what could only be described as puzzlement, a slight deviation from the normal as if his head were spinning and he were going round in circles.
15   What would the neighbours say about it, he wondered. Never in the history of the village had there been a red door before. For that matter he couldn't remember seeing even a blue door himself, though he had heard of the existence of one.

The morning was breaking all over the village as he looked. Blue smoke was ascending from chimneys, a cock was crowing, belligerent and heraldic, its red claws sunk into the
20   earth, its metallic breast oriental and strange. There was a dew all about him and lying on the fences ahead of him. He recognised that the village would wake to a new morning, for the red door would gather attention to itself.

And he thought to himself, "I have always sought to hide among other people. I agree to whatever anybody tells me to do. If they think I should go to church, I go to church. If they
25   want me to cut peats for them, I do. I have never," he thought with wonder, "been myself." He looked down at his grey fisherman's jersey and his wellingtons and he thought, "I have always worn these things because everybody else does. I have never had the courage to wear what I wanted to wear, for example a coloured waistcoat and a coloured jacket."

The red door stood out against the whiteness of the frost and the glimmerings of snow. It
30   seemed to be saying something to him, to be asking him a question. Perhaps it was pleading with him not to destroy it. Perhaps it was saying, "I don't want to be green. There must be a place somewhere for me as myself. I wish to be red. What is wrong with red anyway?" The door seemed to him to have its own courage.

Page fourteen

MARKS

35 Wine of course was red and so was blood. He drank none of the former and only saw the latter when he cut himself while repairing a fence or working with wood when a nail would prick his finger.

But really was he happy? That was the question. When he considered it carefully he knew that he wasn't. He didn't like eating alone, he didn't like sitting in the house alone, he didn't like having none who belonged to him, to whom he could tell his secret thoughts,

40 for example that such and such was a mean devil and that that other one was an ungrateful rat.

He had to keep a perpetually smiling face to the world, that was his trouble. But the red door didn't do that. It was foreign and confident. It seemed to be saying what it was, not what it thought others expected it to say. On the other hand, he didn't like wellingtons and

45 a fisherman's jersey. He hated them in fact: they had no elegance.

Now Mary had elegance. Though she was a bit odd, she had elegance. It was true that the villagers didn't understand her but that was because she read many books, her father having been a teacher. And on the other hand she made no concessions to anybody. She seemed to be saying, "You can take me or leave me." She never gossiped. She was proud

50 and distant. She had a world of her own.

Questions

13. Look at lines 1—12.

By referring to **at least two** examples, analyse how the language emphasises the differences between the red door and the existing surroundings.   4

14. Look at lines 18—33.

By referring to **at least two** examples, analyse how language is used to highlight the significance of the red door at this moment in Murdo's life.   4

15. Look at lines 37—45.

Analyse how the language reveals Murdo's deep-rooted unhappiness.   2

16. By referring to this extract and to at least one other short story, discuss how Crichton Smith explores the conflict between individuality and conformity.   10

[Turn over

OR

Text 2 — Prose

If you choose this text you may not attempt a question on Prose (Fiction or Non-Fiction) in Section 2.

Read the extract below and then attempt the following questions.

Tartan **by George Mackay Brown**

They crossed a field to the third house, a hovel. From the door they heard muttering and sighing inside. "There's breath in this house," said Kol. He leapt into the middle of the floor with a loud beserk yell, but it might have been a fly buzzing in the window for all the attention the old woman paid to him. "Ah," she was singing over the sheeted dead child on
5   the bed, "I thought to see you a shepherd on Morven, or maybe a fisherman poaching salmon at the mouth of the Naver. Or maybe you would be a man with lucky acres and the people would come from far and near to buy your corn. Or you might have been a holy priest at the seven altars of the west."

There was a candle burning at the child's head and a cross lay on his breast, tangled in his
10 cold fingers.

Arnor, Havard, and Sven crossed themselves in the door. Kol slunk out like an old dog.

They took nothing from that house but trudged uphill to a neat grey house built into the sheer brae.

At the cairn across the valley, a mile away, a group of plaided men stood watching them.

15 At the fourth door a voice called to them to come in. A thin man was standing beside a loom with a half-made web in it. "Strangers from the sea," he said, "you are welcome. You have the salt in your throats and I ask you to accept ale from Malcolm the weaver."

They stood round the door and Malcolm the weaver poured horns of ale for each of them.

"This is passable ale," said Havard. "If it had been sour, Malcolm the weaver, we would
20 have stretched you alive on your loom. We would have woven the thread of eternity through you."

Malcolm the weaver laughed.

"What is the name of this place?" said Arnor.

"It is called Durness," said Malcolm the weaver. "They are good people here, except for the
25 man who lives in the tall house beyond the cairn. His name is Duncan, and he will not pay me for the cloth I wove for him last winter, so that he and his wife and his snovelly-nosed children could have coats when the snow came."

"On account of the average quality of your ale, we will settle matters with this Duncan," said Arnor. "Now we need our cups filled again."

30 They stayed at Malcolm the weaver's house for an hour and more, and when they got up to go Kol staggered against the door. "Doubtless somebody will pay for this," he said thickly.

They took with them a web of cloth without asking leave of Malcolm. It was a gray cloth of fine quality and it had a thick green stripe and a thin brown stripe running up and down and a very thick black stripe cutting across it horizontally. It was the kind of Celtic weave
35 they call tartan.

MARKS

"Take it, take it by all means," said Malcolm the weaver.

"We were going to take it in any case," said Sven.

"Tell us," said Havard from the door, "who is the girl in Durness with black hair and black eyes and a cleft chin?"

40 "Her name is Morag," said Malcolm the weaver, "and she is the wife of John the shepherd. John has been on the hill all week with the new lambs. I think she is lonely."

Questions

17. Look at lines 1—13.

     By referring to **at least two** examples, analyse how the writer uses language to convey the emotional impact of the child's death.   4

18. Look at lines 15—41.

     By referring to **at least two** examples, analyse how the writer uses language to reveal the character **and/or** attitudes of Malcolm the weaver.   4

19. Look at the whole extract.

     By referring closely to the extract, analyse how the characters of **two** of the Vikings are conveyed.   2

20. By referring to this extract and to at least one other short story, discuss how Mackay Brown explores the relationship between the individual and the community.   10

[Turn over

OR

Text 3 — Prose

If you choose this text you may not attempt a question on Prose (Fiction or Non-Fiction) in Section 2.

Read the extract below and then attempt the following questions.

The Trick Is To Keep Breathing by Janice Galloway

On the map, it's called Bourtreehill, after the elder tree, the bourtree, Judas tree; protection against witches. The people who live here call it Boot Hill. Boot Hill is a new estate well outside the town it claims to be part of. There was a rumour when they started building the place that it was meant for undesirables: difficult tenants from other places,

5   shunters, overspill from Glasgow. That's why it's so far away from everything. Like most rumours, it's partly true. Boot Hill is full of tiny, twisty roads, wild currant bushes to represent the great outdoors, pubs with plastic beer glasses and kids. The twisty roads are there to prevent the kids being run over. The roads are meant to make drivers slow down so they get the chance to see and stop in time. This is a dual misfunction. Hardly anyone

10   has a car. If one does appear on the horizon, the kids use the bends to play chicken, deliberately lying low and leaping out at the last minute for fun. The roads end up more conducive to child death than if they had been straight. What they do achieve is to make the buses go slow. Buses are infrequent so the shelters are covered in graffiti and kids hanging from the roofs. Nobody waits in these shelters even when it's raining. It rains a lot.

15   The buses take a long time.

When I was small I always wanted a red front door. This front door is bottle green. The key never surrenders first time. I have to rummage through my bag and every pocket while I stand at the door as though I'm begging to be mugged. The first time we came, there were two sets of numbers on the door; one large and black; the other brass and much smaller.

20   Like this:

13 13

We laughed and left them on, wondering if the previous tenants had been amnesiacs or phobics. When I came back alone, I took both sets off. There are four little holes on the door where they used to be

    •

    •   :   and a

25

different colour of paint underneath. I wondered what had moved away the previous tenants with their amnesia or their phobia. I wondered where they were now. Anyway, I didn't want those numbers on the door: it was a signal I could do without. I was angry I hadn't done it before. The nameplate was something he had bought, so I left it on. It says

30   his name. Not mine.

MARKS

Grit wells up when I open the door. There are always withered leaves in the porch. It seems to sit at the end of a natural tunnel of wind and makes itself difficult even on mild days. Litter accumulates on either side of the porch step: the porch is full of curled, brown leaves. Slaters run frantic in the sudden emptiness overhead while I fight my way inside.
35 This makes me shiver. Every time. I notice a little shell of something dead that's been there for weeks now because I can't pick it up, not even through paper. I hate the feel of them, gritty little packets. Insects make me sick. They have their skeletons outside, too many eyes, unpredictable legs and you can never tell where their mouths are. Spiders are worse. But today there are only the slaters. They disgust me but I'm not afraid of them. I push the
40 letters with my foot till they are well clear of the dead one and pick them up with the tips of my fingers.

A bill from the lawyer, a note from the Health Visitor and a postcard from Marianne.

I've been Whitewater Rafting

The postcard has a picture of a butterfly and a gushing torrent of water in the background.
45 The words on the back are smudged as though some of the water from the front of the card has splashed over and made the ink run. This makes it hard to read but I get the general drift.

> Camping better than anticipated. Leaving for the
> Canadian border tomorrow. Scenery wonderful.
50 > You would hate it. Love   Mxx

I forget about the slaters and try to feel the other continent through the card. It doesn't work. I make tea and check out the livingroom. The spill on the rug is almost dry. I find the bottle open from last night but not the lid. I put an envelope over the neck, sitting the bottle aside so I don't kick it later, then reshape cushions trying to keep my feet on the rug
55 because my shoes make a terrible noise on the floorboards. But things have to be set in place. A lot depends on stillness later and I have to get a lot of moving around out of my system now. Stillness helps when I'm alone. It keeps me contained.

Questions

21. Look at lines 1—15.

    By referring to **at least two** examples, analyse how the writer uses language to convey a negative impression of Bourtreehill.   4

22. Look at lines 16—41.

    By referring to **at least two** examples, analyse how the writer's use of language reveals Joy's anxiety.   4

23. Look at lines 42—57.

    Analyse how the writer's use of language emphasises Joy's attempts to cope with her situation.   2

24. By referring to this extract and to elsewhere in the novel, discuss how Galloway explores the impact of loneliness.   10

OR

Text 4 — Prose

If you choose this text you may not attempt a question on Prose (Fiction or Non-Fiction) in Section 2.

Read the extract below and then attempt the following questions.

Sunset Song by Lewis Grassic Gibbon

In this extract, which is from Part II (Drilling), it is threshing time at Chae Strachan's farm.

Not that they'd much to shout for that winter themselves, the Strachans; folk said it was easy to see why Chae was so strong on Rich and Poor being Equal: he was sore in need of the sharing out to start ere he went clean broke himself. Maybe old Sinclair or the wife were tight with the silver that year, but early as December Chae had to sell his corn, he
5 brought the first threshing of the season down in Kinraddie. John Guthrie and Will were off at the keek of dawn when they saw the smoke rise from the engines, Chris followed an hour later to help Chae's wife with the dinner and things. And faith! broke he might be but he wasn't mean, Chae, when the folk came trampling in to eat there was broth and beef and chicken and oat-cakes, champion cakes they made at the Knapp; and loaf and jelly
10 and dumpling with sugar and milk; and if any soul were that gutsy he wanted more he could hold to the turnip-field, said Chae.

The first three men to come in Chris hardly saw, so busied she was pouring their broth for them. Syne, setting the plates, she saw Alec Mutch, his great lugs like red clouts hung out to dry: and he cried *Ay, Chris!* and began to sup as though he hadn't seen food for a
15 fortnight. Beside him was Munro of the Cuddiestoun, he was eating like a colie ta'en off its chain, Chae's thresh was a spree to the pair of them. Then more trampling and scraping came from the door, folk came drifting in two-three at a time, Chris over-busied to notice their faces, but some watched her and gave a bit smile and Cuddiestoun cried to father, *Losh, man, she's fair an expert getting, the daughter. The kitchen's more her style than the*
20 *College.*

Some folk at the tables laughed out at that, the ill-nature grinned from the faces of them, and suddenly Chris hated the lot, the English Chris came back in her skin a minute, she saw them the yokels and clowns everlasting, dull-brained and crude. Alec Mutch took up the card from Cuddiestoun then and began on education and the speak ran round the tables.
25 Most said it was a coarse thing, learning, just teaching your children a lot of damned nonsense that put them above themselves, they'd turn round and give you their lip as soon as look at you. But Chae was sitting down himself by then and he wouldn't have that. *Damn't man, you're clean wrong to think that. Education's the thing the working man wants to put him up level with the Rich.* And Long Rob of the Mill said *I'd have thought a bit*
30 *balance in the bank would do that.* But for once he seemed right in agreement with Chae — *the more education the more of sense and the less of kirks and ministers.* Cuddiestoun and Mutch were fair shocked at that, Cuddiestoun cried out *Well, well, we'll hear nothing coarse of religion*, as though he didn't want to hear anything more about it and was giving out orders. But Long Rob wasn't a bit took aback, the long rangy childe, he just cocked an
35 eye at Cuddiestoun and cried *Well, well, Munro, we'll turn to the mentally afflicted in general, not just in particular. How's that foreman of yours getting on, Tony? Is he still keeping up with his shorthand?* There was a snicker at that, you may well be sure, and Cuddiestoun closed up quick enough, here and there folk had another bit laugh and said Long Rob was an ill hand to counter. And Chris thought of her clowns and yokels, and was
40 shamed as she thought — Chae and Long Rob they were, the poorest folk in Kinraddie!

MARKS

Questions

25.   Look at lines 1—11.

By referring to **at least two** examples, explain how important aspects of Chae's character are revealed.

3

26.   Look at lines 12—20.

By referring to **at least two** examples, analyse how humour is created.

3

27.   Look at lines 21—40.

By referring to **at least two** examples, analyse how the writer conveys the differing attitudes of those present.

4

28.   By referring to this extract and to elsewhere in the novel, discuss how Grassic Gibbon conveys Chris's conflicting emotions towards the community of Kinraddie.

10

[Turn over

OR

Text 5 — Prose

If you choose this text you may not attempt a question on Prose (Fiction or Non-Fiction) in Section 2.

Read the extract below and then attempt the following questions.

The Cone-Gatherers by Robin Jenkins

In this extract, a storm is brewing.

In the tip of the tall larch they were in a good position to watch the approach of the storm. At the sea end of the loch for the past half hour indigo clouds had been mustering, with rumbles of thunder still distant and half-hearted. More ominous was the river of radiance pouring straight down into the orange mass of the tree. After long excited consultations,
5   the finches had whisked away. The two men were the only living creatures left in the tree tops.

At the very crest, Calum was frightened and exhilarated. He chattered involuntarily, making no sense. Instead of dropping the golden cones safely into his bag he let them dribble out of his hands so that, in the expectancy before the violence of the storm, the
10   tiny stots from one transfigured branch to another could be clearly heard. Several times he reached up and raised his hand, so that it was higher than the tree.

Neil, a little lower down, was fastened by a safety belt. His rheumatism had heralded the rain, so that the climb to the top had been for him a long slow agony which he did not wish to repeat. That was why he did not give the order to go down; he hoped the storm
15   would pass over without striking them. He too was agitated, finding the cones exasperatingly small and his bag insatiable. The belt chafed his waist, and his arms and legs ached. Above all, Calum's meaningless chatters distressed him. He shouted to him several times to stop. Calum only screamed back, not in defiance, but in uncontrollable excitement.

20   Then that cascade of light streaming into the larch ceased, leaving it dark and cold. Black clouds were now overhead. Thunder snarled. Colour faded from the wood. A sough of wind shook the gloomy host of trees. Over the sea flashed lightning. Yet, far to the east, islands of peace and brightness persisted in the sky.

The first few drops of rain fell, as large as cones.

25   "We'd better get down," shouted Neil, and he tugged frantically at the buckle of his belt with his stiff sticky blackened fingers.

Calum slithered down and helped to loose him. He was giggling.

"Whether we go down or not," said Neil, "we'll get soaked to the skin. But up here the lightning might be dangerous."

30   "I don't like the lightning, Neil."

"Nobody does. What's been the matter with you? You're not a child. You've been in a storm before."

MARKS

"Did you see the light, Neil?"

"How could I miss seeing it? It was in my eyes, blinding me."

35 "Was it from heaven, Neil?"

"Heaven?" Neil's shout was astonished and angry. "What are you talking about?"

Calum pressed close to him eagerly.

"Do you mind what you said yon time, Neil? We were in the shed together, with the horse. You said it was always as bright as that in heaven."

40 "In the shed, with the horse? What shed and what horse?"

"It was called Peggy, Neil."

Neil remembered. "But that was more than twenty years ago," he cried.

"Aye, but you said it, Neil. You said heaven was always as bright as that."

His face wet with rain and tears, Neil clung to the tree and shut his eyes.

45 "Maybe I did, Calum," he said.

"And mind what else you said, Neil? You said that was where our mither was. You said that, Neil, in the shed."

"Maybe I did."

Questions

29. Look at lines 1—6.

Analyse how the writer effectively describes the impending storm.   2

30. Look at lines 7—19.

By referring to **at least two** examples, analyse how the writer's use of language conveys Calum's reaction to the storm.   4

31. Look at lines 25—48.

By referring to **at least two** examples, analyse how dialogue is used to convey aspects of the relationship between Calum and Neil.   4

32. By referring to this extract and to elsewhere in the novel, discuss how Jenkins uses symbolism to develop the central concerns of the text.   10

[Turn over

SECTION 1 — SCOTTISH TEXT — 20 marks

Choose ONE text from Drama, Prose or Poetry.

Read the text extract carefully and then attempt ALL the questions for your chosen text.

You should spend about 45 minutes on this Section.

PART C — SCOTTISH TEXT — POETRY

Text 1 — Poetry

If you choose this text you may not attempt a question on Poetry in Section 2.

Read the extract below and then attempt the following questions.

Address To The Deil by Robert Burns

'O Prince! O chief of many thronéd Pow'rs
That led th' embattl'd Seraphim to war—'— Milton.

O Thou! whatever title suit thee—
Auld Hornie, Satan, Nick, or Clootie,
Wha in yon cavern grim an' sootie,
        Clos'd under hatches,
5 Spairges about the brunstane cootie,
        To scaud poor wretches!

Hear me, auld Hangie, for a wee,
An' let poor damnéd bodies be;
I'm sure sma' pleasure it can gie,
10   Ev'n to a deil,
To skelp an' scaud poor dogs like me,
        An' hear us squeel!

Great is thy pow'r, an' great thy fame;
Far kenm'd an' noted is thy name;
15 An' tho' yon lowin' heuch's thy hame,
        Thou travels far;
An' faith! thou's neither lag nor lame,
        Nor blate, nor scaur.

Whyles, ranging like a roarin' lion,
20 For prey, a' holes and corners tryin';
Whyles, on the strong-wind'd tempest flyin',
        Tirlin' the kirks;
Whyles, in the human bosom pryin',
        Unseen thou lurks.

25 I've heard my rev'rend graunie say,
In lanely glens ye like to stray;
Or where auld ruin'd castles grey
        Nod to the moon,
Ye fright the nightly wand'rer's way,
30   Wi' eldritch croon.

MARKS

When twilight did my graunie summon,
To say her pray'rs, douse, honest woman!
Aft 'yont the dyke she's heard you bummin',
                    Wi' eerie drone;
35 Or, rustlin', thro' the boortrees comin',
                    Wi' heavy groan.

Ae dreary, windy, winter night,
The stars shot down wi' sklentin light,
Wi' you, mysel, I gat a fright,
40   Ayont the lough;
Ye, like a rash-buss, stood in sight,
                    Wi' wavin' sough.

The cudgel in my nieve did shake,
Each brist'ld hair stood like a stake,
45 When wi' an eldritch, stoor 'quaick, quaick',
                    Amang the springs,
Awa ye squatter'd like a drake,
                    On whistlin' wings.

Questions

33. Look at lines 1—12.

    By referring to **at least two** examples, analyse how the poet's use of language presents a light-hearted depiction of the Deil.   4

34. Look at lines 13—24.

    Analyse how the poet's use of language portrays the Deil as a powerful being.   2

35. Look at lines 25—48

    By referring to **at least two** examples, analyse how Burns mocks superstitious beliefs.   4

36. By referring to this extract and to at least one other poem by Burns, discuss the poet's use of humour in his exploration of serious issues.   10

[Turn over

OR

Text 2 — Poetry

If you choose this text you may not attempt a question on Poetry in Section 2.

Read the poem below and then attempt the following questions.

Valentine by Carol Ann Duffy

Not a red rose or a satin heart.

I give you an onion.
It is a moon wrapped in brown paper.
It promises light
5 like the careful undressing of love.

Here.
It will blind you with tears
like a lover.
It will make your reflection
10 a wobbling photo of grief.

I am trying to be truthful.

Not a cute card or a kissogram.

I give you an onion.
Its fierce kiss will stay on your lips,
15 possessive and faithful
as we are,
for as long as we are.

Take it.
Its platinum loops shrink to a wedding ring,
20 if you like.
Lethal.
Its scent will cling to your fingers,
cling to your knife.

MARKS

Questions

37. Look at lines 1—5.

    By referring to **at least two** examples, analyse how the poet uses language to challenge **and/or** reinforce traditional stereotypes associated with romantic love.

    4

38. Look at lines 6—17.

    By referring to **at least two** examples, analyse how the poet uses language to suggest a "truthful" view of love.

    4

39. Look at lines 18—23.

    By referring to the poet's use of language, evaluate the effectiveness of these lines as a conclusion to the poem.

    2

40. By referring to this poem and to at least one other poem by Duffy, discuss how the poet explores emotional conflict within an individual.

    10

[Turn over

OR

Text 3 — Poetry

If you choose this text you may not attempt a question on Poetry in Section 2.

Read the poem below and then attempt the following questions.

For my Grandmother Knitting by Liz Lochhead

There is no need they say
but the needles still move
their rhythms in the working of your hands
as easily
5 as if your hands
were once again those sure and skilful hands
of the fisher-girl.

You are old now
and your grasp of things is not so good
10 but master of your moments then
deft and swift
you slit the still-ticking quick silver fish.
Hard work it was too
of necessity.

15 But now they say there is no need
as the needles move
in the working of your hands
once the hands of the bride
with the hand-span waist
20 once the hands of the miner's wife
who scrubbed his back
in a tin bath by the coal fire
once the hands of the mother
of six who made do and mended
25 scraped and slaved slapped sometimes
when necessary.

But now they say there is no need
the kids they say grandma
have too much already
30 more than they can wear
too many scarves and cardigans —
gran you do too much
there's no necessity . . .

MARKS

At your window you wave
35 them goodbye Sunday.
With your painful hands
big on shrunken wrists.
Swollen-jointed. Red. Arthritic. Old.
But the needles still move
40 their rhythms in the working of your hands
easily
as if your hands remembered
of their own accord the pattern
as if your hands had forgotten
45 how to stop.

Questions

41. Look at lines 1—14.

By referring to **at least two** examples, analyse how the poet's use of language conveys a sense of **both** the past and the present.

4

42. Look at lines 15—26.

Analyse how the poet uses the idea of "hands" to convey **two** different stages in the grandmother's past life.

2

43. Look at lines 27—45.

By referring to **at least two** examples, analyse how the poet's use of language creates a bleak mood or atmosphere.

4

44. By referring to this poem and to at least one other poem by Lochhead, discuss how she explores the theme of personal **and/or** social change.

10

[Turn over

OR

Text 4 — Poetry

If you choose this text you may not attempt a question on Poetry in Section 2.

Read the poem below and then attempt the following questions.

Basking Shark by Norman MacCaig

To stub an oar on a rock where none should be,
To have it rise with a slounge out of the sea
Is a thing that happened once (too often) to me.

But not too often — though enough. I count as gain
5   That once I met, on a sea tin-tacked with rain,
That roomsized monster with a matchbox brain.

He displaced more than water. He shoggled me
Centuries back — this decadent townee
Shook on a wrong branch of his family tree.

10 Swish up the dirt and, when it settles, a spring
Is all the clearer. I saw me, in one fling,
Emerging from the slime of everything.

So who's the monster? The thought made me grow pale
For twenty seconds while, sail after sail,
15 The tall fin slid away and then the tail.

MARKS

Questions

45. Look at lines 1—3.

Analyse how the poet's use of language conveys the nature of the encounter.   **2**

46. Look at lines 4—9.

By referring to **at least two** examples, analyse how language is used to suggest the impact of the experience on the speaker.   **4**

47. Look at lines 10—15.

By referring to **at least two** examples, analyse how the poet's language reveals a sense of new understanding.   **4**

48. By referring to this poem and to at least one other poem by MacCaig, discuss how the poet uses symbolism to develop central ideas in his poetry.   **10**

[Turn over

OR

Text 5 — Poetry

If you choose this text you may not attempt a question on Poetry in Section 2.

Read the poem below and then attempt the following questions.

Heroes by Sorley MacLean

I did not see Lannes at Ratisbon
nor MacLennan at Auldearn
nor Gillies MacBain at Culloden,
but I saw an Englishman in Egypt.

5   A poor little chap with chubby cheeks
and knees grinding each other,
pimply unattractive face —
garment of the bravest spirit.

He was not a hit "in the pub
10 in the time of the fists being closed,"
but a lion against the breast of battle,
in the morose wounding showers.

His hour came with the shells,
with the notched iron splinters,
15 in the smoke and flame,
in the shaking and terror of the battlefield.

Word came to him in the bullet shower
that he should be a hero briskly,
and he was that while he lasted,
20 but it wasn't much time he got.

He kept his guns to the tanks,
bucking with tearing crashing screech,
until he himself got, about the stomach,
that biff that put him to the ground,
25 mouth down in sand and gravel,
without a chirp from his ugly high-pitched voice.

No cross or medal was put to his
chest or to his name or to his family;
there were not many of his troop alive,
30 and if there were their word would not be strong.
And at any rate, if a battle post stands,
many are knocked down because of him,
not expecting fame, not wanting a medal
or any froth from the mouth of the field of slaughter.

35 I saw a great warrior of England,
a poor manikin on whom no eye would rest;
no Alasdair of Glen Garry;
and he took a little weeping to my eyes.

MARKS

Questions

49. Look at lines 1—8.

Analyse how the poet's use of language makes it clear that the soldier was not a conventional hero.

2

50. Look at lines 13—26.

By referring to **at least two** examples, analyse how the poet's use of language conveys the hardships suffered by the soldier in battle.

4

51. Look at lines 27—38.

By referring to **at least two** examples, analyse how the poet uses language to create a sense of pity.

4

52. By referring to this poem and to at least one other poem by MacLean, discuss how the poet explores the theme of destruction.

10

[Turn over

OR

Text 6 — Poetry

If you choose this text you may not attempt a question on Poetry in Section 2.

Read the extract below and then attempt the following questions.

Nil Nil by Don Paterson

From the top, then, the zenith, the silent footage:
McGrandle, majestic in ankle-length shorts,
his golden hair shorn to an open book, sprinting
the length of the park for the long hoick forward,
5   his balletic toe-poke nearly bursting the roof
of the net; a shaky pan to the Erskine St End
where a plague of grey bonnets falls out of the clouds.
But ours is a game of two halves, and this game
the semi they went on to lose; from here
10 it's all down, from the First to the foot of the Second,
McGrandle, Visocchi and Spankie detaching
like bubbles to speed the descent into pitch-sharing,
pay-cuts, pawned silver, the Highland Division,
the absolute sitters ballooned over open goals,
15 the dismal nutmegs, the scores so obscene
no respectable journal will print them; though one day
Farquhar's spectacular bicycle-kick
will earn him a name-check in Monday's obituaries.
Besides the one setback — the spell of giant-killing
20 in the Cup (Lochee Violet, then Aberdeen Bon Accord,
the deadlock with Lochee Harp finally broken
by Farquhar's own-goal in the replay)
nothing inhibits the fifty-year slide
into Sunday League, big tartan flasks,
25 open hatchbacks parked squint behind goal-nets,
the half-time satsuma, the dog on the pitch,
then the Boys' Club, sponsored by Skelly Assurance,
then Skelly Dry Cleaners, then nobody;
stud-harrowed pitches with one-in-five inclines,
30 grim fathers and perverts with Old English Sheepdogs
lining the touch, moaning softly.
Now the unrefereed thirty-a-sides,
terrified fat boys with callipers minding
four jackets on infinite, notional fields;
35 ten years of dwindling, half-hearted kickabouts
leaves two little boys — Alastair Watt,
who answers to "Forty", and wee Horace Madden,
so smelly the air seems to quiver above him —
playing desperate two-touch with a bald tennis ball

MARKS

40 in the hour before lighting-up time.
    Alastair cheats, and goes off with the ball
    leaving wee Horace to hack up a stone
    and dribble it home in the rain;
    past the stopped swings, the dead shanty-town
45 of allotments, the black shell of Skelly Dry Cleaners
    and into his cul-de-sac, where, accidentally,
    he neatly back-heels it straight into the gutter
    then tries to swank off like he meant it.

    Unknown to him, it is all that remains
50 of a lone fighter-pilot, who, returning at dawn
    to find Leuchars was not where he'd left it,
    took time out to watch the Sidlaws unsheathed
    from their great black tarpaulin, the haar burn off Tayport
    and Venus melt into Carnoustie, igniting
55 the shoreline; no wind, not a cloud in the sky
    and no one around to admire the discretion
    of his unscheduled exit

Questions

53. Look at lines 1—6 ("From . . . the net;).

     Analyse how the poet's language creates a celebratory mood.   2

54. Look at lines 9—29 ("from here . . . inclines").

     By referring to **at least two** examples, analyse how the poet's use of language creates
     an atmosphere of decline.   4

55. Look at lines 41—57.

     By referring to **at least two** examples, analyse how the poet's use of language
     conveys the tragic situation of **both** the community and the pilot.   4

56. By referring to this extract and to at least one other poem by Paterson, discuss how
     the poet explores the impact of loss.   10

[END OF SECTION 1]

[Turn over

SECTION 2 — CRITICAL ESSAY — 20 marks

Attempt ONE question from the following genres — Drama, Prose Fiction, Prose Non-Fiction, Poetry, Film and Television Drama, or Language.

Your answer must be on a different genre from that chosen in Section 1.

You should spend approximately 45 minutes on this Section.

PART A — DRAMA

> *Answers to questions on Drama should refer to the text and to such relevant features as characterisation, key scene(s), structure, climax, theme, plot, conflict, setting . . .*

1. Choose a play in which a major character behaves in an impulsive **or** calculating **or** emotional manner.

   With reference to appropriate techniques, briefly explain the circumstances surrounding this behaviour and discuss how this behaviour adds to your understanding of the play as a whole.

2. Choose a play in which there is a scene which influences the course of future events.

   With reference to appropriate techniques, explain how the scene influences the course of events and discuss how it contributes to your appreciation of the text as a whole.

3. Choose a play which deals with the theme of honour **or** shame **or** betrayal.

   With reference to appropriate techniques, explain how the dramatist presents the theme and discuss why it is important to your understanding of the play as a whole.

PART B — PROSE FICTION

Answers to questions on Prose Fiction should refer to the text and to such relevant features as characterisation, setting, language, key incident(s), climax, turning point, plot, structure, narrative technique, theme, ideas, description . . .

4. Choose a novel **or** short story in which there is a character who experiences rejection **or** isolation.

   With reference to appropriate techniques, explain the rejection **or** isolation, and discuss how this aspect adds to your appreciation of the text as a whole.

5. Choose a novel **or** short story which has an effective opening **or** conclusion.

   With reference to appropriate techniques, explain why the opening **or** conclusion is effective and discuss how it adds to your appreciation of the text as a whole.

6. Choose a novel **or** short story which deals with the theme of love **or** loss **or** redemption.

   With reference to appropriate techniques, explain how the writer develops this theme, and discuss how it adds to your understanding of the text as a whole.

PART C — PROSE NON-FICTION

Answers to questions on Prose Non-Fiction should refer to the text and to such relevant features as ideas, use of evidence, stance, style, selection of material, narrative voice . . .

Non-fiction texts can include travel writing, journalism, autobiography, biography, essays . . .

7. Choose a non-fiction text in which the writer reports on aspects of war **or** injustice **or** human suffering.

   With reference to appropriate techniques, discuss how the writer engages your interest in these aspects of war **or** injustice **or** human suffering.

8. Choose a non-fiction text which gives you a detailed insight into a place **or** a person's life.

   With reference to appropriate techniques, discuss how the writer successfully engages your interest in the place **or** the person's life.

9. Choose a non-fiction text which makes effective use of humour to make a significant point.

   With reference to appropriate techniques, discuss how the writer uses humour to make the significant point.

PART D — POETRY

> *Answers to questions on Poetry should refer to the text and to such relevant features as word choice, tone, imagery, structure, content, rhythm, rhyme, theme, sounds, ideas . . .*

10. Choose a poem in which the poet challenges accepted beliefs **or** attitudes **or** conventions.

    With reference to appropriate techniques, discuss how the poet's challenge of these accepted beliefs **or** attitudes **or** conventions enhances your appreciation of the poem as a whole.

11. Choose a poem which deals with a powerful emotion.

    With reference to appropriate techniques, discuss how the poet's presentation of this powerful emotion enhances your appreciation of the poem as a whole.

12. Choose a poem which makes effective use of imagery **and/or** sound to convey central concern(s).

    With reference to appropriate techniques, discuss how the poet's use of imagery **and/or** sound contributes to the presentation of the poem's central concern(s).

PART E — FILM AND TELEVISION DRAMA

> *Answers to questions on Film and Television Drama* should refer to the text and to such relevant features as use of camera, key sequence, characterisation, mise-en-scène, editing, music/sound, special effects, plot, dialogue . . .*

13. ... sequence is particularly effective in

    ... w the film or programme makers

14. ... cter faces a significant moment of

    ... the film or programme makers

15. ... make an important contribution

    W... e special effects are used to
    en... a whole.

* "televi... ...es or a serial.

Handwritten note overlaid:

(10) Sailing to byzantium
(11) Sailing to byzantium
(12) Sailing to byzantium
The Second Coming
The Lake Isle of Innisfree
Long legged fly

PART F — LANGUAGE

Answers to questions on Language should refer to the text(s) and to such relevant features as register, accent, dialect, slang, jargon, vocabulary, tone, abbreviation . . .

16. Choose the language of newspaper reporting associated with sport **or** celebrity **or** crime **or** war **or** the environment.

    Identify the key language features and discuss the effectiveness of these features in communicating with the readership.

17. Choose the language of persuasion as used in the world of advertising **or** politics.

    Identify specific examples and discuss to what extent the language is effective.

18. Choose the language associated with a particular group in society which shares a common interest **or** work environment.

    Identify specific examples and discuss the advantages of these language features in aiding communication.

[END OF SECTION 2]

[END OF QUESTION PAPER]

[BLANK PAGE]

DO NOT WRITE ON THIS PAGE

HIGHER

2018

National
Qualifications
SPECIMEN ONLY

S824/76/11

**English
Reading for Understanding,
Analysis and Evaluation — Text**

Date — Not applicable

Duration — 1 hour 30 minutes

Total marks — 30

Read the passages carefully and then attempt ALL questions, which are printed on a separate sheet.

The following two passages focus on the importance of trees.

This Specimen Question Paper replaces the original RUAE section of the official SQA Past Paper 2018, which cannot be reproduced for copyright reasons. The Specimen Question Paper is set and verified by SQA and offers appropriate practice material for Higher English.

Passage 1

Read the passage below and then attempt questions 1 to 6.

In the first passage Janice Turner, writing in The Times newspaper, considers the value of trees.

Watching the tree surgeon from the window, I felt I was witnessing a crime. One I'd authorised, like a Mafia hit. The holm oak — a dense, virulent, evergreen ball — loomed over the garden like a storm cloud. It had to be cut back. But as the chainsaw whined and branches tumbled, I wondered if I really had the right.

5 I'm a resolute city-dweller, but trees seem ever more precious these days, a rebuke to built-in obsolescence, a steady point in a churning world. My pear and apple trees are remnants from when South London orchards ran all the way down to meet the sea. The walnut reaches out a mammoth limb from my neighbour's garden to mine like God's arm on the ceiling of the Sistine Chapel in Rome.

10 They are our living past, clocking up the years, ring by ring. Trees are calming like cathedrals, reassuring us that they will endure even though we will not. No wonder the ancients believed they were gods; there are worse things to worship than a tree.

And this week, reading how some protesters had been arrested trying to prevent ancient woodland being destroyed to make way for a three-mile link road to Hastings, I thought: yes, I'd 15 go to prison for a tree. Indeed, the protesters who are digging tunnels in the mud and standing before the diggers are not 'eco-warriors' or 'hippies'. Among them are young families, retired folk and ordinary dog-walkers. 'Local grandmothers', it was reported, came to swing in giant hammocks strung between the 400-year-old oaks.

But this is their last stand. They can only slow the developers. By March the trees will be felled. 20 Local people have fought for 20 years to save them, but they are on the wrong side of what the government is determined to market as progress, however short-term and dubious the economic benefits. The Chancellor of the Exchequer gave £56·8 million of government money for this very road, which will fill up with extra traffic, as new roads do, and lead in time to a spanking new industrial estate, although Hastings town already has plenty of boarded-up premises from which 25 to trade.

Development versus the trees. The government tells us that those who want to protect open countryside and woodland from being turned into endless Lego-brick estates are not conservationists, they are selfish, privileged people who, sitting comfortably in their own cheaply bought piles, have no care for struggling young couples who can't afford a family home. Anyway, 30 what's a bunch of trees?

But people with no respect for trees show a special kind of arrogance: they think they're bigger than history. I'd argue that cutting down an ancient oak is worse than killing most types of animal. Certainly the more numerous species such as dogs, cows, monkeys or cats. A chainsaw slicing into a 300-year-old trunk is more brutal and grotesque than hunting 100 foxes. Chopping down a fine 35 old tree is more like shooting an elephant or harpooning a whale: the aching poignancy of an enormous creature whose size and strength nonetheless cannot save it. Except even the mightiest mammal can be bred to maturity in a few years. Not so a tree.

Yet it is astonishing, given how much people love them — planting them to mark special moments or honour dead loved ones, measuring their lives by their seasonal changes — that officialdom 40 loathes trees. Insurance companies fretting about subsidence would rather you took them all down just in case. Councils detest them, employing municipal butchers to hack away at whole groves. Embarrassed stumps with a couple of twigs are all that remain.

It's a wonder any tree survives a health and safety audit. One city council tried to remove a whole row of horsechestnuts because conkers fell on cars and children might slip on leaves. Our local
45   primary school cut down a fine tree beneath which generations of children had played, because the new head deemed its twigs and leaves too messy. A posh gardener once suggested we cut down most of our trees and start again with fresh, more groovy varieties. This misunderstood the very point: trees are the antithesis of fickle fashion. But some crass homeowners can't bear the fluff-balls from plane trees messing up their hall carpet or the lime sap puking down on their
50   shiny car bonnets. Neater to reach for the axe. Maybe garden centres should start selling plastic ones: say goodbye to autumnal hell.

Visiting Burma, I learnt that its teak forests were flogged off to China by the generals, who were desperate for quick cash, like a beautiful girl being forced to sell her hair. Iceland is barren because Vikings cut them all down in a year and Peru is logging away its resources.

55   Our country's trees will tumble to make way for the machines of progress. But for how much economic growth is it worth mowing down a wood? Trees are beyond priceless: they are our history inscribed in the natural world. Which rich men, planting beautiful orchards to their own glorious memory, have always known.

Adapted from an article in The Times newspaper, January 2013.

Passage 2

Read the passage below and attempt question 7. While reading, you may wish to make notes on the main ideas and/or highlight key points in the passage.

In the second passage, the science writer Colin Tudge gives his own views on trees.

In New Zealand a few years ago I experienced more powerfully than ever the sheer gravitas of trees: in the presence of the world's largest kauri. Kauris are conifers, the biggest of their family. The great trunk of the kauri rises like a lighthouse out of the gloom: fifteen metres in circumference — it would touch all four walls in an average living room — and straight up,
5   leafless, for twenty metres or so. And then on its great horizontal boughs rests a virtual park, a floating island with an entire ecosystem of ferns and flowers. Kauris are about 2000 years old. For the first 1400 years of the kauri's life, moas strutted their stuff around its base. Moas included the world's tallest-ever birds, like giant emus, which were preyed upon by commensurately huge but
10   short-winged eagles. The moas and their attendant eagles are now long gone. The kauri lives on.

The remaining kauri forest has been horribly reduced these past two hundred years, but the way modern New Zealanders look after the trees that are left to them is a model for all the world. Rare trees are no longer felled but existing planks are prized and meticulously re-cycled. Meanwhile, you can follow slatted wooden paths among the vast conifers. That's conservation;
15   that's intelligent ecotourism.

Similarly, if new farming economies are to come about, then trees must be at the centre of them. Yet, tree-based farming systems have to fight for survival against the massed ranks of the powers-that-be. How ludicrous. The world's most powerful governments have made themselves answerable to the big companies — and they take pride in this. They call it 'realism'.

20   So although the things that need doing seem obvious, governments — and the big corporations whose interests they serve — have a quite different agenda. If we want life to be agreeable or indeed to continue at all we just have to ignore the pressures from our ostensible leaders, and do things the way they should be done: building new ways of life, whatever the pressures from on high. Again, trees show the way.

25   Outstanding among the world's many popular initiatives is the Greenbelt Movement, a campaign among Kenyan women to re-plant trees in places they used to grow. Now they have planted 30 million. They have transformed landscapes and changed entire economies and the whole tenor of life. This kind of thing, very simple, and achieved in the teeth of the modern economy (for who makes money out of it?), contributes far more to human wellbeing than, say, cheap white goods from China, on which the economy of the modern world, egged on by our world leaders, is being
30   built.

The broadest issue of all is the western conceit that we can 'conquer' nature, or indeed control it. This idea truly took off in the 19th century, and yet is taken still as a mark of modernity. In 1879 the poet Gerard Manley Hopkins lamented the felling of poplars: 'O if we but knew what we do/ When we delve or hew — Hack and rack the growing green!' We still don't know what we are
35   doing but the hacking and racking continue more vigorously than ever. The only halfway sane approach if we want this world to remain habitable, is to approach it humbly. Trees teach humility. We need to take the world far more seriously. It would be a good idea to begin with trees.

Adapted from an article published on Colin Tudge's website in 2005.

[END OF SPECIMEN TEXT]

National Qualifications
SPECIMEN ONLY

S824/76/21

English
Reading for Understanding,
Analysis and Evaluation — Questions

Date — Not applicable

Duration — 1 hour 30 minutes

Total mark — 30

Attempt ALL questions.

Write your answers clearly in the answer booklet provided. In the answer booklet, you must clearly identify the question number you are attempting.

Use **blue** or **black** ink.

Before leaving the examination room you must give your answer booklet to the Invigilator; if you do not, you may lose all the marks for this paper.

MARKS

Attempt ALL questions

Total marks — 30

1. Read lines 1—12.

    (a) From the first paragraph, identify **two** feelings the writer had as she watched the tree in her garden being cut back.   2

    (b) By referring to **at least two** examples, analyse how the writer uses language in lines 5—12 to emphasise the importance of trees.   4

2. Read lines 13—18.

    According to the writer, in what ways are the protesters different from how we might expect them to be?   2

3. Read lines 19—25.

    By referring to **at least two** features of language, analyse how the writer conveys her feelings of unhappiness about the Hastings development.   3

4. Read lines 26—37.

    (a) From lines 26—30 identify **two** claims the government makes about the protesters.   2

    (b) By referring to **at least two** features of language in lines 31—37, analyse how the writer conveys the strength of her belief in tree conservation.   4

5. Read lines 38—54.

    (a) Identify any **four** reasons given in these lines for cutting down trees. Use your own words as far as possible.   4

    (b) By referring to **at least one** example, analyse how the writer's use of imagery emphasises her opposition to cutting down trees.   2

6. Evaluate the final paragraph's effectiveness as a conclusion to the passage as a whole.   2

Question on both passages

7. Look at both passages.

    Both writers express their views about the importance of trees.

    Identify **three** key areas on which they agree. You should support the points by referring to important ideas in both passages.

    You may answer this question in continuous prose or in a series of developed bullet points.   5

[END OF SPECIMEN QUESTION PAPER]

National
Qualifications
2018

X724/76/12

English
Critical Reading

FRIDAY, 11 MAY
10:50 AM – 12:20 PM

Total marks — 40

SECTION 1 — Scottish Text — 20 marks

Read an extract from a Scottish text you have previously studied and attempt the questions.

Choose ONE text from either

Part A — Drama   Pages 2–7
or
Part B — Prose   Pages 8–17
or
Part C — Poetry   Pages 18–29

Attempt ALL the questions for your chosen text.

SECTION 2 — Critical Essay — 20 marks

Attempt ONE question from the following genres — Drama, Prose Fiction, Prose Non-Fiction, Poetry, Film and Television Drama, or Language.

Your answer must be on a different genre from that chosen in Section 1.

You should spend approximately 45 minutes on each Section.

Write your answers clearly in the answer booklet provided. In the answer booklet, you must clearly identify the question number you are attempting.

Use **blue** or **black** ink.

Before leaving the examination room you must give your answer booklet to the Invigilator; if you do not, you may lose all the marks for this paper.

SECTION 1 — SCOTTISH TEXT — 20 marks

Choose ONE text from Drama, Prose or Poetry.

Read the text extract carefully and then attempt ALL the questions for your chosen text.

You should spend about 45 minutes on this Section.

PART A — SCOTTISH TEXT — DRAMA

Text 1 — Drama

If you choose this text you may not attempt a question on Drama in Section 2.

Read the extract below and then attempt the following questions.

The Slab Boys by John Byrne

In this extract, from Act 1 of the play, Jack Hogg is showing Alan around and introducing him to colleagues.

	JACK:	This is the Slab Room, Alan . . . where the colours are ground and dished for the Designers . . . you saw the patterns out there. What the lads do, basically, is dole out a quantity of dry colour from those drums over there . . . Persian red, rose pink . . .
5	PHIL:	. . . bile green . . .
	SPANKY:	. . . acne yellow . . .
	JACK:	. . . dump it onto one of these marble slabs, add some gum arabic to prevent it flaking off the paper . . . do we have some gum arabic? Then it's just a matter of grinding . . . (*Demonstrates.*) Bit of a diff from the studio, eh?
10	SPANKY:	Why don't you vamoose, Jacky Boy?
	PHIL:	Yeh, Plooky Chops . . . them boils of yours is highly smittal.
	JACK:	I'm warning you, McCann . . .
	PHIL:	Keep away from me! Hector, fling us over the Dettol!
	JACK:	Jealousy will get you nowhere, McCann . . . just because I'm on a desk.
15	SPANKY:	It's a bloody operating table you want to be on, Jack. That face . . . yeugh.
	PHIL:	You can put in for plastic surgery, you know . . . on the National Health.
	SPANKY:	Or a 'pimplectomy' . . .
	PHIL:	It would only take about six months . . .
	SPANKY:	. . . and a team of surgeons . . .
20	PHIL:	. . . with pliers.
	JACK:	(*to Alan*) I've just got to dodge down the factory . . . have a look at a couple of 'trials' . . . shouldn't be too long. (*to Spanky and Phil*) The boss would like you to show Alan what goes on in here . . . in the way of work. (*to Alan*) Don't worry, you haven't been condemned to spend the rest of the day here . . . I'll
25		have a word with Bobby Sinclair the colour consultant. He could take you through the dyeing process . . .

Spanky collapses into Phil's arms.

See you shortly . . . (*Exits.*)

PHIL: Get a brush and some red paint, Heck.

30 HECTOR: What for?

SPANKY: To paint a cross on the door, stupid. To warn the villagers . . .

HECTOR: What villagers?

PHIL: (*to Alan*) Okay, son, what did you say your name was again?

ALAN: Alan . . . Alan Downie.

35 PHIL: Right, Eamonn . . . let's show you some of the mysteries of the Slab Room. Mr Farrell . . .

SPANKY: Mr Mac?

PHIL: I'm just showing young Dowdalls here some of the intricacies of our work. If you and the boy would care to stand to the one side . . .

40 SPANKY: Certainly. Hector . . .

PHIL: Many thanks. Right, Alec . . . this here is what we call a sink . . . s-i-n-k. Now I don't expect you to pick up all these terms immediately but you'll soon get the hang of it. And this — (*Grabs Hector.*) — is what we cry a Slab Boy . . .

SPANKY: You say it . . . Slab Boy . . .

45 PHIL: Note the keen eye . . . the firm set of the jaw . . .

SPANKY: They're forced up under cucumber frames . . .

MARKS

Questions

1. Look at lines 1–9.

    Analyse how language is used to convey the attitudes of both Jack **and** the slab boys (Phil and Spanky) to the work of the slab room.   2

2. Look at lines 10–26.

    By referring to **at least two** examples, analyse how language is used to convey the hostility felt by both Jack **and** the slab boys (Phil and Spanky) towards each other.   4

3. Look at lines 27–46.

    By referring to **at least two** examples, analyse how humour is used by the slab boys (Phil and Spanky).   4

4. By referring to this extract and to elsewhere in the play, discuss how Byrne explores attitudes to authority.   10

[Turn over

OR

Text 2 — Drama

If you choose this text you may not attempt a question on Drama in Section 2.

Read the extract below and then attempt the following questions.

The Cheviot, the Stag and the Black, Black Oil by John McGrath

In this extract, Loch and Sellar discuss aspects of Highland life and land ownership.

LOCH: The Marquis is not unaware of the responsibility his wealth places upon him, Mr. Sellar. The future and lasting interest and honour of his family, as well as their immediate income, must be kept in view.

     They freeze. A phrase on the fiddle. Two SPEAKERS *intervene between them, speak*
5   *quickly to the audience.*

SPEAKER 1: Their immediate income was over £120,000 per annum. In those days that was quite a lot of money.

SPEAKER 2: George Granville, Second Marquis of Stafford, inherited a huge estate in Yorkshire; he inherited another at Trentham in the Potteries; and he
10   inherited a third at Lilleshall in Shropshire, that had coal-mines on it.

SPEAKER 1: He also inherited the Bridgewater Canal. And, on Loch's advice, he bought a large slice of the Liverpool-Manchester Railway.

SPEAKER 2: From his wife, Elizabeth Gordon, Countess of Sutherland, he acquired three-quarters of a million acres of Sutherland — in which he wanted to invest some
15   capital.

     Another phrase on the fiddle: they slip away.

     SELLAR *and* LOCH *re-animate.*

SELLAR: The common people of Sutherland are a parcel of beggars with no stock, but cunning and lazy.

20 LOCH: They are living in a form of slavery to their own indolence. Nothing could be more at variance with the general interests of society and the individual happiness of the people themselves, than the present state of Highland manners and customs. To be happy, the people must be productive.

SELLAR: They require to be thoroughly brought to the coast, where industry will pay,
25   and to be convinced that they must worship industry or starve. The present enchantment which keeps them down must be broken.

LOCH: The coast of Sutherland abounds with many different kinds of fish. (LOCH *takes off his hat, and speaks directly to the audience.*) Believe it or not, Loch and Sellar actually used these words. (*Puts hat on again.*) Not only white fish,
30   but herring too. With this in mind, His Lordship is considering several sites for new villages on the East Coast — Culgower, Helmsdale, Golspie, Brora, Skelbo and Knockglass — Helmsdale in particular is a perfect natural harbour for a fishing station. And there is said to be coal at Brora.

SELLAR: You will really not find this estate pleasant or profitable until by draining to
35   your coast-line or by emigration you have got your mildewed districts cleared.

They are just in that state of society for a savage country, such as the woods of Upper Canada — His Lordship should consider seriously the possibility of subsidising their departures. They might even be inclined to carry a swarm of dependants with them.

40 LOCH: I gather you yourself Mr. Sellar, have a scheme for a sheep-walk in this area.

SELLAR: The highlands of Scotland may sell £200,000 worth of lean cattle this year. The same ground, under the Cheviot, may produce as much as £900,000 worth of fine wool. The effects of such arrangements in advancing this estate in wealth, civilisation, comfort, industry, virtue and happiness are palpable.

45 *Fiddle in — Tune, 'Bonnie Dundee', quietly behind.*

LOCH: Your offer for this area, Mr. Sellar, falls a little short of what I had hoped.

SELLAR: The present rents, when they can be collected, amount to no more than £142 per annum.

LOCH: Nevertheless, Mr. Sellar, His Lordship will have to remove these people at
50 considerable expense.

SELLAR: To restock the land with sheep will cost considerably more.

Questions

MARKS

5. Look at lines 1—15.

   By referring to **at least two** examples, analyse how language is used to convey both Loch's **and** the Speakers' views of the Marquis' situation.   4

6. Look at lines 18—26.

   Analyse how language is used to create a dismissive tone in these lines.   2

7. Look at lines 27—51.

   By referring to **at least two** examples, analyse how language is used to reveal the characters' apparently positive aims **and** their true attitudes.   4

8. By referring to this extract and to elsewhere in the play, discuss how McGrath uses unusual dramatic techniques to highlight central concerns.   10

[Turn over

OR

Text 3 — Drama

If you choose this text you may not attempt a question on Drama in Section 2.

Read the extract below and then attempt the following questions.

***Men Should Weep* by Ena Lamont Stewart**

This extract is from Act 2, Scene 2.

Alec and Isa are quarrelling in the bedroom: their raised voices are heard off

Isa comes out in a soiled, tawdry negligé with her hair about her shoulders, a cigarette hanging from her lip

ISA:	Aw shut up! I'm sick o yer jawin.

5   *Alec appears behind her, half dressed*

ALEC:	I'm tellin ye, Isa, I'll no staun much mair! I'm jist warnin ye. That's a.
ISA:	An I'm warnin you! If you think I'm gaun on like this a ma life, ye've anither think comin. You're no the only pebble on ma beach, no by a lang chalk. If you want tae keep me, it's time ye wis makin a bit o dough again. I canna live on air.
ALEC:	(*placating*) Come an we'll go tae the dugs the night, Isa; mebbe we'll hae a bit o luck.
ISA:	Aye. *Mebbe.*
ALEC:	Mind the last time I won — —
ISA:	Aye, an I mind the last hauf dizzen times ye lost . . . Whit did ye dae wi yon bag?
ALEC:	I flung it ower a wa.
ISA:	Ye stupid fool! I'm needin a bag.
ALEC:	It's no safe, Isa — ye've got tae get rid o the evidence — the Polis . . .
ISA:	Three quid and a handfu o coppers! A fat lot o use that is tae me. Why the Hell did ye no pick on a toff! We wis in the right district.
ALEC:	She looked like a toff; honest, Isa! She'd on a fur coat . . .
ISA:	Whit kind o fur? Rabbit? You're that dumb ye wouldnae ken. Next time, I'm no jookin up a lane, I'm stayin wi ye.
ALEC:	No ye're no! It's no safe. Ye've got tae be able tae rin fast.
ISA:	Rin! That's a you're guid for. Rinnin. It's aboot time I wis daein the rinnin. I'm sick fed up wi you. If I'd went wi Peter Robb I'd hae a fur coat an it wouldna be rabbit. An he's got a caur . . .
ALEC:	You say Peter Robb tae me again an I'll kill ye! I wull! I'll kill ye!

30   *He gets hold of her by the throat: she makes strangling noises. He panics and drops her*

ISA:	(*frightened first, then angry*) You . . . ! Ma Goad! (*Rubbing her throat*) You'll pey for that!

Page six

	ALEC:	Isa! Did I hurt ye? I didnae mean tae hurt ye — I lost ma heid.
	ISA:	Get oot! Clear aff oot o ma sight!
35	ALEC:	Isa, I'm sorry. I jist see red when ye talk aboot Peter Robb. I canna see naethin but him an you taegether an the way ye wis last night, cairryin oan wi him.
	ISA:	Aye! Ye can use yer hauns a right on a wumman; but if ye wis hauf a man, ye'd have kicked his teeth in last night.
	ALEC:	He's bigger nor me — he'd have hauf-killed me!
40	ISA:	Fancy me mairryin a rat like you. The joke wis on me a right.
	ALEC:	Isa, I'll hae plenty again, you'll see . . . I've a coupla pals that's got ideas . . . wait on, Isa! I'll get ye onythin ye want . . . a fur coat an crockydile shoes — ye said ye wanted crockydile shoes — I proamise, Isa! I proamise! If ye'll stay wi me . . . I love ye, Isa; honest, I dae. I love ye.
45	ISA:	*Love!* Hee-haw! There's nae sich a thing. There's wantin tae get intae bed wi someone ye fancy . . . or wantin someone'll let ye lie in yer bed an no have tae work; but there's nae love. No roon aboot here, onyway. Don't kid yersel.
50	ALEC:	(*trying to take her in his arms*) That's no true! I love ye. I'm no fit for onythin when ye're oot o ma sight. I'm . . . lost waitin on ye comin back. I get tae thinkin . . . an wonderin whaur ye are . . . and if — —
	ISA:	If I'm behavin masel? Well, hauf the time, I'm no.
	ALEC:	Isa!
55	ISA:	Aw shut up! (*She pushes him away*) Ye're aye wantin tae slobber ower me. If ye wis onythin decent tae look at it wouldna be sae bad, but ye're like somethin that's been left oot a night in the rain. G'on blow! I canna staun yer fumblin aboot — unless I'm canned. Get oot ma way. I'm gonnae get dressed.

She slams the bedroom door in his face

He stands looking at it

Questions

MARKS

9. Look at lines 1—28.

    By referring to **at least two** examples, analyse how language is used to convey Isa's attitude(s) towards Alec.   4

10. Look at lines 29—44.

    By referring to **at least two** examples, analyse how both dialogue **and** stage directions reveal the extreme nature of Alec's treatment of Isa.   4

11. Look at lines 45—58.

    Analyse how language is used to create a cynical tone in these lines.   2

12. By referring to this extract and to elsewhere in the play, discuss how Lamont Stewart explores the theme of love.   10

SECTION 1 — SCOTTISH TEXT — 20 marks

Choose ONE text from Drama, Prose or Poetry.

Read the text extract carefully and then attempt ALL the questions for your chosen text.

You should spend about 45 minutes on this Section.

PART B — SCOTTISH TEXT — PROSE

Text 1 — Prose

If you choose this text you may not attempt a question on Prose (Fiction or Non-Fiction) in Section 2.

Read the extract below and then attempt the following questions.

The Painter by Iain Crichton Smith

We felt a certain responsibility towards him also since he was sickly, and many maintained that he wouldn't live very long, as he was so clever. So our houses were decorated with his colourful paintings and if any stranger came to the village we always pointed to the paintings with great pride and mentioned the painter as one of our greatest assets. No
5 other village that we knew of had a painter at all, not even an adult painter, and we had a wonderful artist who was also very young. It is true that once or twice he made us uncomfortable for he insisted on painting things as they were, and he made our village less glamorous on the whole than we would have liked it to appear. Our houses weren't as narrow and crooked as he made them seem in his paintings, nor did our villagers look so
10 spindly and thin. Nor was our cemetery, for instance, so confused and weird. And certainly it wasn't in the centre of the village as he had placed it.

He was a strange boy, seeming much older than his years. He hardly ever spoke and not because there was anything wrong with him but because it seemed as if there was nothing much that he wished to say. He dressed in a very slapdash manner and often had holes in
15 the knees of his trousers, and paint all over his blouse. He would spend days trying to paint a particular house or old wall or the head of an old woman or old man. But as we had a lot of old people in the village, some who could play musical instruments — especially the melodeon — extremely well, he didn't stand out as a queer person. There is, however, one incident that I shall always remember.

20 Our village of course was not a wholly harmonious place. It had its share of barbarism and violence. Sometimes people quarrelled about land and much less often about women. Once there was a prolonged controversy about a right of way. But the incident I was talking about happened like this. There was in the village a man called Red Roderick who had got his name because of his red hair. As is often the case with men with red hair he was also a
25 man of fiery temper, as they say. He drank a lot and would often go uptown on Saturday nights and come home roaring drunk, and march about the village singing.

He was in fact a very good strong singer but less so when he was drunk. He spent most of his time either working on his croft or weaving in his shed and had a poor thin wife given to bouts of asthma whom he regularly beat up when it suited him and when he was in a
30 bad temper. His wife was the daughter of Big Angus who had been a famous fisherman in his youth but who had settled down to become a crofter and who was famed for his great strength though at this time he was getting old. In fact I suppose he must have been about

35 seventy years old. His daughter's name was Anna and during the course of most days she seemed to be baking a lot without much result. You would also find her quite often with a dripping plate and a soggy dishcloth in her hand. She had seven children all at various stages of random development and with running noses throughout both summer and winter.

40 It must be said that, when sober, Red Roderick was a very kind man, fond of his children and picking them up on his shoulders and showing them off to people and saying how much they weighed and how clever and strong they were, though in fact none of them was any of these things, for they were in fact skinny and underweight and tending to have blotches and spots on their faces and necks. In those moments he would say that he was content with his life and that no one had better children or better land than he had. When he was sunny-tempered he was the life and soul of the village and up to all sorts of

45 mischief, singing songs happily in a very loud and melodious voice which revealed great depth of feeling. That was why it seemed so strange when he got drunk. His whole character would change and he would grow violent and morose and snarl at anyone near him, especially the weakest and most inoffensive people.

MARKS

Questions

13. Look at lines 1—19.

By referring to **at least two** examples, analyse how language is used to convey the community's differing attitudes to the painter.   4

14. Look at lines 20—26.

Analyse how language is used to create an impression of the community in these lines.   2

15. Look at lines 27—48.

By referring to **at least two** examples, analyse how language is used to convey contrasting aspects of Red Roderick's character.   4

16. By referring to this extract and to at least one other short story, discuss how Crichton Smith explores the theme of isolation.   10

[Turn over

OR

Text 2 — Prose

If you choose this text you may not attempt a question on Prose (Fiction or Non-Fiction) in Section 2.

Read the extract below and then attempt the following questions.

The Bright Spade **by George Mackay Brown**

That winter the gravedigger was the busiest man in the island.

They got the thin harvest in and then the wind squatted in the east, a winter witch, and blew the island gray with her breath.

James of Moss died in the last week of October. Jacob dug his grave and got a bottle of
5   whisky for it from the widow of Moss. This death was not unexpected. James of Moss had been ill with dropsy all summer; he had clung to life like the last tattered leaf on a branch.

The gravedigger had hardly sobered up when he was called to the house of Maria of Graystones. There Maria lay as stiff and pale as a candle. He dug her grave near the wall of the kirk. Maria's nephew gave him a goose.

10   There was not much food in the island even at the beginning of winter, and the ale was sour and thin.

In early November the laird's youngest son was thrown from his horse at the bridge and broke his neck. 'This will need a deep grave,' said Jacob. He threw up many fine white bones, the laird's ancestors, with his spade. The laird gave him half a guinea, and a dram
15   both before and after the funeral.

Late November and early December brought death to Samuel Ling the fisherman, Jean the wife of Ebenezer of Ness, and the boy with the hare lip from the Quarry. They were all poor people and Jacob got nothing at all for his work but a box of coarse tobacco snuff from Ebenezer of Ness. 'I suppose I'll be glad of somebody to bury me when my time
20   comes,' said Jacob, and sneezed heroically for a month till the snuff was finished.

It was a hard winter, and nobody expected most of the old people and the sickly people to see the spring.

At harvest Kirstie had given birth to a daughter, just three months after she had married Amos of the Glebe. Kirstie and Amos raged at each other so much, both before and after
25   the birth, that there wasn't a bowl or a dish unbroken in the cupboard. In the season of snow and small fires the infant breathed her last; she died the week before Christmas. Jacob dug a small grave in the east corner of the kirkyard. He got a shilling from Kirstie and a pocket-full of potatoes from Amos. The day after the funeral Kirstie left Amos and went back to her parents' house. She never lived with Amos again.

30   The day after New Year a Dutch ship went ashore at the Red Head. Unfortunately the ship had no cargo; she was in ballast, bound for Labrador. Seven bodies were found on the shore next morning. The minister asked Jacob to dig one large grave for the foreigners.

'Who will pay my fee?' said Jacob.

'I don't know that,' said the minister, 'for the next-of-kin are in the Low Countries.'

35   In the end Jacob agreed to dig their grave for three spars of timber from the wrecked ship and half a barrel of oil out of the hold.

MARKS

Questions

17. Look at lines 1—11.

By referring to **at least two** examples, analyse how language is used to create a bleak atmosphere.

4

18. Look at lines 12—36.

By referring to **at least two** examples, analyse how language is used to explore the idea of death.

4

19. Look at the whole extract.

Analyse how language is used to convey **two** aspects of Jacob's character.

2

20. By referring to this extract and to at least one other short story, discuss how Mackay Brown uses characters as metaphorical and/or symbolic figures.

10

[Turn over

OR

Text 3 — Prose

If you choose this text you may not attempt a question on Prose (Fiction or Non-Fiction) in Section 2.

Read the extract below and then attempt the following questions.

The Trick Is To Keep Breathing by Janice Galloway

In this extract Joy receives a visit from the Health Visitor.

I rearrange things, placing chairs over the bald patches of the rug, sweeping the boards. It never looks as good as I'd like.

By twenty past I'm running along the twisty road between the houses to the shop for biscuits. She likes biscuits. I get different ones each time hoping they are something else
5 she will enjoy. I can't choose in a hurry. I can't be trusted with custard creams so deliberately don't get them. Chocolate digestives are too expensive. I wait for too long in the queue while a confused little kid tries to bargain for his father's cigarettes with the wrong money, so I have to run back clutching fig rolls and iced coffees and nearly drop the milk. I get flustered at these times, but I know I'll manage if I try harder. These visits are
10 good for me. Dr Stead sends this woman out of love. He insisted.

    I said, I'm no use with strangers.

    He said, But this is different. Health Visitors are trained to cope with that. He said she would know what to do; she would find me out and let me talk. *Make me* talk.

HAH

15 I'm putting on the kettle, still catching my breath when she comes in without knocking and frightens me. What if I had been saying things about her out loud? I tell her to sit in the livingroom so I can have time to think.

    Tray

          jug

20   sweeteners

                    plates

                         cups and saucers

                             another spoon

                                 christ

25 the biscuits

the biscuits

I burst the wrap soundlessly and make a tasteful arrangement. I polish her teaspoon on my cardigan band. No teapot. I make it in the cup, using the same bag twice, and take it through as though I've really made it in a pot and just poured it out. Some people are sniffy
30 about tea-bags. It sloshes when I reach to push my hair back from falling in my eyes and I suddenly notice I am still wearing my slippers dammit.

Never mind. She smiles and says

Well!

35 This is to make out the tea is a surprise though it isn't. She does it every time. We sit opposite each other because that's the way the chairs are. The chairs cough dust from under their sheets as she crosses her legs, thinking her way into the part. By the time she's ready to start I'm grinding my teeth back into the gum.

HEALTH VISITOR So, how are you/how's life/what's been happening/anything interesting to tell me/what's new?

40 PATIENT   Oh, fine/nothing to speak of.

I stir the tea repeatedly. She picks a piece of fluff off her skirt.

HEALTH VISITOR Work. How are things at work? Coping?

PATIENT   Fine. [Pause] I have trouble getting in on time, but getting better.

45 I throw her a little difficulty every so often so she feels I'm telling her the truth. I figure this will get rid of her quicker.

HEALTH VISITOR [Intensifying] But what about the day-to-day? How are you coping?

PATIENT   OK. [Brave smile] I manage.

HEALTH VISITOR The house is looking fine.

PATIENT   Thank-you. I do my best.

50 This is overdone. She flicks her eyes up to see and I lower mine. She reaches for a biscuit.

HEALTH VISITOR These look nice. I like a biscuit with a cup of tea.

We improvise about the biscuits for a while, her hat sliding back as she chews. She doesn't like the tea. Maybe she eats so many biscuits just to get rid of the taste.

HEALTH VISITOR Aren't you having one? They're very good.

55 PATIENT   No, thanks. Maybe later. Having lunch soon.

She goes on munching, knowing I don't want her to be here/that I do want her to be here but I can't talk to her.

MARKS

Questions

21. Look at lines 1—10.

    By referring to **at least two** examples, analyse how the writer's use of language creates a sense of tension before the visit.   3

22. Look at lines 11—33.

    By referring to **at least two** examples, analyse how the writer's use of language conveys Joy's anxiety about the visit.   3

23. Look at lines 34—57.

    By referring to **at least two** examples, analyse how the writer's use of language conveys the artificiality of the situation.   4

24. By referring to this extract and to elsewhere in the novel, discuss how Galloway explores Joy's difficulties with social interaction.   10

OR

Text 4 — Prose

If you choose this text you may not attempt a question on Prose (Fiction or Non-Fiction) in Section 2.

Read the extract below and then attempt the following questions.

Sunset Song by Lewis Grassic Gibbon

This extract is from Part IV (Harvest).

Different from the old Rob he looked, she thought, but thought that carelessly, hurried to be in to young Ewan. But she stopped and watched him swing down the rigs to Ewan by the side of his horses, Ewan with his horses halted on the side of the brae and the breath of them rising up like a steam. And she heard Ewan call *Ay, man, Rob,* and Rob call *Ay, man,*
5 *Ewan,* and they called the truth, they seemed fine men both against the horizon of Spring, their feet deep laired in the wet clay ground, brown and great, with their feet on the earth and the sky that waited behind. And Chris looked at them over-long, they glimmered to her eyes as though they had ceased to be there, mirages of men dreamt by a land grown desolate against its changing sky. And the Chris that had ruled those other two selves of
10 herself, content, unquestioning these many months now, shook her head and called herself daft.

That year's harvest fell sharp away, but the price of corn made up for it, other prices might rise but farming folk did well. So it went in the winter and into the next year too, Ewan took in a drove of Irish steers to eat up the lush green grass of nineteen-sixteen. They grew
15 fat and round in the shortest while, Chris proud to see them, so many beasts had Blawearie. You'd hardly believe 'twas here father had chaved and fought for a living the way he did; but that was before the War.

For it still went on, rumbling its rumours like the thunder of summer beyond the hills. But nobody knew now when it would finish, not even Chae Strachan come home, a soldier all
20 the way from the front, as they called it; in the orra-looking khaki he came, with two stripes sewn on his arm, he said they had made him a corporal. He came up to Blawearie the night he got home and scraped his feet on the scraper outside and came dandering into the kitchen as aye he had done, not knocking but crying through the door *Ay, folk, are you in?*

25 So there was Chae, Chris gave a loud gasp to see him, Chae himself, so altered you'd hardly believe it, Chae himself, thin, his fine eyes queered and strained somehow. Even his laugh seemed different, hearty as it was, and he cried *God, Chris, I'm not a ghost yet!* and syne Chris and Ewan were shaking his hands and sitting him down and pouring him a dram and another after that. And young Ewan came running to see and cried *soldier!* and Chae
30 caught him and swung him up from the floor and cried *Chris's bairn — God, it can't be, I mind the day he was born, just yesterday it was!*

Young Ewan took little to strangers, most, not frightened but keep-your-distance he was, but he made no try to keep distant from Chae, he sat on his knee as Chris spread them supper and Chae spoke up about things in the War, it wasn't so bad if it wasn't the lice. He
35 said they were awful, but Chris needn't be feared, he'd been made to stand out in the close by Kirsty and strip off everything he had on, and fling the clothes in a tub and syne get into another himself. So he was fell clean, and God! he found it a change not trying to reach up his shoulders to get at some devil fair sucking and sucking the life from his skin.

And he gave a great laugh when he told them that, his old laugh queerly crippled it was.
40 And Ewan asked what he thought of the Germans, were they truly coarse? And Chae said he
was damned if he knew, he'd hardly seen one alive, though a body or so you saw now and
then, gey green and *feuch! there's a supper on the table!* Well, out there you hardly did
fighting at all, you just lay about in those damned bit trenches and had a keek at the soil
they were made of. And man, it was funny land, clay and a kind of black marl, but the
45 French were no good as farmers at all, they just pleitered and pottered in little bit parks
that you'd hardly use as a hanky to wipe your neb.

MARKS

Questions

25. Look at lines 1—11.

By referring to **at least two** examples, analyse how the writer's use of language
creates a dreamlike atmosphere.   3

26. Look at lines 12—17.

By referring to **at least two** examples, analyse how the writer's use of language
creates a sense of prosperity.   3

27. Look at lines 25—46.

By referring to **at least two** examples, analyse how language is used to convey the
impact of the War on Chae.   4

28. By referring to this extract and to elsewhere in the novel, discuss how Grassic
Gibbon uses symbolism to explore the central concerns of the text.   10

[Turn over

OR

Text 5 — Prose

If you choose this text you may not attempt a question on Prose (Fiction or Non-Fiction) in Section 2.

Read the extract below and then attempt the following questions.

The Cone-Gatherers by Robin Jenkins

In this extract from chapter five, Duror's presence threatens the cone-gatherers.

In the tree here was Calum's happiness. Here were his friends the finches, safe from the hawk scouting above. The ground of snares and stumbles was far below. In the loch the seals were playing, with audible splashes. In a nearby Douglas fir cushat doves were crooning. Above all, his brother beside him was singing. So much present joy was there for
5   him he did not have to look forward. He did not wonder, as Neil sometimes did, whether the cones he was gathering would be fertile; nor did he see the great trees born from this seed in his hands being toppled down in fifty years' time to make ammunition boxes for that generation's war. He was as improvident as the finches to whom he had fed more than half of his morning slice of bread.

10   Yet it was he who first saw the gamekeeper approaching through the sunshine and shadow of the wood, with his three glossy dogs running silently in front. In agitation he stretched over to touch Neil, and point.

Neil paused in his singing and picking to watch Duror. The latter, he thought, must be on a patrol of the wood, looking for deer or foxes or weasels to shoot. Even if he saw their
15   ladder against the tree, and from it learned where they were, he would still pass by. While they were gathering cones, they were none of his business: his own mistress had given them permission.

'It's all right,' he murmured to Calum. 'He's got nothing to do with us. He'll pass by.'

Indeed, as he watched the gamekeeper now in and now out of sight on the dappled ground
20   among the trees, he felt the sympathy he could never withhold when he saw any human being alone in a vast place, on a hillside say, or here in a wood. Unlike his brother, he saw nature as essentially hostile; and its resources to take away a man's confidence were immense. He felt sure, for instance, that the gamekeeper treading on the withered leaves must be thinking of his sick wife.

25   In a clearing Duror halted, laid down his gun, took his binoculars out of their case, and trained them on the top of the larch.

Neil knew that they must be clearly visible; it seemed to him typical of nature that the foliage was gone which would have hidden them. It took an effort to go on picking cones. He told Calum to keep on picking too. He objected to this spying on them, but would not
30   show it even by stopping work.

Calum could not concentrate on the cones. He became like an animal in danger with no way of escape. He began to whimper, and tilting over in a panicky attempt to hide from that distant scrutiny he let some cones dribble out of his bag.

'What's the matter with you?' asked Neil. 'Aye, I ken he's looking at us. But where's the
35   harm in that? He's just doing his work, like you and me. Maybe he's not looking at us at all. Maybe it's that hawk we saw that he's looking at. Didn't I tell you, that if we keep out of his way, he can't harm us? Well, we're out of his way up here.'

Calum was not reassured; he still whimpered and cowered, like a dog in the presence of someone who has been cruel to it.

40 Neil's own fear suddenly increased. He became angry.

'What are you moaning for?' he demanded. 'I ken he doesn't like us, but we don't like him either. This wood doesn't belong to him; it belongs to the lady and she's given us permission to climb the trees and pick the cones. You heard Mr Tulloch say it. As long as we don't saw branches off and injure the trees, nobody would interfere with us, he said.
45 Have we ever sawn any branches off?'

He repeated that last question in a passion of resentment, for on most trees the best harvest of cones was on the tips of branches too far out from the trunk to be reached. If sawing was permitted, then those branches, so small as hardly to be noticed, could be dropped to the ground where it would be easy and safe to strip them of every cone. The
50 trees' wounds would soon heal, the yield of cones would be doubled, and the strain on arms, legs, and back would be greatly relieved.

'The trees are more precious than we are,' he added bitterly.

MARKS

Questions

29. Look at lines 1—9.

     Analyse how the writer's use of language conveys 'Calum's happiness'.   2

30. Look at lines 10—33.

     By referring to **at least two** examples, analyse how the writer's use of language conveys the impact of Duror's presence on both Calum **and** Neil.   4

31. Look at lines 34—52.

     By referring to **at least two** examples, analyse how the writer's use of language gives a clear impression of Neil's character.   4

32. By referring to this extract and to elsewhere in the novel, discuss how Jenkins explores the theme of power.   10

[Turn over

SECTION 1 — SCOTTISH TEXT — 20 marks

Choose ONE text from Drama, Prose or Poetry.

Read the text extract carefully and then attempt ALL the questions for your chosen text.

You should spend about 45 minutes on this Section.

PART C — SCOTTISH TEXT — POETRY

Text 1 — Poetry

If you choose this text you may not attempt a question on Poetry in Section 2.

Read the poem below and then attempt the following questions.

A Man's A Man For A' That by Robert Burns

Is there, for honest poverty
    That hangs his head, and a' that;
The coward slave, we pass him by,
    We dare be poor for a' that!
5 For a' that, and a' that,
    Our toils obscure, and a' that,
The rank is but the guinea's stamp,
    The Man's the gowd for a' that.

What though on hamely fare we dine,
10   Wear hoddin grey, and a' that;
Gie fools their silks, and knaves their wine,
    A man's a man for a' that!
For a' that, and a' that,
    Their tinsel show, and a' that;
15 The honest man, though e'er sae poor,
    Is king o' men for a' that!

Ye see yon birkie, ca'd a lord,
    Wha struts, and stares, and a' that;
Though hundreds worship at his word,
20   He's but a coof for a' that.
For a' that, and a' that,
    His riband, star, and a' that,
The man of independent mind
    He looks and laughs at a' that.

25 A king can mak a belted knight,
    A marquis, duke, and a' that;
But an honest man's aboon his might,
    Guid faith, he maunna fa' that!
For a' that, and a' that,
30   Their dignities, and a' that,
The pith o' sense, and pride o' worth,
    Are higher rank than a' that.

Then let us pray that come it may —
    As come it will for a' that —
35 That sense and worth, o'er a' the earth,
    May bear the gree, and a' that.
For a' that, and a' that,
    It's coming yet for a' that,
That man to man, the world o'er,
40   Shall brothers be for a' that!

MARKS

Questions

33. Look at lines 1—8.

    By referring to **at least two** examples, analyse how the poet's use of language conveys his views on poverty.   4

34. Look at lines 9—32.

    By referring to **at least two** examples, analyse how the poet's use of language conveys his contempt for wealth and/or status.   4

35. Look at lines 33—40.

    Analyse how the poet's use of language creates an inspirational tone.   2

36. By referring to this poem and to at least one other poem, discuss how Burns uses contrast to explore central concerns.   10

[Turn over

OR

Text 2 — Poetry

If you choose this text you may not attempt a question on Poetry in Section 2.

Read the poem below and then attempt the following questions.

Originally by Carol Ann Duffy

We came from our own country in a red room
which fell through the fields, our mother singing
our father's name to the turn of the wheels.
My brothers cried, one of them bawling, *Home,*
5 *Home*, as the miles rushed back to the city,
the street, the house, the vacant rooms
where we didn't live any more. I stared
at the eyes of a blind toy, holding its paw.

All childhood is an emigration. Some are slow,
10 leaving you standing, resigned, up an avenue
where no one you know stays. Others are sudden.
Your accent wrong. Corners, which seem familiar,
leading to unimagined pebble-dashed estates, big boys
eating worms and shouting words you don't understand.
15 My parents' anxiety stirred like a loose tooth
in my head. *I want our own country*, I said.

But then you forget, or don't recall, or change,
and, seeing your brother swallow a slug, feel only
a skelf of shame. I remember my tongue
20 shedding its skin like a snake, my voice
in the classroom sounding just like the rest. Do I only think
I lost a river, culture, speech, sense of first space
and the right place? Now, *Where do you come from?*
strangers ask. *Originally?* And I hesitate.

MARKS

Questions

37. Look at lines 1—8.

    Analyse how the poet uses language to convey the emotional impact of the journey on the speaker **and/or** her family.

    2

38. Look at lines 9—16.

    By referring to **at least two** examples, analyse how language is used to convey the speaker's alienation from her new surroundings.

    4

39. Look at lines 17—24.

    By referring to **at least two** examples, analyse how language is used to convey a sense of acceptance of the speaker's situation.

    4

40. By referring to this poem and at least one other by Duffy, discuss how the poet explores concerns about identity.

    10

[Turn over

OR

Text 3 — Poetry

If you choose this text you may not attempt a question on Poetry in Section 2.

Read the poem below and then attempt the following questions.

Some Old Photographs by Liz Lochhead

weather evocative as scent
the romance of dark stormclouds
in big skies over the low wide river
      of long shadows and longer shafts of light

5 of smoke
     fabulous film-noir stills of Central Station
of freezing fog silvering the chilled, stilled parks
    of the glamorous past
    where drops on a rainmate are sequins
10   in the lamplight, in the black-and-white

your young, still-lovely mother laughs, the
hem of her sundress whipped up
by a wind on a beach before you were even born

all the Dads in hats
15 are making for Central at five past five
in the snow, in the rain, in the sudden *what-a-scorcher*,
in the smog, their
belted dark overcoats white-spattered by the starlings

starlings swarming
20 in that perfect and permanent cloud
above what was
never really this photograph
but always all the passing now
and noise and stink and smoky breath of George Square

25 wee boays, a duchess, bunting, there's a
big launch on the Clyde
and that boat is yet to sail

MARKS

Questions

41.　Look at lines 1—10.

By referring to **at least two** examples, analyse how the poet's language conveys the enjoyment gained from looking at the photographs.

4

42.　Look at lines 11—18.

By referring to **at least two** examples, analyse how the poet's language creates a nostalgic mood.

4

43.　Look at lines 19—27.

Analyse how the poet's language challenges what is presented in the photographs.

2

44.　By referring to this poem and to at least one other poem, discuss how Lochhead explores important aspects of life through everyday objects **and/or** situations.

10

[Turn over

OR

Text 4 — Poetry

If you choose this text you may not attempt a question on Poetry in Section 2.

Read the poem below and then attempt the following questions.

***Sounds of the Day* by Norman MacCaig**

When a clatter came,
it was horses crossing the ford.
When the air creaked, it was
a lapwing seeing us off the premises
5 of its private marsh. A snuffling puff
ten yards from the boat was the tide blocking and
unblocking a hole in a rock.
When the black drums rolled, it was water
falling sixty feet into itself.

10 When the door
scraped shut, it was the end
of all the sounds there are.

You left me
beside the quietest fire in the world.

15 I thought I was hurt in my pride only,
forgetting that,
when you plunge your hand in freezing water,
you feel
a bangle of ice round your wrist
20 before the whole hand goes numb.

MARKS

Questions

45. Look at lines 1—9.

By referring to **at least two** examples, analyse how the poet uses language to build a sense of anticipation. 4

46. Look at lines 10—12.

Analyse how the poet's use of language creates a turning point. 2

47. Look at lines 13—20.

By referring to **at least two** examples, analyse how imagery **and/or** tone is used to convey the speaker's situation at this point. 4

48. By referring to this poem and to at least one other poem by MacCaig, discuss how relationships are used to develop key themes. 10

[Turn over

OR

Text 5 — Poetry

If you choose this text you may not attempt a question on Poetry in Section 2.

Read the extract below and then attempt the following questions.

Screapadal by Sorley MacLean

Screapadal in the morning
facing Applecross and the sun,
Screapadal that is so beautiful,
quite as beautiful as Hallaig.
5   No words can be put on beauty,
no picture, music or poem made for it.

Screapadal in May
when the young bracken is
but half a foot in height,
10   hardly above the grass.

Screapadal the sheep-pen and the cattle-fold
with walls to the south and west and north,
and to the east the sea-sound
over to the Sanctuary of Maol Rubha.

15   There is a half-dead memory of Maol Rubha
but only the dead written names
of the children, men and women
whom Rainy put off the land
between the north end of the Rock
20   and the Castle built for MacSwan
or for Mac Gille Chaluim
for violence and refuge.

Green, red-rocked and yellow
knolls to the horizon of the Carn Mor
25   in the west above the brae
coming down to green meadows,
and the pine wood dark and green
north right to the Castle
and the light-grey rocks beyond it.

30   And to the south the end of Creag Mheircil
hundreds of feet above the grass,
towers, columns and steeples
with speckled light-grey bands,
limestone whiteness in the sun.

35   A steep brae with scree-cairns
to the east down from the end of the Rock
under birch, rowan and alder,

and the Church of Falsehood in high water
when the spring tide is at its height.

40 It was not its lies that betrayed the people
in the time of the great pietist,
Rainy, who cleared
fourteen townships
in the Island of the Big Men,
45 Great Raasay of the MacLeods.

Rainy left Screapadal without people,
with no houses or cattle, only sheep,

MARKS

Questions

49. Look at lines 1—22.

    By referring to **at least two** examples, analyse how the poet's language conveys a contrast in atmosphere within these lines.   4

50. Look at lines 23—34.

    Analyse how the poet uses language to create a vivid sense of place.   2

51. Look at lines 35—47.

    By referring to **at least two** examples, analyse how the poet's language makes clear his sympathy for the people of Screapadal.   4

52. By referring to this extract and to at least one other poem by MacLean, discuss how he explores change in relation to people **and/or** places.   10

[Turn over

OR

Text 6 — Poetry

If you choose this text you may not attempt a question on Poetry in Section 2.

Read the poem below and then attempt the following questions.

The Ferryman's Arms **by Don Paterson**

About to sit down with my half-pint of Guinness
I was magnetized by a remote phosphorescence
and drawn, like a moth, to the darkened back room
where a pool-table hummed to itself in the corner.
5   With ten minutes to kill and the whole place deserted
I took myself on for the hell of it. Slotting
a coin in the tongue, I looked round for a cue —
while I stood with my back turned, the balls were deposited
with an abrupt intestinal rumble; a striplight
10 batted awake in its dusty green cowl.
When I set down the cue-ball inside the parched D
it clacked on the slate; the nap was so threadbare
I could screw back the globe, given somewhere to stand.
As physics itself becomes something negotiable
15 a rash of small miracles covers the shortfall.
I went on to make an immaculate clearance.
A low punch with a wee dab of side, and the black
did the vanishing trick while the white stopped
before gently rolling back as if nothing had happened,
20 shouldering its way through the unpotted colours.

The boat chugged up to the little stone jetty
without breaking the skin of the water, stretching,
as black as my stout, from somewhere unspeakable
to here, where the foaming lip mussitates endlessly,
25 trying, with a nutter's persistence, to read
and re-read the shoreline. I got aboard early,
remembering the ferry would leave on the hour
even for only my losing opponent;
but I left him there, stuck in his tent of light, sullenly
30 knocking the balls in, for practice, for next time.

MARKS

Questions

53. Look at lines 1—10.

    By referring to **at least two** examples, analyse how the poet's use of language conveys an unsettling atmosphere.   4

54. Look at lines 11—20.

    Analyse how the poet's use of language conveys the speaker's attitude at this point.   2

55. Look at lines 21—30.

    By referring to **at least two** examples, analyse how the poet uses imagery to convey the central concern(s).   4

56. By referring to this poem and to at least one other poem, discuss how Paterson explores the challenges of human experience.   10

[Turn over

[END OF SECTION 1]

SECTION 2 — CRITICAL ESSAY — 20 marks

Attempt ONE question from the following genres — Drama, Prose Fiction, Prose Non-Fiction, Poetry, Film and Television Drama, or Language.

Your answer must be on a different genre from that chosen in Section 1.

You should spend approximately 45 minutes on this Section.

PART A — DRAMA

*Answers to questions on **drama** should refer to the text and to such relevant features as characterisation, key scene(s), structure, climax, theme, plot, conflict, setting . . .*

1. Choose a play which focuses on a relationship which is destructive **or** is in crisis.

   By referring to appropriate techniques, explain the nature of the relationship and discuss how it contributes to your appreciation of the play as a whole.

2. Choose a play in which a character has a weakness **or** flaw.

   By referring to appropriate techniques, explain the importance of this weakness **or** flaw and discuss how it contributes to your appreciation of the play as a whole.

3. Choose a play which explores the theme of truth and lies, **or** good and evil, **or** appearance and reality.

   By referring to appropriate techniques, explain how the dramatist presents this theme and discuss how it contributes to your appreciation of the play as a whole.

PART B — PROSE FICTION

*Answers to questions on **prose fiction** should refer to the text and to such relevant features as characterisation, setting, language, key incidents(s), climax, turning point, plot, structure, narrative technique, theme, ideas, description . . .*

4. Choose a novel **or** short story in which there is a complex character for whom the reader has some sympathy.

    With reference to appropriate techniques, explain the nature of the complexity and discuss how your response to this character adds to your appreciation of the text as a whole.

5. Choose a novel **or** short story in which important human values are explored.

    With reference to appropriate techniques, explain how these values are explored and discuss how this adds to your appreciation of the text as a whole.

6. Choose a novel **or** short story in which the setting in time **and/or** place is important to your understanding of the text.

    By referring to appropriate techniques, explain the nature of the setting and discuss how it is important to your understanding of the text as a whole.

PART C — PROSE NON-FICTION

*Answers to questions on **prose non-fiction** should refer to the text and to such relevant features as ideas, use of evidence, stance, style, selection of material, narrative voice . . .*

7. Choose a non-fiction text which has an emotional **and/or** intellectual appeal for the reader.

    With reference to appropriate techniques, discuss how the writer has created this emotional **and/or** intellectual appeal.

8. Choose a non-fiction text which has made you think differently about an important moral **or** social issue.

    With reference to appropriate techniques, discuss how the writer has caused you to view the issue differently.

9. Choose a non-fiction text which provides fresh understanding of a group of people, **or** a way of life, **or** an important figure.

    With reference to appropriate techniques, discuss how the writer has provided this insight.

PART D — POETRY

Answers to questions on **poetry** should refer to the text and to such relevant features as word choice, tone, imagery, structure, content, rhythm, rhyme, theme, sounds, ideas . . .

10. Choose a poem which deals with an issue of importance to human experience.

    With reference to appropriate techniques, explain how the issue is presented and discuss how it enhances your appreciation of the poem.

11. Choose a poem which creates a mood of hope **or** despair **or** mystery.

    With reference to appropriate techniques, explain how the mood is created and discuss how it enhances your appreciation of the poem as a whole.

12. Choose a poem in which the ending is important in highlighting central concerns.

    With reference to appropriate techniques, explain how the ending highlights central concerns and discuss how it enhances your appreciation of the poem as a whole.

PART E — FILM AND TELEVISION DRAMA

Answers to questions on **film and television drama*** should refer to the text and to such relevant features as use of camera, key sequence, characterisation, mise-en-scène, editing, music/sound, special effects, plot, dialogue . . .

13. Choose a film **or** television drama in which there is a sequence which is particularly moving **or** humorous **or** shocking.

    With reference to appropriate techniques, discuss how the film or programme makers succeed in engaging the viewer's emotions or reactions.

14. Choose a film **or** television drama in which setting in time **and/or** place is important to the development of the central concerns.

    With reference to appropriate techniques, discuss how the setting in time **and/or** place enhances your appreciation of the film or television drama as a whole.

15. Choose a film **or** television drama in which the viewer feels engaged with a character who is flawed **or** vulnerable.

    With reference to appropriate techniques, discuss how the film or programme makers succeed in creating engagement with the character, and how this adds to your appreciation of the film or television drama as a whole.

* 'television drama' includes a single play, a series or a serial.

PART F — LANGUAGE

> *Answers to questions on **language** should refer to the text and to such relevant features as register, accent, dialect, slang, jargon, vocabulary, tone, abbreviation . . .*

16. Choose language which is intended to persuade you to buy products, **or** to agree with a particular point of view.

    Identify specific examples of language use, and discuss to what extent they are effective.

17. Choose the language associated with digital communications.

    Identify specific language features, and discuss their effectiveness as a means of communication.

18. Choose the spoken **or** written language typically used by a particular vocational **or** leisure group.

    Identify specific language features, and discuss their contribution to efficient communication within the group.

[END OF SECTION 2]

[END OF QUESTION PAPER]

[BLANK PAGE]

DO NOT WRITE ON THIS PAGE

HIGHER

Answers

PAPER 1 — READING FOR UNDERSTANDING, ANALYSIS AND EVALUATION

Marking Instructions for each question

Passage 1

Question		Expected Answer(s)	Max Mark	Additional Guidance
1.		For full marks there should be comments on at least two examples. Possible answers are shown in the "Additional Guidance" column.	2	Possible answers: • Emphatic/categorical nature of opening sentence conveys the topic in an unequivocal manner • "hugely important" conveys the gravity of the topic • Use of question/repeated use of questions invites the reader to think about the topic • Humorous tone created, e.g. mockery of their lack of basic political awareness • Use of stereotypical teenage concerns leads the reader to agree or disagree with the writer • Climactic nature of final sentence
2.	(a)	Candidates must attempt to use their own words. No marks for straight lifts from the passage. 2 marks may be awarded for detailed/insightful comment. 1 mark for more basic comment. Possible answers are shown in the "Additional Guidance" column.	2	Possible answers: Writer's viewpoint: • Assumption that today's teenagers will be just like her generation ("my younger self") • No idea how to make important decisions/lack of awareness or knowledge ("clueless") • Preoccupied with relationships with contemporaries ("increased obsession with their peer group") • Distracted/influenced by technology ("unpatrolled access to social media", "constant barrage of entertainment") Scientific research: • The teenage brain is not fully formed ("undeveloped teenage brain") • (Inadequate frontal lobes means) higher order thinking/judgements are challenging for teenagers ("think in the abstract...impulses") • Teenagers' inability to make personal choices precludes them from influencing issues affecting other people ("life-changing decisions for themselves")
	(b)	For full marks there should be comments on at least two examples. 2 marks may be awarded for detailed/insightful comment plus quotation/reference. 1 mark for more basic comment plus quotation/ reference. 0 marks for quotation/reference alone. Possible answers are shown in the "Additional Guidance" column.	4	Possible answers: • The delaying of the final clause of the first sentence ("when I would have agreed .... status quo") suggests the plausibility of the case against lowering the voting age • "clueless" suggests an inability to make responsible decisions • "(increased) obsession" suggests an irrational fixation with social standing • "unpatrolled" suggests the potential damage of unlimited access/malign influence of social media on young people • "constant" suggests the unremitting distraction of media products • "barrage", an intense military bombardment, suggests the destructive influence of the media • The list "social media... entertainment" suggests range of lifestyle features on which they place greater importance

Question		Expected Answer(s)	Max Mark	Additional Guidance
2.	(b)	*(continued)*		• "disengagement" suggests an apathetic attitude towards politics • "smartphone-fixated" suggests the supposedly trivial/self-absorbed nature of the teenagers' concerns • "undeveloped" suggests that the brain is not fully functioning/is not capable of fully undertaking a task • The list "enables us to think in the abstract … control our impulses" suggests the seeming amount/variety of mental processes teenagers can't properly engage in
3.		2 marks may be awarded for detailed/insightful comment. 1 mark for more basic comment. Possible answers are shown in the "Additional Guidance" column.	2	Possible answers: The example of Malala's achievements at such a young age is used to show that young people should be allowed to vote/challenge the view that young people are too irrational or immature. Someone with Malala's qualities could not vote in the UK elections merely because of age shows how ridiculous the age restriction is/adults with ridiculous views can vote, yet someone like Malala would not be allowed to. Candidates could approach this question in a number of ways (e.g. Malala reference acts as a link between negative views of young people and more positive views).
4.		For full marks, candidates must deal with both word choice and sentence structure, but not necessarily in equal measure. 2 marks may be awarded for detailed/insightful comment plus quotation/reference. 1 mark for more basic comment plus quotation/reference. 0 marks for quotation/reference alone. Possible answers are shown in the "Additional Guidance" column.	4	Possible answers: Word choice: • "scarcely (exempt)" suggests a scathing condemnation of adult failings • "limited brain power/inadequately brained" suggests adults' lack of intelligence • "incivility" suggests the rude behaviour exhibited by adults • "tantrums" suggests immature outbursts of temper • "profanity" suggests the offensive nature of the language used by adults • "prejudice" suggests the intolerance displayed by adults • "time-wasting" suggests a lack of commitment/ desire to shirk work • "unedifying" suggests setting a poor example • "illiterate" suggests lack of sophistication in opinion • "non-taxpaying" suggests devious, unwilling to accept civic responsibilities • "ignorant" suggests ill-mannered/lack of awareness Sentence structure: • Parenthesis "as politicians must hope" emphasises/ isolates the writer's point about political hypocrisy • List "incivility, tantrums, …. tabloid websites" emphasises the variety/scale of the unacceptable behaviour exhibited by adults (a comment on the anti-climactic nature of the list, introducing a mocking tone is also possible) • Parallel sentence structure of the lists "sport, music, creating computer software" and "incivility, tantrums, … tabloid websites" to emphasise the negative behaviour of adults in comparison to teenagers

Question	Expected Answer(s)	Max Mark	Additional Guidance
4.	*(continued)*		• Parallel sentence structure of the lists "incivility, tantrums, … tabloid websites" and "inadequately brained, illiterate, non-taxpaying or ignorant" to reinforce the negative behaviour exhibited by adults • Climactic nature of final sentence culminating in condemnatory use of "chilling"
5.	2 marks may be awarded for detailed/ insightful comment. 1 mark for more basic comment. Possible answers are shown in the "Additional Guidance" column.	3	Possible answers: • From their earliest years they have been exposed to technological advances • They have the capacity to absorb a variety of sources to establish their own outlook on important issues • They have enough knowledge of how the media works not to be taken in by those who try to deceive them
6.	For full marks there should be comments on at least two examples. 2 marks may be awarded for detailed/ insightful comment plus quotation/reference. 1 mark for more basic comment plus quotation/reference. 0 marks for quotation/reference alone. Possible answers are shown in the "Additional Guidance" column.		Possible answers: • Sequence "No … Yes … But" builds to climactic turnaround emphasising the positive qualities of teenagers • Positioning of "But" in the paragraph/sentence to indicate change to positive view of teenagers • Parenthesis of "idealism … open-mindedness" to identify/clarify the "more loveable teenage qualities" • List of "loveable teenage qualities" to emphasise the scale/variety of qualities • "idealism" suggests lack of cynicism/belief in making the world a better place • "energy" suggests passion and commitment to making a difference • "sense of injustice" suggests their desire to right wrongs in the world • "open-mindedness" suggests their tolerance and lack of prejudice • "starved" suggests that at the moment politics is in dire need of/sorely lacks/is deprived of the positive qualities young people exhibit • "inject some life" suggests the rejuvenating effect of young people on political debate OR the sudden force/strength/impact of their introduction into political debate
7.	For full marks candidates must deal with both tone and contrast, but not necessarily in equal measure. 2 marks may be awarded for detailed/ insightful comment plus quotation/reference. 1 mark for more basic comment plus quotation/reference. 0 marks for quotation/reference alone. Possible answers are shown in the "Additional Guidance" column.	4	Possible answers: Tone: • Conversational tone of "Naturally" suggests shared understanding between writer and reader about validity of teenage concerns • Tongue-in-cheek tone. "If voting has to be rationed …" Writer uses humour to approach the topic in a subversive manner • Ironic tone of "only have a year to wait" builds on previous examples of irony e.g. the reference to "epistocracy"/the irony of the powers of old and teenage voters, to mock the opposing viewpoint • Blunt, matter-of-fact tone of "We could compromise" suggests the initial plausibility of this solution • Incredulous tone created by listing the responsibilities currently conferred ("after they have already married … fight for their country") highlights the absurdity/inconsistencies of current policy • Scathing tone of "believe they know so much better" underlines the arrogance of adults

Question	Expected Answer(s)	Max Mark	Additional Guidance
7.	*(continued)*		• Sarcasm/mockery of the final sentence ("doing our young people a great big favour") to suggest the absurdity of not recognising a teenager's right to vote Contrast: • Development of old vs young argument — old allowed to vote but not around to live with the consequences, young not allowed to vote but have to live with the consequences • List of fairly trivial things ("fireworks") contrasted with life-changing decisions ("donated an organ") — stresses random/illogical nature of what people are and are not allowed to do • Final sentence emphasises the contrast between adults who consider themselves superior set against the young people whose rights are being denied

Passage 2

Question	Expected Answer(s)	Max Mark	Additional Guidance
8.	Candidates can use bullet points in this final question, or write a number of linked statements. Key areas of disagreement are shown in the grid. Possible answers are shown in the "Additional Guidance" column.	5	The following guidelines should be used: 5 marks — identification of three key areas of disagreement with detailed/insightful use of supporting evidence 4 marks — identification of three key areas of disagreement with appropriate use of supporting evidence 3 marks — identification of three key areas of disagreement 2 marks — identification of two key areas of disagreement 1 mark — identification of one key area of disagreement 0 marks — failure to identify any key areas of disagreement and/or misunderstanding of the task **NB** A candidate who identifies only two key areas of disagreement may be awarded up to a maximum of 4 marks, as follows: • 2 marks for identification of two key areas of disagreement **plus** **either** • a further mark for appropriate use of supporting evidence to a total of 3 marks **or** • a further 2 marks for detailed/insightful use of supporting evidence to a total of 4 marks A candidate who identifies only one key area of disagreement may be awarded up to a maximum of 2 marks, as follows: • 1 mark for identification of one key area of disagreement • a further mark for use of supporting evidence to a total of 2 marks

	Areas of Disagreement	Passage 1	Passage 2
1.	Intellectual ability	Teenagers are capable of intellectual maturity, for example reference to Malala	Young people may have political knowledge but not the intellectual development of an adult, for example the writer refers to her daughter
2.	Areas of political debate	Teenagers would focus on issues of relevance to them like student debt, minimum wage	Debate will continue to focus on traditional areas of concern like the economy and the NHS
3.	Independence of thought	As part of iGeneration, they have developed an independent political stance	Influenced by parents to turn out to vote
4.	Response to manipulation	Too media aware to be taken in by politicians/spin doctors	Susceptible to media manipulation by cynical politicians
5.	Commitment	Potential to sustain long term commitment to political issues, for example the environment	Give up on voting very quickly
6.	Responsibilities/rights	Teenagers already have a large number of rights/responsibilities and therefore should be allowed to vote	Teenagers have a limited number of rights/responsibilities and therefore should not be allowed to vote
7.	Impact of teenage voters	Teenager voters would invigorate/energise political life	Teenage voters would be detrimental/would make no difference to the political process

PAPER 2 — CRITICAL READING

SECTION 1 — Scottish Text

For all Scottish Texts, marking of the final question, for 10 marks, should be guided by the following generic instruction in conjunction with the specific advice given for the question on each Scottish Text:

Candidates can answer in bullet points in this final question, or write a number of linked statements.

0 marks for reference/quotation alone.

Up to 2 marks can be achieved for identifying elements of commonality as identified in the question.

A further 2 marks can be achieved for reference to the extract given.

6 additional marks can be awarded for discussion of similar references to at least one other part of the text (or other story or poem) by the writer.

In practice this means:

Identification of commonality (2) (e.g.: theme, characterisation, use of imagery, setting, or any other key element …)

From the extract:

1 × relevant reference to technique/idea/feature (1)
1 × appropriate comment (1)
(maximum of 2 marks only for discussion of extract)

From at least one other text/part of the text:

2 marks for detailed/insightful comment plus quotation/reference

1 mark for more basic comment plus quotation/reference

0 marks for quotation/reference alone

(Up to 6 marks).

Detailed Marking Instructions for each question

SECTION 1 — Scottish Text

PART A — SCOTTISH TEXT — DRAMA

Text 1 — *Drama* — *The Slab Boys* by John Byrne

Question	Expected Answer(s)	Max Mark	Additional Guidance
1.	2 marks may be awarded for detailed/ insightful comment plus quotation/reference. 1 mark for more basic comment plus quotation/reference. 0 marks for quotation/reference alone.	2	Possible answers include: • Challenging/obstructive: "What're you wanting him for?" • Assertive: repetition of "I'll take it." • Taking control away from Jack: "That's all right. I'll take it." • Defiant: "I'll take it, I said."/"I'm authorised!" • No respect for Jack/ignoring him shown by *"(Exits.)"* to take the call when Jack has said not to
2.	2 marks may be awarded for detailed/ insightful comment plus quotation/reference. 1 mark for more basic comment plus quotation/reference. 0 marks for quotation/reference alone.	4	Possible answers include: • Sadie's incongruous casting of herself as a martyr: "Too bloody soft, that's my trouble..." • Incongruity of reference to casters instead of feet. • Lucille's shocked overreaction to finding Sadie in the slab room: "Waaaahh! God!" • Play on word "shy": Sadie means "fifteen bob shy" whereas Lucille thinks she means lacking in confidence (opposite of what Spanky is) • Ludicrousness of description of Sadie's husband's antics at last year's dance — "leapfrogging over ... beehive hairdo" • Juxtaposition of Lucille's question about leg injury sustained during this behaviour
3.	For full marks both Sadie and Lucille should be covered but not necessarily in equal measure. 2 marks may be awarded for detailed/ insightful comment plus quotation/reference. 1 mark for more basic comment plus quotation/reference. 0 marks for quotation/reference alone.	4	Possible answers include: Sadie: • Critical of men/contemptuous/thinks they are useless: reference to negative connotations of "real rubbish" and "dross" • Impossibility of finding a decent man: anti-climactic effect of "sift through the dross ... real rubbish" • Blames her choice of husband for her disappointment with life: dismissive tone of "all you've got to show's bad feet and a display cabinet" Lucille: • She is confident in her own chance of finding a better man than Sadie's: powerful rebuttal of Sadie's viewpoint of men "They're not all like that, for God's sake" • Determined not to define herself by choice of man: confident assertion of "Not this cookie, Lucille Bentley ... Woman of the World"
4.	Candidates can answer in bullet points in this final question, or write a number of linked statements.	10	Up to 2 marks can be achieved for identifying elements of commonality as identified in the question, i.e. the role of women. A further 2 marks can be achieved for reference to the extract given. 6 additional marks can be awarded for discussion of similar references to at least one other part of the text by the writer. <u>In practice this means:</u> Identification of commonality (2) E.g. play is mainly about men/the male experience of work/thwarted ambition (1) but women important in terms of what they represent/the relationships they offer to the men (1)

Question	Expected Answer(s)	Max Mark	Additional Guidance
4.	*(continued)*		From the extract:
			2 marks for detailed/insightful comment plus quotation/reference;
			1 mark for more basic comment plus quotation/reference;
			0 marks for quotation/reference alone;
			Maximum of 2 marks only for discussion of extract.
			E.g. Lucille represents the confident young woman who sees herself as independent/equal to any man and does not need to validate herself through a relationship **(2)**
			From at least one other part of the text:
			as above for up to 6 marks
			Possible references include:
			• Lucille "every slab boy's dream" — she is seen as a traditional representation of femininity/objectified in terms of her desirability **(2)**
			• Phil's mother — source of worry for Phil/reverse of the nurturing role of mother, e.g. his story about her breakdown and its impact on him **(2)**
			• Lucille provides the motivation/cause of the extreme mockery of Hector: he is dressed up ridiculously to impress her **(2)**
			• Sadie's role as "surrogate mother" providing food (tea trolley cakes) and nagging the slab boys to behave properly **(2)**
			• Sadie is represented as a clichéd/stock female character in a male-dominated world, providing humour in the play on the receiving end of Phil and Spanky's banter/scene where she hits Phil on the head **(2)**

Text 2 — *Drama — The Cheviot, the Stag and the Black, Black Oil* by John McGrath

Question	Expected Answer(s)	Max Mark	Additional Guidance
5.		2	Possible answers include:
			Tone:
			• Astonishment
			• Incredulity
			• Outrage
			Analysis:
			• Dismissive nature of "Re" contrasts with the serious nature of the accusation
			• Repeated use of questions suggests inability to believe they could think this of him
			• "Can you believe" emphasises the unlikely nature of the accusation
			• Repetition of "no" emphasises the obvious lack of motivation
6.	2 marks are awarded for detailed/insightful comment plus quotation/reference.	4	Possible answers include:
	1 mark for more basic comment plus quotation/reference.		Language:
	0 marks for quotation/ref alone.		• Use of "Therefore" implies unquestioning acceptance of Sellar's defence
			• Understatement of the crimes with language such as "ignored a custom"
			• Directing the jury with phrases such as "I would ask them ..."
			• Using language which suggests the crime — damaged property ("barns" and "the burning of the house of Chisholm") — whilst ignoring the deaths of the tenants

Question	Expected Answer(s)	Max Mark	Additional Guidance
6.	*(continued)*		• "contradictory nature" contrasts with "real evidence" suggesting that the judge gives greater credence to evidence which defends Sellar • Use of "And … And …" suggests an accumulation of evidence for Sellar's defence • He directs the jury to ignore contradictory evidence and focus on character assessment with references to the accused "humanity" and being "in all cases … most humane" • The inappropriately friendly greeting, "hello, Archie" suggests he is complicit in Sellar's defence
7.	2 marks are awarded for detailed/insightful comment plus quotation/reference. 1 mark for more basic comment plus quotation/reference. 0 marks for quotation/ref alone.	4	Possible answers include: • "Every reformer of mankind" suggests he/those he works for are bringing about grand-scale improvement as many others have before • "errors, frauds and quackery" suggests that he dismisses the opposition as duplicitous and mistaken: • "at bottom" suggests the fundamental truth/ rightness of what the reformers are doing • "patience" suggests resilience and commitment in the face of adversity • His references to "zeal and enthusiasm" present the reformers as being motivated, committed and dynamic • "generous" suggests reformers are selflessly working for the good of mankind • "exertions" suggests the tireless efforts to make improvements • "public yet unostentatious" suggests generosity combined with modesty • "distresses of the widow, the sick and the traveller" list of clichéd examples of needy people to emphasise Sutherland's wide-ranging philanthropic role
8.	Candidates may choose to answer in bullet points in this final question, or write a number of linked statements.	10	Up to 2 marks can be achieved for identifying elements of commonality as identified in the question, i.e. McGrath's presentation of authority A further 2 marks can be achieved for reference to the extract given. 6 additional marks can be awarded for discussion of similar references to at least one other part of the text by the writer. In practice this means: Identification of commonality **(2)** E.g. the self-seeking nature of authority in a variety of guises **(1)** Their cruel treatment of the people over whom they should exercise stewardship **(1)** From the extract: 2 marks for detailed/insightful comment plus quotation/reference; 1 mark for more basic comment plus quotation/ reference; 0 marks for quotation/reference alone. Maximum of 2 marks only for discussion of extract. E.g. The judge's involvement with the defence illustrates collusion within the establishment **(2)** Sellar's speech shows hypocrisy by presenting the inhumane actions of Lord and Lady Stafford in a positive light **(2)**

Question	Expected Answer(s)	Max Mark	Additional Guidance
8.	*(continued)*		From elsewhere in the text: as above for up to 6 marks Possible answers include: • List of Sutherland's estates, properties and sources of wealth, e.g. "huge estate in Yorkshire", "a large slice of the Liverpool-Manchester Railway" suggests his self- serving, selfish and materialistic view of his privileges as a lord **(2)** • Hypocrisy of Sellar and Loch in lamenting the problems of the lifestyle of the crofters as an excuse to remove them and exploit the land they live on **(2)** • Cruelty and violence towards vulnerable crofters shown in example of old woman and her grandchildren forced to live in an exposed sheep-cot when their home was seized **(2)** • Sinister behaviour of Lord Crask and Lady Phosphate turning guns on audience to show threat their kind pose "We'll show you we're the ruling class" **(2)** • Sutherland's attempts to manipulate the people into enlisting suggests that they are seen as a resource to be exploited, not people to be respected **(2)**

Text 3 — *Drama — Men Should Weep* by Ena Lamont Stewart

Question	Expected Answer(s)	Max Mark	Additional Guidance
9.	For full marks, both relationships should be covered but not necessarily in equal measure. 2 marks awarded for detailed/insightful comment plus quotation/reference. 1 mark for a more basic comment plus quotation/reference. 0 marks for quotation/reference alone.	4	Possible answers include: Relationship with Maggie: • "…gives Maggie a pat" — gesture suggests an easy intimacy between them • "they exchange warm smiles" — suggests their affection is mutual, natural, spontaneous • "Ye dry, John? I'll pit the kettle on." — suggests Maggie anticipates his needs and wants to care for him • "He didna mean onythin." — Maggie's assertion is an attempt to justify his behaviour, to keep the peace with Lily Relationship with Lily: • "turning to Lily" — lack of respect shown by the fact John only acknowledges Lily after being in the room some time • "with as much of a smile as he can muster" — suggests being polite to Lily requires considerable effort on his part, is not natural or easy • "An how's Lil?" — suggests deliberate provocation by using a form of her name he knows she dislikes • "Don't you two stert up!" — Maggie's remark shows an awareness of repeated confrontations between John and Lily/highlights childish nature of John's behaviour towards Lily • "Goad help us!" — John finds Lily's constant criticism and undermining of him tiresome/irritating/exasperating

Question	Expected Answer(s)	Max Mark	Additional Guidance
10.	For full marks both Lily and Maggie should be covered, though not necessarily in equal measure. 2 marks awarded for detailed/insightful comment plus quotation/reference. 1 mark for a more basic comment plus quotation/reference. 0 marks for quotation/reference alone.	4	Possible answers: Lily: • Ridicules him by presenting an idealised vision of the domestic world he believes men would create. "if you was a wumman"/"everythin just perfect"/"the weans a washed and pit tae bed at six"/"everythin' spick an span"/"naethin tae dae till bedtime but twiddle yer thumbs" • Points out the impracticalities of his ideas in the face of the reality of the demands placed on Maggie every day "hoose-fu o weans"/"and a done aul granny tae look after." • Emphatic nature of "And ony wumman'll tell ye" undermines his status as a man Maggie: • Mocks his ability to do anything useful around the house despite his claims that he could organise things more efficiently. "Ye should see him tryin tae mak the breakfast on a Sunday; ye'd get yer kill." • Highlights his inability to multi-task when he actually tries to do household chores. "If he's fryin bacon, he's fryin bacon, see? ... intae the pan a at the same time." Lily and Maggie • Mock John, showing how silly they think his ideas are by throwing his words back at him in unison. "He'd hae a system!"
11.		2	Possible answers include: • Lily is annoyed by John's insinuation that she is expecting the Morrisons to feed her • She feels a lack of appreciation for the fact that she often provides the family with food/has brought the tin of beans • She is annoyed by John's suggestion that she would chase after a man if she had the opportunity • She is annoyed at their ingratitude in the light of the fact that (their son) Alec still owes her money
12.	Candidates may choose to answer in bullet points in this final question, or write a number of linked statements.	10	Up to 2 marks can be achieved for identifying elements of commonality as identified in the question, i.e. John's role within the family. A further 2 marks can be achieved for reference to the extract given. 6 additional marks can be awarded for discussion of similar references to at least one other part of the text by the writer. In practice this means: Identification of commonality **(2)** E.g. John conforms to assumptions about the male role within the family **(1)** however he often does not fulfil this traditional role and feels frustrated/despondent as a result **(1)** From the extract: 2 marks for detailed/insightful comment plus quotation/reference; 1 mark for more basic comment plus quotation/reference; 0 marks for quotation alone. Maximum of 2 marks only for discussion of extract

Question	Expected Answer(s)	Max Mark	Additional Guidance
12.	*(continued)*		E.g. John's obvious consideration for Maggie does not stop him from accepting her assumption that she should make him tea when he comes in, although she is exhausted **(2)**
			From elsewhere in the text:
			as above for up to 6 marks
			Possible answers include:
			• John's willingness to share in Maggie's household duties is very limited/he sees domestic work as very much the preserve of women Maggie: "Ye couldna even wash up a dish for me!"
			• John sees his role as father of Jenny is to protect her and be respected shown by his anger when she is out in the close with a man
			• He feels ashamed of his inability to provide for the family "Ye end up a bent back and a heid hanging wi shame for whit ye canna help."
			• He responds to Isa's flirtation/criticism of Maggie even though this is a betrayal of his wife for feelings which are much more superficial
			• He is proud and happy when he is able to provide for the family, in the traditional male role for example the Christmas present of the red hat for Maggie in Act 3 - a reminder of their "courting" days

PART B – SCOTTISH TEXT – PROSE

Text 4 – *Prose – The Crater* by Iain Crichton Smith

Question	Expected Answer(s)	Max Mark	Additional Guidance
13.	2 marks awarded for detailed/insightful comment plus quotation/reference. 1 mark for more basic comment plus quotation/reference. 0 marks for quotation/reference alone.	2	Possible answers include: • Repetition of questions suggests his nervousness/confusion/frustration at a situation he cannot control • "We're like a bunch of actors" – comparison suggests a sense of unreality • Emphatic statement/repetition of "I'm" "I'm leading these men, I'm an officer" suggests self-doubt as he is trying to convince/reassure himself • "a huge mind breeding thought after thought" – suggests that he believes that something/someone beyond earthly beings must be controlling their actions
14.	2 marks awarded for detailed/insightful comment plus quotation/reference. 1 mark for more basic comment plus quotation/reference. 0 marks for quotation/reference alone.	4	Possible answers include: • "I am frightened." – simple statement/child-like language suggests the sudden realisation of the danger that he is in • Repetition of "fear" reinforces the pervasive nature of the feeling • "It was an older fear"/"the fear of being buried"/"the fear of wandering" use of repetition/word choice to emphasise the deep-rooted atavistic nature of the fear • "grey figures like weasels" symbolises the unknown/unnatural/indeterminate nature of the threat • Reference to "web"/"spiders" – primitive fears/idea of being trapped

Question	Expected Answer(s)	Max Mark	Additional Guidance
15.	2 marks awarded for detailed/insightful comment plus quotation/reference. 1 mark for more basic comment plus quotation/reference. 0 marks for quotation/reference alone.	4	Possible answers include: • Sequence of "thrustings", "hackings", "scurryings", "flowing" suggests unrelenting nature of the action • "thrustings and flashes" — dramatic language emphasises sudden combat/forceful violence • "scurryings and breathings as of rats" — evokes primitive fears • "Back. They must get back." — urgency of short sentences/repetition emphasises panic • "Mills bombs, hackings ..." — listing of horrors emphasises the range of danger they are in • "Over the parapet. They were over the parapet. Crouched they had run and scrambled" — staccato nature of sentence structure creates a sense of relief that they were safe for the moment • "Wright ... one arm seemed to have been shot off" use of ellipsis emphasises his sudden realisation of the horror of combat • "all those dead moons" description of desolate landscape evocative of death/emptiness is ever present
16.	Candidates can answer in bullet points in this final question, or write a number of linked statements.	10	Up to 2 marks can be achieved for identifying elements of commonality as identified in the question — i.e. the impact of extreme situations on characters A further 2 marks can be achieved for reference to the extract given. 6 additional marks can be awarded for discussion of similar references to at least one other part of the text. <u>In practice this means:</u> Identification of commonality (2) E.g. extremity of situation can bring out positive qualities in a character (1) and/or bring about their destruction (1) From the extract: 2 marks for detailed/insightful comment plus quotation/reference; 1 mark for more basic comment plus quotation/ reference; 0 marks for quotation/reference alone. E.g. Sergeant Smith's practical, phlegmatic response to war is underlined by his matter of fact comment to the soldier who has lost his arm, focusing on the positive benefits (2) From at least one other text/part of the text: as above for up to 6 marks Possible answers include: • *In Church* when Colin MacLeod is faced with the threat of death from the 'priest' during his sermon we see his growing sense of unease and stoicism • *The Telegram* the thin woman's quiet heroism, coping with (apparent) reality of the bad news of her son's death as the elder seems to be approaching her house — she is able to comfort the fat woman at that moment • *The Painter* William Murray's detached attitude of the artist is developed as he coolly observes the fight and the emotional reactions of the villagers — isolates him further

Question	Expected Answer(s)	Max Mark	Additional Guidance
16.	*(continued)*		• *Mother and Son* the mother's unrelenting criticism of her adult son creates tension in the household resulting in his feelings of hopelessness and despair • *The Red Door* the mysterious painting of Murdo's door prompts him to consider the difficulty — and attractiveness - of breaking away from the conformity of his community.

Text 5 — *Prose — The Whaler's Return* by George Mackay Brown

Question	Expected Answer(s)	Max Mark	Additional Guidance
17.	Up to 2 marks awarded for detailed/insightful comment plus quotation/reference. 1 mark for more basic comment plus quotation/reference. 0 marks for quotation/reference alone.	4	Possible answers include: • "standing at a mirror … drove a pin through it" her actions reveal her vanity, determined focus on her appearance • "yellow hair … fine burnished knot" — build-up of 'golden' images suggests attractive, almost magical/captivating quality • "At last she got a fine …" suggests the length of time she spends on her hair and the length of time he watches her • Use of the list with repeated use of "and" emphasises her snobbish attitude towards the working men • "Out of her pretty mouth she spat on the stone floor" — contrast between daintiness of "pretty mouth" and coarseness of "spat" emphasises her unpleasant action which contrasts with her lovely appearance
18.	Up to 2 marks awarded for detailed/insightful comment plus quotation/reference. 1 mark for more basic comment plus quotation/reference. 0 marks for quotation/reference alone.	4	Possible answers include: • "wearing his decent suit" suggests he is pleased he is looking his best in order to impress her • "smiled at him sweetly" suggests the special nature of the moment because of the perceived approval/acceptance by 'unattainable' barmaid • "touched rims" suggests intimacy/gentle coming together • "whisky trembled" suggests nervous, tremulous excitement • "transported" — shows intensity of experience for flaws taken beyond normality • "glittered at him with eyes, teeth, hair, rings" word choice/listing suggests the all-encompassing nature of her allure
19.		2	Possible answers include: • "shame" because he was being dishonest about what he is in order to be accepted • "resentment" because he has been unfairly rejected/humiliated/missed his opportunity

Question	Expected Answer(s)	Max Mark	Additional Guidance
20.	Candidates can answer in bullet points in this final question, or write a number of linked statements.	10	Up to 2 marks can be achieved for identifying elements of commonality as identified in the question, i.e. the importance of journeys, both literal and metaphorical. A further 2 marks can be achieved for reference to the extract given. 6 additional marks can be awarded for discussion of similar references from at least one other short story. <u>In practice this means:</u> Identification of commonality **(2)** E.g.: journeys can be physical challenges for survival **(1)** and these are mirrored by metaphorical journeys as a rite of passage **(1)** From the extract: 2 marks for detailed/insightful comment plus quotation/reference; 1 mark for more basic comment plus quotation/reference; 0 marks for quotation alone. E.g. The episode in the bar, when Flaw's deception is rewarded with humiliation, is a learning moment on his journey to fulfilment **(2)** From at least one other text: as above for up to 6 marks Possible answers include: • *The Eye of the Hurricane* – Cpt. Stevens' speech on the 'voyage' of life is a quiet moment in the final storm of his life • *A Time to Keep* – journey through the year in time and life involving marriage, birth, death and rebirth • *Tartan* – the Vikings' journey across the island seeking treasure: allegorical journey meeting the human condition in the form of death, fear, betrayal... • *The Bright Spade* – the men set off on a physical/metaphorical journey into the snow to save the community which leads to their heroic, but pointless, deaths • *The Bright Spade* – the community's journey through winter reflects the harsh nature of life and the ever-present threat of death faced by the community

Text 6 – *Prose – The Trick Is To Keep Breathing* **by Janice Galloway**

Question	Expected Answer(s)	Max Mark	Additional Guidance
21.	2 marks may be awarded for detailed/insightful comment plus quotation/reference. 1 mark for more basic comment plus quotation/reference. 0 marks for quotation/reference alone.	3	Possible answers include: • Word-choice shows attempt to think positively, e.g. "cheap"/"opened up"/"fresh" • "it also meant travel"/"it made me feel free" suggests the idea of freedom as the bus stop is outside the door • Repetition – "my own place, my home" emphasises she is pleased/proud to possess the cottage/be independent • Sentence structure – lists the number and variety of domestic chores she undertook to try to be positive about her new home "I papered ... the place fresh" • Use of short sentences makes it sound matter-of-fact/keeping her emotions in check – "The parting wasn't bitter. We wanted to be civilised and polite" • "I figured they were good signs. Everybody needs to cry now and then" – she turns a negative into a positive

Question	Expected Answer(s)	Max Mark	Additional Guidance
22.	Up to 2 marks awarded for detailed, insightful comment plus quotation/reference. 1 mark for more basic comment plus quotation/reference. 0 marks for quotation/reference alone.	3	Possible answers include: • Word-choice "uneasy" suggests her feelings of concern as she is worried/uncomfortable • Word-choice "tried" suggests she did not succeed in forgetting/continues to be concerned • Personification of the mushroom — "where it had settled"/"left a little pink trail like anaemic blood"/"baby mushrooms"/"just to let them alone in case"/"dangerous"/emphasises that she sees them as almost human/actions are deliberately menacing • "LOOK" in bold and/or capitals emphasises her panic • Minor sentence "In case" suggests they are a real threat
23.	Candidates should deal with both sides of the contrast but not necessarily in equal measure. Up to 2 marks awarded for detailed, insightful comment plus quotation/reference. 1 mark for more basic comment plus quotation/reference. 0 marks for quotation/reference alone.	4	Possible answers include: Cottage: • "Dry rot." abrupt statement/repetition/positioning at the start of both paragraphs emphasises the scale and the extent of the problem • "Sinister" emphasises that Joy sees the dry rot as something evil/deliberately menacing • Metaphor "eaten from the inside by this thing" emphasises that she sees her cottage as a victim of something alien/evil/monstrous • "multiply ... as we slept" emphasises the sense of menace as the rot creeps up on them while they are vulnerable • Word choice "silent spores" also increases the feeling of an invisible evil presence • Word choice "creeping red clouds" emphasises the silent predatory nature of the rot/like it is alive House: • Word choice "cheerful"/"bright" emphasises the attractiveness of and happiness within the house • "full of windows" gives the impression of openness and light • Emphasis on colour — "yellow walls and white woodwork" is bright/cheerful symbolising a new start
24.	Candidates may choose to answer in bullet points in this final question, or write a number of linked statements.	10	Up to 2 marks can be achieved for identifying elements of commonality as identified in the question, i.e. the impact of Joy's relationship with Michael A further 2 marks can be achieved for reference to the extract given. 6 additional marks can be awarded for discussion of similar references from at least one other part of the text. In practice this means: Identification of commonality (2) E.g. Michael brings a short period of happiness to Joy (1) and, therefore, his sudden, tragic death is all the more shocking for her (1). From the extract: 2 marks for detailed/insightful comment plus quotation/reference; 1 mark for more basic comment plus quotation/reference; 0 marks for quotation alone.

Question	Expected Answer(s)	Max Mark	Additional Guidance
24.	*(continued)*		E.g. throughout the extract Joy repeats "We" to suggest a sense of unity/belonging as she feels protected and complete when she is with Michael **(2)**
			From at least one other part of the text: as above for up to 6 marks
			Possible answers include:
			• The effect of Michael's death and its contribution to Joy's depression — reference to the flashbacks of Michael's drowning convey the still-present horror of that experience
			• The effect on her ability to cope with day to day life, e.g. work — the Head Teacher doesn't want her to make a fuss when Michael's wife is invited to the Memorial Service
			• Her casual relationships with men following Michael's death reveal her difficulties in coping with his loss
			• Her unwillingness to accept Michael's death shows the power of the relationship, still, in her life, e.g. deliberately spilling his aftershave to create a sense of his presence
			• Her anorexia develops after Michael's death and this allows her some control — she realises she has gone past her time for eating/she bakes but doesn't eat any of it

Text 7 — *Prose — Sunset Song* by Lewis Grassic Gibbon

Question	Expected Answer(s)	Max Mark	Additional Guidance
25.	2 marks awarded for detailed/insightful comment plus quotation/reference. 1 mark for more basic comment plus quotation/reference. 0 marks for quotation/reference alone.	4	Possible answers include:
			• "a cold and louring day" — sense of gloom is heightened by the combination of the two adjectives
			• "under the greyness" — dullness which seems all-encompassing
			• "squelched" — onomatopoeic word which catches the gurgling and sucking sound when walking in wet mud emphasising the sodden conditions she's walking through
			• "oozing" — again suggests the unpleasantness of the gradual flow of a smell of decay from the wet earth
			• "sodden" — suggests a thorough soaking which adds to the disagreeable impression of the conditions
			• "sheltered" is contrasted with "drenched" to highlight the extent of the rain damage to the crops
			• The very long sentence from "The wet fields" to "*endures*" gives a sense of the much wider world beyond, which is emphasised by the constant movement south to several places beyond Chris's immediate world
			• "ancient tower that the Pictish folk had reared" suggests Chris's awareness of the achievements of settlers long ago
			• "below the hands of the crofter folk" shows Chris's awareness of previous generations of farmers working this land
			• "Standing Stones" their presence provides a link with ancient times emphasising her sense of connection to the many generations before (and their worship)
			• General awareness that people are transient — "they lasted but as a breath" — but the landscape remains constant

Question	Expected Answer(s)	Max Mark	Additional Guidance
26.	2 marks awarded for detailed/insightful comment plus quotation/reference. 1 mark for more basic comment plus quotation/reference. 0 marks for quotation/reference alone.	4	Possible answers include: • "weeping"/"stricken and frightened" suggests Chris has now realised that her plans to leave the land were foolish and she recognises that the land is part of who she is • "she could never leave it" sums up what Chris has realised/accepted about her relationship with the land • "this life ... acrid" — repeated use of "and" shows a build up of all the challenging aspects of the constant physical effort which Chris (ironically) does not want to leave behind • "bound and held as though they had prisoned her here" suggests no possibility of escape • "fine bit plannings" suggests Chris's plans had been childish and vague, without a basis in reality • "the dreamings of a child" suggests that Chris's plans were unrealistic, fantasy, immature • "over toys it lacked" suggests a peevish desire for a passing childish phase • "toys that would never content it when it heard the smore of a storm ..." suggests that Chris's previous plans were part of a childish world of playthings which cannot compare to the more lasting pleasures of nature and farming the land • "She could no more teach a school than fly" suggests how unrealistic her dreams were by comparing them to the fantasy idea of flying • "for all the fine clothes and gear she might get and hold" suggests that her desire to pursue her education was at least in part a desire for superficial possessions • "hated and loved" explains the dilemma that Chris has with the land
27.	2 marks awarded for detailed/insightful comment plus quotation/reference. 1 mark for more basic comment plus quotation/reference. 0 marks for quotation/reference alone.	2	Possible answers include: • *"Mighty be here, Chris, where are you going?"* — Auntie's words suggest she feels she should have power over Chris/treats her as though she were a child who needs to ask permission • *"I'm away to Stonehaven to see Mr Semple, can I bring you anything?"* — Chris' determination to make her own decisions and establish her independence • *"Away to Stonehive? What are you jaunting there for? I'll transact any business you have"* — Uncle Tam reacts as though Chris is wasting time on an outing, when he, as the man, should deal with business/legal matters
28.	Candidates can answer in bullet points in this final question, or write a number of linked statements.	10	Up to 2 marks can be achieved for identifying elements of communality as identified in the question, i.e. the idea that "nothing endures". A further 2 marks can be achieved for reference to the extract given. 6 additional marks can be awarded for discussion of similar references to at least one other part of the text by the writer. <u>In practice this means:</u> Identification of commonality **(2)** E.g. Chris's life undergoes constant change as a result of family deaths and changes in her circumstances. **(1)** just as the farming community changes as a result of the devastating effects of the war **(1)**

Question	Expected Answer(s)	Max Mark	Additional Guidance
28.	*(continued)*		From the extract: 2 marks for detailed/insightful comment plus quotation/reference; 1 mark for more basic comment plus quotation/reference; 0 marks for quotation alone. E.g. Chris's growing independence reflects her transition from child to woman when she makes a mature decision to stay on the land and stands up to her Aunt and Uncle who try to dictate what she should do **(2)**. From at least one other part of the text: as above for up to 6 marks Possible answers include: • The death of Jean Guthrie forces Chris to relinquish her childhood dreams and educational aspirations and adopt the role of the woman of the house • The impact of the war on the landscape with the felling of the trees leads to soil erosion making the land harder to farm • Post-war economic exploitation of the land leads to the loss of small farms and the crofters' way of life • The mechanisation of farming, e.g. at the harvest demonstrates agricultural change and progress and the emergence of a new technological world • The end of an era as indicated in the "Morning Star" eulogy suggesting the end of a way of life, culture and a community

Text 8 — *Prose — The Cone-Gatherers* by Robin Jenkins

Question	Expected Answer(s)	Max Mark	Additional Guidance
29.	2 marks awarded for detailed/insightful comment plus quotation/reference. 1 mark for more basic comment plus quotation/reference. 0 marks for quotation/reference alone.	4	Possible answers include: • "yew trees" suggests evil/death as they are often found in graveyards • "dark caverns" suggests underground places (possibly idea of Hades?) where Roderick cannot see/place which is creepy/frightening/dangerous … • "evil presences" extremity of word choice suggests someone/something undefined there to do wrong/cause hurt/create danger • "lurker" suggests someone watching and waiting with harmful intent • "No sunshine" negative term suggests darkness/cold and, therefore, connotations of evil/danger • Reference to Roderick's feelings suggests sinister atmosphere as he is uneasy, e.g. "cold"/"frightened"/"sick at heart". These suggest he is clearly upset/rattled/scared by the presence in the wood
30.	2 marks awarded for detailed/insightful comment plus quotation/reference. 1 mark for more basic comment plus quotation/reference. 0 marks for quotation/reference alone.	4	Possible answers include: • Roderick begins to work out what is going on in Duror's mind, e.g. he realises Duror is spying on the cone-gatherers to collect evidence of their "wrong-doing" (although he does not realise how sinister Duror's thoughts actually are, yet he is closer to the truth than any of the other characters) • He recognises some of the hypocrisy/irony in Duror's thinking — "Duror himself shot deer on Sundays", yet he might use working on a Sunday as an example of the cone-gatherers' "wrong-doing"

Question	Expected Answer(s)	Max Mark	Additional Guidance
30.	*(continued)*		• He is insightful enough to recognise that Duror dislikes the cone-gatherers and wants them removed from the wood: "Why then did he hate the cone-gatherers and wish to drive them away?" • Roderick has an understanding of the "struggle between good and evil" — and recognises the cone-gatherers as good and Duror as evil • He understands that "Good did not always win" based on his reading (references to Christian from *The Pilgrim's Progress* and Sir Galahad's struggles) • He recognises there is something wrong with Duror — "Had Duror gone mad" — and links this to the "change" his mother and Mrs. Morton had been discussing • He makes the link between Duror and the "perils in the wood" which Mrs. Morton had warned him about: without understanding fully, intuitively, he is the closest to understanding what is going on with Duror
31.	2 marks may be awarded for a detailed/ insightful comment plus reference. 1 mark should be awarded for a more basic comment plus reference. 0 marks for reference/quotation alone.	2	Possible answers include: • Duror's presence is responsible for Roderick hiding rather than going to the cone-gatherers' hut as intended • Duror is responsible for Roderick's feelings of fear • Roderick's thoughts and fears involve Duror — his imaginings and his attempt to work out why Duror thinks and acts as he does • Duror motivates Roderick to think about the battle between good and evil
32.	Candidates may answer in bullet points in this final question, or write a number of linked statements.	10	Up to 2 marks can be achieved for identifying elements of commonality as identified in the question, i.e. the conflict between good and evil. A further 2 marks can be achieved for reference to the extract given. 6 additional marks can be awarded for discussion of similar references to at least one other part of the text by the writer. In practice this means: Identification of commonality **(2)** E.g. Conflict between good and evil is symbolised through Duror's irrational hatred of the innocent Calum **(1)** Calum has an affinity with nature whereas Duror destroys it **(1)** From the extract: 2 marks for detailed/insightful comment plus quotation/reference; 1 mark for more basic comment plus quotation/ reference; 0 marks for quotation alone. E.g. Roderick works out that the cone-gatherers represent goodness and Duror evil shown by his perceptive reaction to Duror's presence outside the hut and is beginning to understand that the struggle between good and evil never ends **(2)** From at least one other text/part of the text: as above for up to 6 marks

Question	Expected Answer(s)	Max Mark	Additional Guidance
32.	*(continued)*		Possible answers include: • References to the war as an influence of evil, destroying the landscape/many men/families contrasts with the gentleness of Calum/nature as a life force • Calum is presented as a Christ-like figure of goodness, sacrificed in a Biblical way at the end of the novel whereas Duror is presented as evil in his thoughts and deeds, e.g. lurking at the start of the novel • Roderick is presented as the future of hope/goodness, having inherited a sense of fairness and justice from his grandfather and mother — his desire to be like the cone gatherers identifies him with Calum's innocence • Lady Runcie-Campbell's faith is presented as goodness as this encourages her to visit Peggy Duror/be lenient towards the cone-gatherers following the deer drive/weeps at the end of the novel, yet she sends the cone-gatherers into the storm rather than allowing them to stay in the beach-hut — corrupted by Duror • Mr. Tulloch's continued support of the cone-gatherers is seen as good; he demonstrates fairness and justice following the deer drive and their expulsion from the beach-hut and at the end when Lady Runcie-Campbell insists they rescue Roderick from the tree — this contrasts with influence of Duror

PART C – SCOTTISH TEXT – POETRY

Text 9 – *Poetry – A Poet's Welcome to His Love-Begotten Daughter; The First Instance that entitled him to the Venerable Appellation of Father* by Robert Burns

Question	Expected Answer(s)	Max Mark	Additional Guidance
33.	2 marks awarded for detailed/insightful comment plus quotation/reference. 1 mark for more basic comment plus quotation/reference.	2	Possible answers include: • "Thou's welcome, wean" suggests warm/congratulatory/proud tone in defiance of convention • "My sweet wee" acknowledges ownerships/suggests intimacy and protectiveness • "My (sweet wee) lady!" — deliberately gives the child status despite the circumstances of her birth • "Daddy" — familiar/informal title underlines the closeness of the bond he acknowledges between them • "mishanter fa' me" — determination not to feel shame/embarrassment
34.	2 marks awarded for detailed/insightful comment plus quotation/reference. 1 mark for more basic comment plus quotation/reference.	4	Possible answers include: • "fornicator" — blunt statement of their accusation showing his refusal to be intimidated/troubled by it • "kintry clatter" — reduces the accusations to trivial gossip/alliteration emphasises the noisy meaninglessness of it • "the mair they talk, I'm kent the better" — balance in the comparatives suggests relishing his notoriety • "clash!" makes all the gossip seems like discordant noise/climactic nature of positioning at end of the short line

Question	Expected Answer(s)	Max Mark	Additional Guidance
34.	*(continued)*		• "auld wife's tongue's" belittling connotations — people who think like this are old-fashioned/out of touch/not worth listening to • "I hae fought for"/"Baith kirk and queir" defiant tone emphasises his determination to take them on/individual taking on authority and institution
35.	2 marks awarded for detailed/insightful comment plus quotation/reference. 1 mark for more basic comment plus quotation/reference. 0 marks for quotation/reference only.	4	Possible answers include: • "Tho' I should be the waur bestead…bienly clad" juxtaposition/contrast of "I" and "thou" to emphasise his commitment to support her, whatever the cost to himself • Word choice of "brat" and "wedlock's bed" emphasises his defiant attitude in the face of social convention • "fatherly I kiss and daut thee" use of terms of physical tenderness as an expression of his love for her/the attention he lavishes on her • "Thy mither's person, grace an' merit" list of conventional female virtues emphasises his loyalty and commitment to the baby's mother despite the circumstances • "An' thy poor, worthless daddy's spirit" word choice creates self-deprecating humour showing that he doesn't take himself too seriously
36.	Candidates can answer in bullet points in this final question, or write a number of linked statements.	10	Up to 2 marks can be achieved for identifying elements of commonality as identified in the question, i.e. Burns' treatment of the religious and/or moral concerns of his time A further 2 marks can be achieved for the reference to the extract given. 6 additional marks can be awarded for discussion of similar references in at least one other poem by Burns. In practice this means: Identification of commonality (2) E.g. Burns challenges/criticises the rigid/intrusive/hypocritical aspects of moral/religious beliefs of his time (1) while presenting a warmer, more human alternative (1) From the extract: 2 marks for detailed/insightful comment plus quotation/reference; 1 mark for more basic comment plus quotation/reference; 0 marks for quotation/reference alone. E.g. "But be a loving father to thee, And brag the name o' 't." demonstrates his love for and commitment to her, as well as his pride, despite the criticism he will face from those representing conventional religion and morality (2) From at least one other text: as above for up to 6 marks Possible references include: • *Address to the Deil* — humorous, ironic speaker/persona is appropriate for poet's satirical critique of Calvinism • *A Man's A Man For A' That* — a spokesman, champion of equality and fraternity speaking as the voice of a community/nation as he criticises the hierarchical nature of society • *Holy Willie* — creation of self-righteous character who justifies his own sins as an apt vehicle for his critique of the perceived religious hypocrisy of the time

Question	Expected Answer(s)	Max Mark	Additional Guidance
36.	*(continued)*		• *Tam O'Shanter* — character of moralising, commentating narrator allows Burns to point out the vagaries of human nature/undermine the apparent moral 'message' of the poem • *To a Mouse* uses the symbol of the homeless mouse to make a comment about the suffering of the tenant farmers of his day.

Text 10 – *Poetry* – *Mrs Midas* by Carol Ann Duffy

Question	Expected Answer(s)	Max Mark	Additional Guidance
37.	Both sides of the contrast must be dealt with for full marks but not necessarily in equal measure. 2 marks awarded for detailed/insightful comment plus quotation/reference. 1 mark for more basic comment plus quotation/reference. 0 marks for quotation/reference alone.	4	Possible answers include: Stanza 1 — the atmosphere of ordinariness/security suggested by: • "poured a glass of wine/started to unwind/relaxed" all suggest the routine process of starting to enjoy the free time at the end of the day • "kitchen filled … itself" conveys the domesticated/homely environment • "blanching the windows/opened one/wiped the other" suggest the mundane activities involved in the preparation of the meal Stanza 2 — the atmosphere of extraordinariness/threat/disbelief suggested by: • "visibility poor/dark" signals a change in mood from previous stanza to one of mystery • "twig in his hand … gold" suggests a supernatural occurrence • "pear … like a lightbulb" suggests the unnatural appearance of her husband • "fairy lights" the incongruity of putting these up in September/connotations of something magical
38.	2 marks awarded for detailed/insightful comment plus quotation/reference. 1 mark for more basic comment plus quotation/reference. 0 marks for quotation/reference alone.	2	Possible answers include: • "He drew the blinds" the furtive action suggests a concealment/attempt to isolate them from the outside world • "strange, wild, vain" conveys her confusion/concern at the change in his demeanour • "spitting out the teeth … rich" suggests the negative effects of his greed/inappropriateness of his behaviour at the table • "shaking hand" demonstrates the anxiety she feels over his actions • "glass, goblet, golden chalice" suggests the stages of the unnatural transformation of the glass before her eyes
39.	2 marks awarded for detailed/insightful comment plus quotation/reference. 1 mark for more basic comment plus quotation/reference. 0 marks for quotation/reference alone.	4	Possible answers include: • "I finished the wine/I made him sit" highlights her practical nature/ability to regain her composure • Sequencing of "I made/I locked/I moved" suggests she quickly takes control of the situation demonstrating her strength of character/domineering nature • "The toilet I didn't mind" shows her pride in material possessions/keeping up appearances • Use of statement/(rhetorical) questions "I couldn't believe my ears"/"But who has …/about gold?" suggests her no-nonsense approach to life's problems • "keep his hands to himself … lock the cat in the cellar … At least … smoking for good" all suggest a humorous side to her character in being able to make light of such a serious situation

Question	Expected Answer(s)	Max Mark	Additional Guidance
40.	Candidates can answer in bullet points in this final question, or write a number of linked statements.	10	Up to 2 marks can be achieved by identifying elements of commonality as identified in the question, i.e. attempts of characters to cope with life-changing situations. A further 2 marks can be achieved for reference to the text given. 6 additional marks can be awarded for discussion of similar references to at least one other poem by the poet. <u>In practice this means:</u> Identification of commonality **(2)** E.g. Duffy presents characters who develop various coping "strategies" either consciously or unconsciously **(1)** some more successful in allowing them to accept or move on, whilst others are still struggling **(1)** From this extract: 2 marks for detailed/insightful comment plus quotation/reference; 1 mark for more basic comment plus quotation/reference; 0 marks for quotation/reference alone. E.g. she attempts to cope by using humour to make light of the horrifying implications of the situation **(2)** From at least one other text: as above for up to 6 marks Possible comments include: • *Anne Hathaway* she focuses on happy memories of when her husband was alive and the depth of their passionate love for one another to cope with the pain of her loss • *Havisham* the speaker imagines violent acts against her one time lover in order to cope with the rejection she feels but is still stuck in the past • *War Photographer* the inability of the photographer to rid himself of his experiences in warzones despite his attempts to adopt a professional distance • *Originally* the speaker attempts to adapt her language in order to fit in to her new environment but feels a sense of loss as a result of this • *Valentine* the speaker attempts to cope with the loss of her illusions about love by rejecting the clichés of love in favour of a more cynical view

Text 11 — *Poetry — The Bargain* by Liz Lochhead

Question	Expected Answer(s)	Max Mark	Additional Guidance
41.	At least two examples should be included for full marks. 2 marks awarded for detailed/insightful comment plus quotation/reference. 1 mark for more basic comment plus quotation/reference. 0 marks for quotation/reference alone.	4	Possible answers include: • "river fast and high" suggests the relationship isn't going smoothly/could run into trouble • "You and I" Individual personal pronouns separated by "and" suggests that even though they seem physically together, they are drifting apart • "twitch and fret" — connotations of unsettled, jumpy. Refers not only to the police horses but the speaker's awareness of her failing relationship • "rubbing the wrong way" — beginnings of disagreement/discomfort of being in the crowd echoes their feelings towards each other

Question	Expected Answer(s)	Max Mark	Additional Guidance
41.	*(continued)*		<ul><li>"ready to let fly" — the impending violence of the fans suggests conflict/her fear that her lover is preparing to leave her</li><li>"looking back, looking forward" — repetition to highlight the uncertainty in the relationship/don't know whether to look to the past or the future</li></ul>
42.	2 marks awarded for detailed/insightful comment. 1 mark for more basic comment. 0 marks for quotation/reference alone.	2	Possible answers include:<ul><li>Alliteration of "b" in "but the boy…beautiful Bakelite/Bush" suggests energy/upbeat attitude of boy to activity</li><li>Positive connotations of "beautiful/Bakelite" suggests bright, upbeat mood</li><li>Fast pace/internal rhyme of "buttonpopping stationhopping" suggests enthusiastic enjoyment of music</li><li>List of three positive aspects of boy's experience in "doesn't miss a beat", "sings along", "it's easy" suggests the boy's happiness</li></ul>
43.	At least two examples should be included for full marks. 2 marks awarded for detailed/insightful comment plus quotation/reference. 1 mark for more basic comment plus quotation/reference. 0 marks for quotation/reference alone.	4	Possible answers include:<ul><li>"splintering city" — suggests city is broken or divided, just as the relationship is fractured</li><li>"wintry bridges" — cold and uninviting, which suggests the distance/lack of connection in the relationship</li><li>"black" — suggests neglect and poverty in this area, which reflects the deteriorating nature of the relationship</li><li>"every other tenement … on its gable end" — pun suggests the open and frank nature of the people which contrasts with lack of openness in the relationship now</li><li>"I know it's cold" — pathetic fallacy suggests lack of harmony/closeness in their relationship</li><li>"wet dog reek … damp clothes" — emphasises the unpleasant smell which permeates the area, symbolic of the state of their relationship</li></ul>
44.	Candidates can answer in bullet points in this final question, or write a number of linked statements.	10	Up to 2 marks can be achieved for identifying elements of commonality as identified in the question, i.e. Lochhead's exploration of the theme of difficult relationships. A further 2 marks can be achieved for reference to the extract given. 6 additional marks can be awarded for discussion of similar references to at least one other poem. In practice this means: Identification of commonality **(2)** E.g. Lochhead explores the various problems in relationships **(1)** and in doing this gives us new insights/increases our understanding of universal human problems **(1)** From the poem: 2 marks for detailed/insightful comment plus quotation/reference; 1 mark for more basic comment plus quotation/reference; 0 marks for quotation/reference alone. E.g. the projection of the disintegrating relationship onto the surroundings "splintering city … wintry bridges" **(2)**

Question	Expected Answer(s)	Max Mark	Additional Guidance
44.	*(continued)*		OR The portrayal of the tension/uncertainty within the relationship "looking back … which way" **(2)** From at least one other text: as above for up to 6 marks Possible answers include: • *My Rival's House* the difficult relationship of the speaker and her prospective mother-in-law due to her overprotectiveness of her son "this son she bore … never can escape" • *My Rival's House* the awkwardness and insecurity of the speaker in the face of the unwelcoming attitude of the rival "I am all edges, a surface, a shell" • *Last Supper* the bitterness and resentment as a result of the disintegration of a relationship "betrayal with a kiss" • *Last Supper* the predatory nature of the spurned as they seek new relationships "get hungry and go hunting again" • *For my Grandmother Knitting* repetition of "there is no need" emphasises the grandmother's diminishing importance within the family

Text 12 — *Poetry — Memorial* by Norman MacCaig

Question	Expected Answer(s)	Max Mark	Additional Guidance
45.	2 marks awarded for detailed/insightful comment plus quotation/reference. 1 mark for more basic comment plus quotation/reference.	3	Possible answers include: • Blunt/matter-of-fact opening statements convey the simple truth that her death surrounds him • Repetition of "everywhere" and/or "dies" reinforces the fact that he cannot escape from this • Present tense shows it is still vivid in his mind • Patterned list of phrases "no sunrise … mountain" emphasises the inescapable nature of her death as these are places not usually associated with death. Placement of "but" after the list highlights the pleasure he previously took has become tainted by her death • Paradox "silence of her dying sounds" conveys the devastating impact of her death as its intensity blocks out everything else. It, in itself, is his only focus • Imagery of "carousel of language" is intricate and candidates may consider it in different ways. Sensible interpretations should be rewarded which link/contrast it to the ideas suggested by "the silence of her dying". E.g. the frivolous, noisy, joyous nature of a fairground; the endless, circular movement which has no purpose other than to entertain; the connotations of childhood freedom and innocence • Imagery of "web" connotes: a deadly trap possibly suggesting his grief is so powerful it eliminates all other emotions/interconnectedness or interwoven human emotions — no escape from absolute quiet • Word choice/imagery of "stitches" further illustrates that his despair is so firmly secured in his psyche that all future happiness will be overpowered/vanquished

Question	Expected Answer(s)	Max Mark	Additional Guidance
45.	*(continued)*		• Candidates may also make a case for "web/stitches" having more positive connotations, e.g. of his memories of happier times being secured/fastened/locked away. As before, sensible interpretations, which are justified with evidence, should be considered • Rhetorical question "How can …" creates a pessimistic tone highlighting that his grief is so prevalent he can see no escape • Word choice of "clasp" suggests a tight grip showing the close bond and the strength of his feelings towards his loved one. Thus, this conveys the impact her death has had on him • Imagery of "thick death" portrays death as something impenetrable which he can never break through or recover from emotionally • Word choice of "intolerable distance" conveys his feelings on the inevitable, unbearable barrier between the living and the dead. Highlights his wider beliefs about the finality of death being a gap which can never be bridged
46.	2 marks awarded for detailed/insightful comment plus quotation/reference. 1 mark for more basic comment plus quotation/reference.	4	Possible answers include: • Repetition/echoing in opening line "she grieves … grief" informs of her sympathy/comfort for him in his sorrow, thus reinforcing their love • Present tense of "dying" and "she tells me" conveys his vivid recollection that at the end of her life she was still concerned about the impact, on him, of her death • References to nature "bird … fish" are contradictions of the normal order of things. He sees death as a reversal of existence and so their relationship has been permanently altered./Equally death is being presented as part of the natural cycle of things symbolised by the bird and the fish • Imagery of "crocus is carved ….shapes my mind" offers a brief respite in mood as he appreciates her invocation of nature to highlight that death is part of the circle of life. As such, her death inspires him to be more creative in his work/be precise in the words he uses • The dash/"But" introduces a contrast/change of mood to one of melancholy about his loved one being forever lost to him • Word choice of "black words" continues this mood and hints at his despair about the finality of death forever separating them • Oxymoron "sound of soundlessness" echoes his anguish in stanza 1 about the intense nature of his all-consuming grief • Word choice of "that name" is vague and unspecific highlighting his view of the implausibility of reunion after death • Imagery of "nowhere …. continuously going into" is ambiguous in nature conveying his bleak outlook that her death is a never-ending journey with no certainty or hopeful conclusion

Question	Expected Answer(s)	Max Mark	Additional Guidance
47.	2 marks awarded for detailed/insightful comment plus quotation/reference. 1 mark for more basic comment plus quotation/reference.	3	Possible answers include: • "she can't stop dying" shows how her death is constantly on his mind. The present (continuous) tense illustrates its vividness and clarity which threatens to overwhelm him • "she makes me" conveys their bond and the strength of his love for her, which will prevail through time • "elegy" shows he has become a living testament to the profound nature of grief as an elegy would usually be written as a tribute to her. Instead he subverts the notion to show how profound his melancholy is • "masterpiece" normally relates to an outstanding piece of work/impressive creation. This satirically conveys his belief that his grief is so penetrating it has transformed him into a work of art/treasure/monument • "true fiction" – oxymoron suggests that unlike a story, his anguish is real and links to the "ugliness of death" to convey his horror and anger regarding his fundamental belief in the reality of the situation • "sad music" sums up the central idea about the pervasive nature of grief and despair. The pessimistic ending highlights the all-consuming nature of grief and how it remains forever with him
48.	Candidates may choose to answer in bullet points in this final question, or write a number of linked statements.	10	Up to 2 marks can be achieved for identifying elements of commonality as identified in the question, i.e. reaction to suffering A further 2 marks can be achieved for reference to the extract given. 6 additional marks can be awarded for discussion of similar references to at least one other poem. In practice this means: Identification of commonality **(2)** E.g. reaction to suffering is part of the human condition **(1)** can be experienced as life-affirming or life-denying **(1)** From the poem: 2 marks for detailed/insightful comment plus quotation/reference; 1 marks for more basic comment plus quotation/reference; 0 marks for quotation alone. E.g. the all-consuming and enduring impact of his grief "Everywhere I go she dies" **(2)** From at least one other text: as above for up to 6 marks Possible answers include: • *Visiting Hour* the speaker's denial/numbness in reaction to severity of the patient's condition and his refusal to accept the inevitable • *Aunt Julia* the speaker's mental pain and regret over the loss of his Aunt and all that she represents in terms of Scotland's heritage • *Assisi* the beggar's reaction to physical suffering: acceptance and gratitude for the little he has in the face of neglect and hypocrisy

Question	Expected Answer(s)	Max Mark	Additional Guidance
48.	*(continued)*		• *Sounds of the Day* the speaker underestimates the depth and enduring nature of his suffering when the relationship ends • *Visiting Hour* the all-consuming despair felt by the speaker at the futility of his efforts to communicate with or to alleviate the suffering of his loved one

Text 13 — *Poetry — Shores* by Sorley MacLean

Question	Expected Answer(s)	Max Mark	Additional Guidance
49.	2 marks awarded for detailed/insightful comment plus quotation/reference. 1 mark for more basic comment plus quotation/reference. 0 marks for quotation/reference alone.	4	Possible answers include: • Sense of immense scale of the landscape conveyed by place names, word choice of "ocean", reference to "between Scotland and Tiree" • Use of Gaelic place names in English translation emphasises speaker's appreciation of the depth of history/his sense of heritage • The enormity of the physical landscape suggested by personification/comparison with a giant of "great white mouth"/"two hard jaws" • "while the ocean was filling … forever" suggests speaker is appreciative of the never ending power of nature • "Prishal bowed his stallion head" comparison to intimidating, wild, elemental force • Use of hyperbole: of "between the world and eternity" emphasises his sense of wonder at the vast timeless quality of nature
50.	2 marks awarded for detailed/insightful comment plus quotation/reference. 1 mark for more basic comment plus quotation/reference. 0 marks for quotation/reference alone.	4	Possible answers include: • "till doom"/"measuring sand, grain: by grain"/"for the sea draining drop by drop" geological timescale to highlight depth of speaker's commitment, devotion and patience • "And if … Mull"/"And if … Moidart" — parallel structure and references to places that he wishes they could be together in, suggests that his strong love for these places is mirrored in his love for the person/wishes to share them with his lover • "that wide solitude … wait there forever" extreme nature of the vocabulary emphasises that even in this vast, empty setting he is willing to wait for his lover • "a synthesis of love" suggests the link between his love for sea and land and love for his woman • Reference to "ocean and sand" emphasises the never ending nature of his love by comparison with never- ending natural phenomena/gives a sense of his love as elemental, like the force of nature itself
51.	Candidates may choose to comment on either language or ideas or both. 2 marks awarded for detailed/insightful comment plus quotation/reference. 1 mark for more basic comment plus quotation/reference. 0 marks for quotation/reference alone.	2	Possible answers include: Language: • Personification of "unhappy" contrasting the sea with his own contented state as conveyed in the rest of the poem • Nature is shown as powerful/threatening "surging sea"/"dragged the boulders"/"threw them over us" as it was earlier • Promise of "I would build the rampart wall" reaffirms his desire to preserve his love from threats and make sure that it will endure • Threat is described as "an alien eternity" linking back to the idea of infinite time and its sublime power

Question	Expected Answer(s)	Max Mark	Additional Guidance
51.	*(continued)*		Ideas: • Desire to protect his love emphasises the strong feelings that he has conveyed in the rest of the poem for his lover • Nature as a powerful, frightening force is emphasised here, and in the rest of the poem • Eternity of his love is compared to the eternity of natural, elemental forces
52.	Candidates can answer in bullet points in this final question, or write a number of linked statements.	10	Up to 2 marks can be achieved for identifying elements of commonality as identified in the question, i.e. discuss how MacLean explores the impact of time on human experience. A further 2 marks can be achieved for reference to the extract given. 6 additional marks can be awarded for discussion of similar references to at least one other poem by the poet. <u>In practice this means:</u> Identification of commonality **(2)** E.g.: human experience is essentially transitory **(1)** but aspects of life, e.g. love, appreciation of nature have greater permanence **(1)** From the extract: 2 marks for detailed/insightful comment plus quotation/reference; 1 mark for more basic comment plus quotation/reference; 0 marks for quotation/reference alone. E.g. declaration of love which will never end – the constant quality of his love emphasised by comparisons with measuring the sea "drop by drop" and the sand, "grain by grain" **(2)** From at least one other text: as above for up to 6 marks Possible answers include: • *Screapadal* the elemental beauty of the place has outlived its human occupation, which is essentially ephemeral • *An Autumn Day* death in war can be sudden and without warning or time and opportunity to prepare • *I Gave You Immortality* the immortality bestowed by the celebration of love in the poem contrasts with actual human response of the woman • *Heroes* youth, inexperience of the soldier who is killed emphasises the lack of heroism/common vulnerability of humanity and transience of human life • *An Autumn Day* the indifference of nature to the suffering of humanity shown in the passing of a whole day as the men's bodies lie in the sunshine

Text 14 — *Poetry* — *The Thread* by Don Paterson

Question	Expected Answer(s)	Max Mark	Additional Guidance
53.	2 marks awarded for detailed/insightful comment plus quotation/reference. 1 mark for more basic comment plus quotation/reference.	4	Possible answers include: • "Made his landing … so hard … ploughed" echoes a crash landing suggesting his arrival on earth was potentially life-threatening • positioning of "so hard" emphasises the intensity of the danger • "ploughed straight back into the earth" alludes to the burial of the dead suggesting the fragility of life • "They caught him" conveys the medical team's active role/intervention in saving his life • "by the thread" suggests how precarious his survival was • "pulled him up" suggests last minute intervention to save his life
54.	2 marks awarded for detailed/insightful comment plus quotation/reference. 1 mark for more basic comment plus quotation/reference.	2	Possible answers include: • "I thank what higher will" suggests his continuing gratitude for the intervention of a benign force guiding their destiny/looking after them • structure of "to you and me and Russ" suggests a unified, cohesive group • "great twin-engined … us" suggests the stability and resilience of the family grouping • "roaring" suggests life and vitality of the family • "somehow" suggests the miraculous nature of his survival • "out-revving … universe" suggests immense energy and power of the family unit and their activities
55.	2 marks awarded for detailed/insightful comment plus quotation/reference. 1 mark for more basic comment plus quotation/reference.	4	Possible answers include: • "All that trouble … dead" reprises the trauma of the boy's birth • "all I thought … week" contrasts with the present happiness • "thread holding all of us" returns to fragility of life/ suggests bond which holds family together • "look at our tiny house" concludes flight metaphor suggesting take-off/elation/joy • "tiny house" symbolic of vulnerability/closeness of small family unit • "white dot … mother waving" suggests the traditional, supportive role of the mother within the family unit

Question	Expected Answer(s)	Max Mark	Additional Guidance
56.	Candidates may choose to answer in bullet points in this final question, or write a number of linked statements.	10	Up to 2 marks can be achieved for identifying elements of commonality as identified in the question, i.e. the fragility of human life.
			A further 2 marks can be achieved for reference to the extract given.
			6 additional marks can be awarded for discussion of similar references to at least one other poem by the poet.
			In practice this means: Identification of commonality **(2)** E.g. the threat of death is ever-present in our sense of ourselves as human beings **(1)** anticipation/survival of this threat can be a powerful force at all stages of life **(1)**
			From the extract: 2 marks for detailed/insightful comment plus quotation/reference; 1 mark for more basic comment plus quotation/reference; 0 marks for quotation/reference alone. E.g. image of the 'thread' fastening Jamie to life reinforces the sense of the fragile and precarious nature of life as death is always a possibility **(2)**
			From at least one other text: as above for up to 6 marks
			Possible answers include:
			• *Nil Nil* reference to gall stone — all that's left of pilot — kicked into gutter emphasises how casually life can be disposed of and a human being can be reduced to an object • *The Ferryman's* Arms speaker waiting for the ferryman — reference to Greek mythology — ferry journey to afterlife suggests sense that we as living human beings are waiting for death/passing the time until the inevitability of death happens • *Nil Nil* decline of football team from (modest) glory days to no one coming to see their match creates a nihilistic picture of the inevitable decline of humanity towards death • *11.00: Baldovan* the boys' return to world where they no longer feel part of things/world seems to have changed suggests sense that life moves on without us and individuals are forgotten and dispensable • *Waking with Russell* the speaker, faced with the vulnerability of his new born child, commits himself to nurture and protect him from danger.

Section 2 – CRITICAL ESSAY
Supplementary marking grid

	Marks 20–19	Marks 18–16	Marks 15–13	Marks 12–10	Marks 9–6	Marks 5–0
Knowledge and understanding	thorough knowledge and understanding of the text	secure knowledge and understanding of the text	clear knowledge and understanding of the text	adequate knowledge and understanding of the text	limited evidence of knowledge and understanding of the text	very little knowledge and understanding of the text
The critical essay demonstrates:	perceptive selection of textual evidence to support line of argument which is fluently structured and expressed	detailed textual evidence to support line of thought which is coherently structured and expressed	clear textual evidence to support line of thought which is clearly structured and expressed	adequate textual evidence to support line of thought, which is adequately structured and expressed	limited textual evidence to support line of thought which is structured and expressed in a limited way	very little textual evidence to support line of thought which shows very little structure or clarity of expression
	perceptive focus on the demands of the question	secure focus on the demands of the question	clear focus on the demands of the question	adequate focus on the demands of the question	limited focus on the demands of the question	very little focus on the demands of the question
Analysis **The critical essay demonstrates:**	perceptive analysis of the effect of features of language/filmic techniques	detailed analysis of the effect of features of language/filmic techniques	clear analysis of the effect of features of language/filmic techniques	adequate analysis of the effect of features of language/filmic techniques	limited analysis of the effect of features of language/filmic techniques	very little analysis of features of language/filmic techniques
Evaluation **The critical essay demonstrates**	committed evaluative stance with respect to the text and the task	engaged evaluative stance with respect to the text and the task	clear evaluative stance with respect to the text and the task	adequate evidence of an evaluative stance with respect to the text and the task	limited evidence of an evaluative stance with respect to the text and the task	very little evidence of an evaluative stance with respect to the text and the task
Technical Accuracy The critical essay demonstrates:	few errors in spelling, grammar, sentence construction, punctuation and paragraphing the ability to be understood at first reading				significant number of errors in spelling, grammar, sentence construction, punctuation and paragraphing which impedes understanding	

HIGHER ENGLISH
2017

PAPER 1 — READING FOR UNDERSTANDING, ANALYSIS AND EVALUATION

Marking Instructions for each question

Passage 1

Question		Expected Response	Max Mark	Additional Guidance
1.	(a)	Read lines 1—12. Analyse how the writer's word choice in lines 1—3 emphasises the "conventional wisdom" that reading books is better than playing video games. 2 marks may be awarded for reference plus detailed/insightful comment; 1 mark for reference plus more basic comment; 0 marks for reference alone. Possible answers are shown in the "Additional Guidance" column. (Marks may be awarded 2 or 1 + 1)	2	Possible answers include: • "enriches" suggests that reading adds to one's knowledge, awareness; is rewarding, beneficial; improves one • "the mind" suggests reading is influencing something greater than just the brain; it influences our consciousness: thought, perception, emotions and imagination • "deadens" suggests video games make kids less aware, less sensitive, less vigorous; they make kids think less; lifeless • "zoning out" suggests video games make kids detached from people and things around them, unresponsive, unstimulated
	(b)	Explain in your own words "the question" the writer asks in line 6 about "other forms of culture". Candidates must attempt to use their own words. No marks for straight lifts from the passage. 2 marks may be awarded for detailed/insightful comment plus quotation/reference; 1 mark for basic comment plus quotation/ reference; 0 marks for quotation/reference alone.	2	Possible answers include: • The writer is asking if these other forms of culture involve discrete thinking skills/have qualities which benefit, stimulate, challenge, stretch our minds in ways which are different from — but just as important as — reading
	(c)	By referring to at least two features of language in lines 8—12 ("Where … books"), analyse how the writer emphasises the contrast between his positive view of "other forms of culture" and the negative view held by "most critics". 2 marks may be awarded for reference plus detailed/insightful comment; 1 mark for reference plus more basic comment; 0 marks for reference alone. Possible answers are shown in the "Additional Guidance" column. (Marks may be awarded 2 + 2, 2 + 1 + 1, 1 + 1 + 1 + 1)	4	Possible answers include: *Imagery* • "(progressive) story": just as a "story" is a developing, organised narrative, so the writer sees the positive influence of popular culture as gradual, logical, coherent, interesting … • "our brains sharper": just as sharpening involves giving cutting tools a better edge, this suggests making our brains keener, more accurate … • "we soak in": soaking in is a process of absorption, of taking in as much liquid as possible; this suggests we become immersed in popular culture, that its influence is natural, irresistible, all-consuming, profound, deep … • "(lowbrow) fluff": fluff is light, downy material (for example, small pieces of wool); its use suggests critics believe popular culture is light, trivial, worthless, superficial, irrelevant, trifling … • "honing": just as honing is a (refined) process of giving cutting tools a perfect edge, this suggests gradually making our brains as sharp as possible, more and more precise, accurate, productive … *Word choice* • "allege" suggest doubt, calls the critics' views into question • "dumbing down" suggests popular culture offers people a reduced intellectual challenge **or** is responsible for making people less educated, less intelligent, more lowbrow

Question		Expected Response	Max Mark	Additional Guidance
1.	(c)	*(continued)*		• "progressive" suggests developing, advancing, moving forward steadily, leading to improvement • "steadily" suggests reliable, consistent progress • "imperceptibly" suggests change is gradual, subtle • "sharper" suggests keener, more precise, more accurate • "soak in" suggests it's not a superficial process; influence is deep; we are fully engaged, absorbed • "dismissed" suggests brushed aside, considered beneath contempt, irrelevant, unimportant, trivial • "lowbrow" suggests vulgar, anti-intellectual, uncultured, plebeian • "fluff" suggests worthless, trivial, inconsequential, superficial • "honing" suggests sharpening, perfecting, refining *Sentence structure* • Balanced structure/contrast of "Where ... story" allows the writer to trump the critics' argument; this is heightened by the greater certainty of his "see" set against the dubious nature of what they "allege" • Use of colon to introduce a full development of his "progressive story" argument • Use of parenthesis "but ... imperceptibly" to explain that this positive development is so gradual that it's easy for the less astute (like the critics) to miss it • Positioning of "I hope to persuade you" at the start of the final sentence alerts the reader to the fact that the writer is about to make what he believes is his most important point • Positioning of "increasingly" just before his key statement stresses that the point he is about to make is more and more relevant, true • Balanced nature of final statement, hinging on the "just as important as" comparison stresses skills developed by popular culture are of a comparable standard to the skills developed by reading
2.		By referring to lines 13–19, analyse how the writer uses both sentence structure and imagery to convey the difficulty of playing video games. For full marks there must be reference to both features. 2 marks may be awarded for reference plus detailed/insightful comment; 1 mark for reference plus more basic comment; 0 marks for mere identification of a feature of sentence structure. Possible answers are shown in the "Additional Guidance" column. (Marks may be awarded 2 + 2, 2 + 1 + 1, 1 + 1 + 1 + 1)	4	Possible answers include: *Sentence structure* • The positioning of **and/or** rhythmic/repetitive nature of "And the first and last thing" conveys the definitive 'Alpha and omega' nature of this phrase, especially when placed at the start of the sentence, suggests the difficulty of video games is a fundamental point to the writer • Use of parenthesis "the thing ... hear" adds to the mystery, adds to the dramatic build-up to the final announcement of video games' difficulty • Additional phrase "sometimes maddeningly" has two functions: again adds to the build-up **and/or** ramps up the notion of extreme difficulty that "fiendishly" has introduced

Question		Expected Response	Max Mark	Additional Guidance
2.		*(continued)*		• Use of climax in the sentence "The dirty … fun." — the somewhat awkward/unusual construction of this sentence is designed to stress the "not having fun" element of its conclusion • Repetition of the "you may be" structure stresses — and this is heightened by the use of the inclusive direct address — the variety of problems playing video games may cause • Repetition of adjectives ("frustrated", "confused", "disorientated", "stuck") — rat-a-tat run of adjectives suggests 'the sea of troubles' playing video games may involve • Anticlimax of "you may be stuck" in its definitive downbeat simplicity, it is a stark summation of the seemingly insoluble challenge these games present • Use of the continuous tense in final sentence — an argument might be made that this reflects the ongoing, nagging nature of the problems involved *Imagery* • "wrestling": just as wrestling involves close, physical combat with a single opponent, so it suggests a demanding, exhausting battle with an unforgiving enemy • "worrying a loose tooth": just as this involves the constant working away at a persistent physical annoyance, so it suggests that the difficulties presented by video games are nagging frustrations that constantly prey on one's mind • "stuck": just as to be stuck is to be fixed immovably, so it suggests being trapped in a situation which offers no escape • "dirty little secret": usually used in the realms of ethics or morality, a deliberate attempt to hide the truth, a cover-up of some sort, a hidden scandal; used in relation to the difficulty of video games, it heightens the potentially damaging nature of this feature, suggests it is a very negative feature that is deliberately glossed over
3.		Read lines 20–33. Identify three reasons why "reward" is so important to the learning process involved in playing video games. Use your own words as far as possible. Candidates must attempt to use their own words. No marks for straight lifts from the passage. (Marks awarded 1 + 1 + 1)	3	Possible answers include: • People are hard-wired to respond strongly to rewards • People find rewards a great stimulus to action, learning etc. • Video games are designed to be full of rewards • Rewards in video games are precise, with clear outcomes (explanation of "clearly defined") • The rewards are attractive • The rewards are presented in a variety of forms • Players are constantly reminded about the rewards • The rewards are vitally important to achieving success in the games • The rewards are more intense, striking, colourful than in real life • Players aren't always aware that they are learning (explanation of "without realising …")

Question		Expected Response	Max Mark	Additional Guidance
4.		Read lines 34–47. Identify two criticisms and two defences the writer makes of video games. Candidates must attempt to use their own words. No marks for straight lifts from the passage. (Marks awarded 1 + 1 + 1 + 1) NB Maximum 2 marks awarded for criticism and 2 marks awarded for defence.	4	Possible answers include: *Criticisms* • The games may seem attractive but the attractions flatter to deceive, are rather superficial, blind one to the truth (explanation of "dazzled") • The games are addictive (explanation of "hooked") • The subject matter is infantile, petty, puerile, trivial … (explanation of "actual content … childish") • Unnecessarily threatening, unjustifiably scary (explanation of "gratuitously menacing" – but explanation of "menacing" alone: 0) • The subject matter is very limited **and/or** moves between the two extremes of violence and childish fantasy (explanation of "alternates … princess-rescuing") • The games are violent (explanation of "drive-by shooting") • The games are pure fantasy (explanation of "princess-rescuing") *Defences* • The activities involved are beneficial for mental training/development ("good for the brain") • The skills developed will be of use in other spheres ("come in handy elsewhere") • It resembles learning algebra, which might seem pointless and abstract but exercises the brain • Like chess, games might seem very basic (and aggressive in concept), but they are every bit as cerebral and mind-developing as chess; they develop strategic, tactical thinking
5.	(a)	Read lines 48–54. Explain in your own words the key distinction the writer makes between reading a novel and playing a video game. Candidates must attempt to use their own words. No marks for straight lifts from the passage. (Marks awarded 1 + 1)	2	Possible answers include: *reading a novel* • Can get us thinking in a creative way, transport us to in different situation (explanation of "activate our imagination") • Can affect our feelings, arouse passions (explanation of "conjure up powerful emotions") *playing a game* • Makes you explore, study carefully (explanation of "analyse") • Makes you weigh up options (explanation of "choose") • Makes you evaluate options (explanation of "priotitise") • Makes you reach a conclusion (explanation of "decide")

Question		Expected Response	Max Mark	Additional Guidance
5.	(b)	Analyse how the writer's use of language in lines 50–54 ("From … strategies") conveys the contrast between what a gamer looks like from "the outside" and what is happening "inside the gamer's mind". For full marks there must be reference to both "outside" and "inside". 2 marks may be awarded for reference plus detailed/insightful comment; 1 mark for reference plus more basic comment; 0 marks for reference alone. Possible answers are shown in the "Additional Guidance" column. (Marks may be awarded 2 + 2, 2 + 1 + 1, 1 + 1 + 1 + 1)	4	Possible answers include: *the gamer from "the outside"* • "looks like" suggests this may be an unreliable perspective, a superficial, unquestioning way to approach an analysis of gamers • "fury" suggests the gamer is behaving in an impulsive, uncontrolled way; everything is being done at top speed, in a blur of unthinking activity • "clicking" suggests mindless, repetitive activity • "shooting" suggests destructive, homicidal activity • "clicking and shooting" automatic, unthinking, mechanical, robotic, repetitive … • The general simplicity of the penultimate sentence (especially when compared to the much more complex final sentence) heightens the impression that this is a naïve, simplistic way to view gamers *the gamer on the inside* • "peer" suggests an active approach involving close examination • "turns out" suggests a sense of some kind of revelation, surprise, discovery • "another creature" suggests something mysterious, surprising, unexpected, interesting but hard to define, a new form of life we didn't know existed • Use of colon introduces a detailed description of the full range of intellectual activities involved in gaming • Balance/repetition of "some of them" stresses range of activities involved • Contrast in "snap judgements … long-term strategies" shows range of important decision-making skills involved from quick, smart thinking to overall planning • "judgements" suggests wise, fair thinking • "strategies" suggests considered, creative thinking

Passage 2

Question	Expected Response	Max Mark	Additional Guidance
6.	Look at both passages. The writers disagree about video games. Identify three key areas on which they disagree. You should support the points by referring to important ideas in both passages. You may answer this question in continuous prose or in a series of developed bullet points. Candidates can use bullet points in this final question, or write a number of linked statements. Approach to marking is shown in the "Additional Guidance column. Key areas of disagreement are shown in the grid below. Other answers are possible.	5	The following guidelines should be used: 5 marks — identification of three key areas of agreement with detailed/insightful use of supporting evidence 4 marks — identification of three key areas of agreement with appropriate use of supporting evidence 3 marks — identification of three areas of agreement 2 marks — identification of two key areas of agreement 1 mark — identification of one key area of agreement 0 marks — failure to identify any key areas of agreement and/or misunderstanding of the task NB A candidate who identifies only two key areas of agreement may be awarded up to a maximum of 4 marks, as follows • 2 marks for identification of two key areas of agreement plus **either** • a further mark for appropriate use of supporting evidence to a total of 3 marks **or** • a further 2 marks for detailed/insightful use of supporting evidence to a total of 4 marks A candidate who identifies only one key area of agreement may be awarded up to a maximum of 2 marks, as follows: • 1 mark for identification of one key area of agreement • a further mark for use of supporting evidence to a total of 2 marks

	Area of Disagreement	Steven Johnson	Boris Johnson
1.	General status	They are viewed as pointless, but they are not	They are harmful, narcotically addictive
2.	Intellectual benefits	They develop the brain in a number of ways	They require no thought or effort
3.	Educational benefits	High level thinking skills are developed	They may pretend to be educational but are totally lacking in educational value; a threat to literacy
4.	The challenge involved	They can appear simple but are often very complex The process is more important than the (often simplistic) content	They encourage slovenly behaviour and thinking
5.	The reward(s) involved	They are at times extremely hard unlike other entertainment, pleasure is not immediate	They offer immediate and simple pleasures

PAPER 2 – CRITICAL READING

SECTION 1 – Scottish Text

- Candidates should gain credit for their understanding, analysis and evaluation of the extract and either the whole play or novel, or other poems and short stories by the writer.
- In the final 10-mark question the candidate should answer the question in either a series of linked statements, or in bullet points.

Detailed Marking Instructions for each question

PART A – SCOTTISH TEXT – DRAMA

Text 1 – *Drama – The Slab Boys* by John Byrne

Question	Expected Answer(s)	Max Mark	Additional Guidance
1.	2 marks awarded for detailed/insightful comment plus quotation/reference; 1 mark for more basic comment plus quotation/reference; 0 marks for quotation/reference alone. Possible answers are shown in the "Additional Guidance" column. (Marks may be awarded 2 + 1, 1 + 1 + 1)	3	Possible answers include: • Spanky's hesitation in e.g. "We'd like to present this little...er... this token of ...er..." suggests sympathy for loss of his job and awkwardness about being sincere now, due to their previously mocking behaviour towards him • "Are you going to shut your face...Shorty?" offhand and insulting vocabulary suggest the familiar exasperation expressed towards Hector, despite current sympathy for him • Spanky's skirting around the subject/use of euphemism to describe losing his job, "We know it's come as a bit of a surprise...you having to leave" suggests attempt to be tactful and not embarrass or hurt Hector • Phil's unsuccessful attempt to be more articulate than Spanky – "What Spanky ... och, here" suggests he, too, feels uncomfortable in the unusual role of kindness towards Hector
2.	2 marks awarded for detailed/insightful comment plus quotation/reference; 1 mark for more basic comment plus quotation/reference; 0 marks for quotation/reference alone. Possible answers are shown in the "Additional Guidance" column. (Marks may be awarded 2 + 2, 2 + 1 + 1, 1 + 1 + 1 + 1)	4	Possible answers include: • Hector's comical repetition of "Eh?" emphasises his lack of understanding as Phil and Spanky try to commiserate with him for the (supposed) loss of his job • Repetition of "Till you get another job" by Phil and Spanky, culminating in climax of their saying it together builds up sense of their frustration that he does not seem to understand what they are commiserating with him about • Hector's statement of "I've already got another job" is a bathetic moment, echoing their repeated statements about his needing another job • Phil's question "Is there a mobile Broo outside?" emphasises the absurdity of the idea that he might have another job already • Spanky and Phil's exclamation in unison, "What????" is a comical climax which conveys their incredulity that he has been promoted • Hector's comment that he feels unwell is echoed by Spanky, "Me too", with the contrasting meaning: Spanky is sickened that Hector should be promoted; Hector feels sick with excitement

Question	Expected Answer(s)	Max Mark	Additional Guidance
3.	2 marks awarded for detailed/ insightful comment plus quotation/reference; 1 mark for more basic comment plus quotation/reference; 0 marks for quotation/ reference alone. Possible answers are shown in the "Additional Guidance" column. (Marks may be awarded 2 + 1, 1 + 1 + 1)	3	Possible answers include: • Repetition of questions: "...guess what?...how about that?" suggests his excitement about starting work and/or insensitivity to the fact that he is given this chance because of Phil losing his job • "Where are the gum crystals kept again?" matter of fact question suggests that he is getting started right away, with no regard for the trauma being suffered by Phil • "Oh...message on..." broken sentences said while looking for gum crystals suggests his offhand attitude to the message which is so important to Phil/his selfish interest in small concerns of his own rather than vital issues of others • Blunt statement of "You didn't get in" suggests his indifference to the blow this message will cause for Phil/an element of enjoyment of Phil's devastation • "...something like that..." lack of specific detail conveys how unimportant this information is to him/dismissive approach to something so important to another person
4.	Candidates may choose to answer in bullet points in this final question, or write a number of linked statements. Possible answers are shown in the "Additional Guidance" column.	10	Up to 2 marks can be achieved for identifying elements of commonality as identified in the question, i.e. theme of opportunity. A further 2 marks can be achieved for reference to the extract given. 6 additional marks can be awarded for discussion of similar references to at least one other part of the text. In practice this means: Identification of commonality (2) e.g. Opportunity is not equally or fairly available: it depends on factors such as social class, education, family connections (1) Lack of real opportunity leads to feelings of cynicism and disillusion, exemplified by the attitudes of Phil and Spanky (1) From the extract: 2 marks for detailed/insightful comment plus quotation/reference; 1 mark for more basic comment plus quotation/reference; 0 marks for quotation alone. e.g. Phil, though talented, is rejected by the art college, therefore not given the opportunity to develop his talent: there is a sense that this background, from 'Feegie', and lack of formal education is held against him (2) From at least one other part of the text: as above for up to 6 marks Possible answers include: • Phil and Spanky resent the lack of opportunities open to them since joining the slab room, claiming that they would be rewarded more if they were masons • Frustration of the slab boys at being stuck in the slab room, with no desk in sight, is clear e.g. Spanky who has been in the slab room for three years and, at the end, is told he might get a desk in eighteen months • Alan, with his education, social class and family commitments has expectations of greater opportunity e.g. he is not over-impressed with his salary of £3 (which is a lot of money to the slab boys) • Opportunities in love also come to those with more money etc., shown by Lucille agreeing to go to the Staffie with Alan, as long as he picks her up in his father's car • Jack accuses Phil and Spanky of destroying Hector's opportunities by mocking him for his eagerness to learn : he wants to give Hector a chance as a designer

Text 2 — *Drama — The Cheviot, the Stag and the Black, Black Oil* by John McGrath

Question	Expected Answer(s)	Max Mark	Additional Guidance
5.	For full marks candidates should deal with both characters but not necessarily in equal measure. 2 marks awarded for detailed/insightful comment plus quotation/reference; 1 mark for more basis comment plus quotation/reference; 0 marks for quotation/reference alone. Possible answers are shown in the "Additional Guidance" column. (Marks may be awarded 2 + 2, 2 + 1 + 1, 1 + 1 + 1 + 1)	4	Possible answers include: Lady Phosphate • Reference to Queen implies personal friendship, suggesting over-inflated sense of her own importance • Repetition of "what?" affectation suggests social posturing/shallowness of character • Over-blown and clichéd language — "divine", "rugged beauty", "abound" — suggests lack of sincerity/pretentiousness • Use of literary quotation "Oh listen … sound" to convey supposed intellectual superiority/lack of authenticity Lord Crask • "Has your ladyship sampled the salmon?" shows eagerness to ingratiate/impress • Unnecessary use of full title to stress status/joint membership of upper classes suggests his pride and arrogance • "120,000 acres … most of it" — comical juxtaposition of large figure with comment on true extent of land suggests boastfulness
6.	2 marks awarded for detailed/insightful comment plus quotation/reference; 1 mark for more basic comment plus quotation/reference; 0 marks for quotation/reference alone. Possible answers are shown in the "Additional Guidance" column. (Marks may be awarded 2 + 2, 2 + 1 + 1, 1 + 1 + 1 + 1)	4	Possible answers include: • Lord Crask's misunderstanding of "capital" suggests the upper class's obsession with wealth and power • Comic exchange of "Wapping … Topping … No Wapping" mocks the upper class's/highlights their ridiculous nature • Lord Crask offers Lochinver when Lady Phosphate asks for "a small port", demonstrating his limited understanding/lack of thought for the local population • Lord Crask offers a bush as toilet facilities suggesting that the sophistication of the upper classes is just a veneer/they are no different from anyone else • Reference to Lady Phosphate's "sten gun" — inappropriately over the top for grouse shooting — suggests her lack of regard for the natural environment • Ironic understatement "Thon was a nice wee boy" suggests complete disregard for human life
7.	1 mark for comment plus quotation/reference (x2); 0 marks for quotation/reference alone. Possible answers are shown in the "Additional Guidance" column. (Marks may be awarded 1 + 1)	2	Possible answers include: Local people • Repetition of "We'll clear" suggests their determination to let nothing stand in their way/not to be stopped or criticised • Derogatory use of plural — "the locals" — suggests dismissive/superior attitude to the community Environment • Juxtaposition of "ni-i-ice" with killing of various creatures suggest selfish lack of concern for environment • Pronunciation of "grice" and "trite" suggests unwillingness to learn about the environment

Question	Expected Answer(s)	Max Mark	Additional Guidance
8.	Candidates may choose to answer in bullet points in this final question, or write a number of linked statements. Possible answers are shown in the "Additional Guidance" column.	10	Up to 2 marks can be achieved for identifying elements of commonality as identified in the question, i.e. how the writer explores the issue of social class and its effects. A further 2 marks can be achieved for reference to the extract given. 6 additional marks can be awarded for discussion of similar references to at least one other part of the text. <u>In practice this means:</u> Identification of commonality (2) e.g. land-owning classes in the Scottish Highlands exhibit selfish and exploitative behaviour (1) leading to suffering and destitution of the poor (1) From the extract: 2 marks for detailed/insightful comment plus quotation/reference; 1 mark for more basic comment plus quotation/reference; 0 marks for quotation/reference alone. e.g. the callous killing of the little boy reveals the contemptuous attitude of the upper classes to the local population (2) From at least one other part of the text: as above for up to 6 marks Possible answers include: • Sellar evicts lower classes from their homes and destroys their livelihood, callously referring to them as "a set of savages" • International developers are encouraged as long as they adhere to the laws of capitalism, where the end justifies the means, despite the suffering of the poor in the name of 'progress' • Lord Selkirk, a member of the aristocracy, has a plan to exploit, develop and maximise profits with no regard for the consequences to the local people • Collective solidarity by the dispossessed against the upper classes has met with varying success, particularly at "The Battle of the Braes", emphasising that ultimately they are powerless • Many of the indigent characters are known only by their employment or gender — Ghillie, Aberdonian Rigger, First woman — contrasting with the use of titles and individual names of the upper class characters, showing the anonymity of and disregard for the poor

Text 3 – Drama – Men Should Weep by Ena Lamont Stewart

Question	Expected Answer(s)	Max Mark	Additional Guidance
9.	For full marks, both stage directions and dialogue should be covered but not necessarily in equal measure. 2 marks awarded for detailed/insightful comment plus quotation/reference; 1 mark for a more basic comment plus quotation/reference; 0 marks for quotation/reference alone. Possible answers are shown in the "Additional Guidance" column. (Marks may be awarded 2 + 2, 2 + 1 + 1, 1 + 1 + 1 + 1)	4	Possible answers include: **Stage directions** • "a hard-faced harridan" suggests Lizzie is a mean, cold, aggressive woman • "ignoring the others" suggests Lizzie has no time for social niceties or being pleasant to people • "Mrs Bone goes to help her" suggests Lizzie is quite happy for Granny to struggle on her own whereas Mrs Bone sees the need to lend a hand • "taking the pension book from Mrs Bone" suggests Lizzie's aggressive, greedy personality • "They both stare hard at Lizzie, then shake their heads at each other" suggests their general disbelief/incredulity at Lizzie's attitude towards life **Dialogue** • "An yer pension book?"/"See's a look at it."/"Ye got the money?" suggests Lizzie's mercenary outlook on life • "Well, it's no Maggie's, it's mines" suggests Lizzie's utterly selfish attitude • "If ye're comin tae bide wi me, ye're no comin tae bide *aff* me" suggests Lizzie's greed and/or her determination not to be taken advantage of • "And whit does she think you're gonna live on for the next week? Air?" aggressive questioning reveals her hard-hearted outlook • "Ach, leave...tae feed." Mrs Harris' speech underlines how lacking in compassion or humanity Lizzie is • "I'm no takin...no room in ma hoose" – suggests Lizzie's cold hearted, uncompromising nature • "That's jist whit I said: *anything human*" emphasises that Mrs Bone feels Lizzie is so lacking in compassion and pity that she is scarcely human
10.	2 marks awarded for detailed/insightful comment plus quotation/reference; 1 mark for a more basic comment plus quotation/reference; 0 marks for quotation/reference alone. Possible answers are shown in the "Additional Guidance" column. (Marks may be awarded 2 + 2, 2 + 1 + 1, 1 + 1 + 1 + 1)	4	Possible answers include: • "ye aul miser"/"at fifty percent" suggests outrage at Lizzie's obsession with making money • "A bargain? Frae you?" suggests incredulity that Lizzie could act in a generous manner • "Veloory hat...bird on tap" mockery suggests their contempt for Lizzie's pretensions • "A bit whit? Pinchin?" suggests recognition of Lizzie's true nature • "No roon aboot here ye couldnae. They a ken ye." conveys a contemptuous awareness of Lizzie's reputation
11.	2 marks awarded for a detailed/insightful explanation; 1 mark for a more basic explanation; 0 marks for quotation/reference alone. Possible answers are shown in the "Additional Guidance" column. (Marks may be awarded 2, 1 + 1)	2	Possible answers include: • Granny represents the older generation who are dependent on others • Granny's situation highlights the poverty which often accompanied old age at that time • As a woman, she has no status or independence in the society of the time • She represents the vulnerable in a harsh world as she moves from household to household • Her lack of autonomy highlights the devastating effects of poverty • She represents the difficulty of family responsibility e.g. there is no room for her when Isa and Alec are made homeless

Question	Expected Answer(s)	Max Mark	Additional Guidance
12.	Candidates may choose to answer in bullet points in this final question, or write a number of linked statements. Possible answers are shown in the "Additional Guidance" column.	10	Up to 2 marks can be achieved by identifying elements of commonality as identified in the question, i.e. how the writer develops the theme of community. A further 2 marks can be achieved for reference to the extract given. 6 additional marks can be awarded for discussion of similar references to at least one other part of the text. <u>In practice this means:</u> Identification of commonality (2) e.g. community is important in this society because of the support and compassion people offer each other (1) although they can also be judgmental, opinionated, intrusive (1) From the extract: 2 marks for detailed/insightful comment plus quotation/reference; 1 mark for more basic comment plus quotation/reference; 0 marks for quotation/reference alone. e.g. Mrs Bone and Mrs Harris support Maggie by sitting with Granny while she is waiting to be collected/by defending Maggie from attack by Lizzie and are not afraid to openly pass judgement on Lizzie's behaviour and morals (2) From elsewhere in the text: as above for up to 6 marks Possible answers include: • Maggie's neighbours often help her with Granny, with baby-sitting and the support neighbours offer each other is an integral part of how this impoverished society operates. Maggie says, "Folks like us hev tae depend on their neighbours when they're needin help." • Maggie's neighbours are mostly compassionate and kind: they really worry about Bertie's serious illness; they keep up Granny's spirits; they take pleasure in Maggie's improved fortunes in the final act. As Maggie says, "Oh, they're no bad — they're coorse but kind." • Women play a central role in this community and there is a sense that they share lives which men do not understand or in which men contribute to women's problems • Members of the community are quite open in passing judgements and voicing criticisms of their husbands, of the younger generation, even of Maggie's new hat: "Whit the hell made ye tak *red*?" • Maggie and John worry about community opinions, whereas the younger generation, such as Jenny and Isa, are happy to flout the traditional values that their neighbours largely represent. Jenny says to her father, "Whit do I care whit the neighbours thinks?"

PART B — SCOTTISH TEXT — PROSE

Text 1 — *Prose — The Red Door* by Iain Crichton Smith

Question	Expected Answer(s)	Max Mark	Additional Guidance
13.	For full marks, candidates must deal with both the door and the surroundings, but not necessarily in equal measure. 2 marks awarded for detailed/insightful comment plus quotation/reference; 1 mark for more basic comment plus quotation/reference; 0 marks for quotation/reference alone. Possible answers are shown in the "Additional Guidance" column. (Marks may be awarded 2 + 2, 2 + 1 + 1, 1 + 1 + 1 + 1)	4	Possible answers include: Door • "painted very lovingly" suggests care had been taken to ensure the door looked beautiful and was not just functional • "shone with a deep inward shine" suggests that the door stood out against its backdrop/had an alluring quality which radiated from within • "looked like a picture/work of art" suggests the door was attractive and now had an importance of its own • "stood out" suggests the door was striking/out of the ordinary Surroundings • "wasn't at all modern/old" suggests the house was dated/behind the times • "intertwined...rusty pipes like snakes" conveys the idea that the house was in need of maintenance/had been neglected • Imagery "intertwined/snake" suggests the house was constricting/restraining its occupant • "drab landscape" implies that it was uninspiring/dull/gloomy set against the brightness of the door • Dismissal of more harmonious colours "blue/green" highlights the surroundings were now tedious/uninspiring to Murdo
14.	2 marks awarded for detailed/insightful comment plus quotation/reference; 1 mark for more basic comment plus quotation/reference; 0 marks for quotation/reference alone. Possible answers are shown in the "Additional Guidance" column. (Marks may be awarded 2 + 2, 2 + 1 + 1, 1 + 1 + 1 + 1)	4	Possible answers include: • "morning was breaking/blue smoke was ascending" symbolises that the new day for the villagers was a new beginning for Murdo • "a cock was crowing" biblical allusion to signal Murdo's 'betrayal' of his current way of life • "belligerent and heraldic...metallic breast" military connotations suggest that a new assertive/combative spirit had been awakened in Murdo • "oriental and strange" suggests that this feeling was foreign and unfamiliar to him • Murdo's inner dialogue "I have always/I go/I do..." conveys his admission of his disillusionment with his life up to this point • "never had the courage...coloured waistcoat/jacket" reveals Murdo's realisation of his long held desire to be an individual/be different from others/stand out from the crowd • "whiteness of the frost...glimmerings of snow" contrast emphasises the striking physical impact of the door and the symbolic significance of a new beginning for Murdo • "seemed to have its own courage" personification represents Murdo's inner thoughts and wishes

Question	Expected Answer(s)	Max Mark	Additional Guidance
15.	2 marks awarded for detailed/insightful comment plus quotation/reference; 1 mark for more basic comment plus quotation/reference; 0 marks for quotation/reference alone. Possible answers are shown in the "Additional Guidance" column. (Marks may be awarded 2, 1 + 1)	2	Possible answers include: • Use of the question "was he happy?" highlights his uncertainty/doubts about his current way of life • Repetition of "he didn't like" emphasises the level of his discontent/frustration with his situation • "had to keep...smiling face" conveys his inner conflict over the image he projected to others • Climactic nature of "hated them" reveals the strength and depth of his true feelings
16.	Candidates may choose to answer in bullet points in this final question, or write a number of linked statements.	10	Up to 2 marks can be achieved by identifying elements of commonality as identified in the question, i.e. Crichton Smith's exploration of the conflict between individuality and conformity. A further 2 marks can be achieved for reference to the extract given. 6 additional marks can be awarded for discussion of similar references to at least one other short story by Crichton Smith. In practice this means: Identification of commonality (2) e.g. Crichton Smith shows that the impact of trying to fit in with one's surroundings (1) can cause some to suffer and deny their true feelings whilst others find the courage to break free (1) From the extract: 2 marks for detailed/insightful comment plus quotation/reference; 1 mark for more basic comment plus quotation/reference; 0 marks for quotation/reference alone. e.g. the discovery of the red door acts as a catalyst for Murdo to begin a new life where he can be true to himself (2) From at least one other text: as above for up to 6 marks Possible comments include: • *The Telegram* the thin woman has lived in the village for many years yet she is isolated by others as she does not make the same choices as them • *The Painter* William challenges the conventions of the village by painting a realistic picture of the fight and is ostracised as a result • *Mother and Son* John feels trapped by his overbearing, critical mother but is compelled by a sense of duty to stay with her thus denying his true self • *In Church* the 'priest' is a deserter who becomes a murderer as he could not conform to the expectations of war • *The Crater* the need to conform to the expected nature of an officer leads Robert to conceal his fears on the battlefield

Text 2 — *Prose — Tartan* by George Mackay Brown

Question	Expected Answer(s)	Max Mark	Additional Guidance
17.	2 marks awarded for detailed/ insightful comment plus quotation/ reference; 1 mark for more basic comment plus quotation/reference; 0 marks for quotation/reference alone. Possible answers are shown in the "Additional Guidance" column. (Marks may be awarded 2 + 2, 2 + 1 + 1, 1 + 1 + 1 + 1)	4	Possible answers include: • "muttering and sighing" suggests ongoing nature of deep grief/despair at loss of the future • Contrast between Kol's energy "leapt...loud beserk yell" and the stillness and quiet in the room • "might have been a fly buzzing...paid to him" comparison with "fly buzzing" conveys how completely unimportant/ irrelevant the Viking raid — normally an event of fear and danger — is in comparison to loss of child • Parallel structure of the old woman's sentences "I thought to see you a shepherd...Or maybe you would be a man...Or you might have been a holy priest" suggests repetitive chant to convey the primal sense of grief • "...shepherd...fisherman...man with lucky acres...holy priest" conveys the range of possible futures/hope which have been destroyed by the child's death • "cross...tangled in his cold fingers" conveys bleak finality of the human loss by creating a picture of the child's fingers, already cold • "crossed themselves in the door": simple description of the Vikings' action conveys the sense that even they are awed and moved by his death • "slunk out like a dog" suggests Kol's shame at the inappropriateness of his leap into the room
18.	2 marks awarded for detailed/ insightful comment plus quotation/ reference; 1 mark for more basic comment plus quotation/reference; 0 marks for quotation/reference alone. Possible answers are shown in the "Additional Guidance" column. (Marks may be awarded 2 + 2, 2 + 1 + 1, 1 + 1 + 1 + 1)	4	Possible answers include: • "Strangers from the sea...you are welcome...I ask you to accept ale" exaggerated nature of welcome, under the circumstances i.e. they are Viking raiders, suggests insincerity/attempt to manipulate them • "They are good people here, except for the man who lives..." use of "they" distances himself from the other people of Durness/sees himself as superior and in a position to judge the others • "he will not pay me for the cloth I wove for him last winter" accusatory tone by which he attempts to gain the support of the Vikings against one of his own community • "he and his wife and his snovelly-nosed children" dismissive and distasteful description of Duncan's family suggests his feelings of superiority towards them • "Take it, take it by all means" repetition of "take it" suggests his eagerness to please the Vikings, to ingratiate himself with them • "John has been on the hill all week...I think she is lonely" apparently simple statement of facts suggests her isolation and vulnerability and even hints at the idea that she is sexual prey, indicating how low and disloyal his attitude is
19.	1 mark for comment plus quotation/ reference (x2); 0 marks for quotation/reference alone. Possible answers are shown in the "Additional Guidance" column. (Marks awarded 1 + 1)	2	Possible answers include: • Havard's 'retrospective' threat to Malcolm: "If it (the ale) had been sour, we would have stretched you..." suggests his aggression/bullying quality (though perhaps said in a jocular way) • Arnor's decision to "settle matters" with Duncan on behalf of Malcolm, along with "Now we need our cups filled again" suggests his desire to be seen as in command • Kol's staggering, combined with his bravado claim "Doubtless somebody will pay for this" suggests his boastful and belligerent attitude • Sven's reply to Malcolm's offer of the tartan cloth: "We were going to take it in any case" suggests his determination to show Malcolm who is in charge, despite Malcolm's attempts to manipulate/be courteous

Question	Expected Answer(s)	Max Mark	Additional Guidance
20.	Candidates may choose to answer in bullet points in this final question, or write a number of linked statements. Possible answers are shown in the "Additional Guidance" column.	10	Up to 2 marks can be achieved for identifying elements of commonality as identified in the question, i.e. the relationship between the individual and the community. A further 2 marks can be achieved for reference to the extract given. 6 additional marks can be awarded for discussion of similar references to at least one other short story by Mackay Brown. In practice this means: Identification of commonality (2) e.g. Individuals will usually show loyalty and commitment to the community (1) though some will rebel against or betray the community values to achieve their own fulfilment/achieve their own ends (1) From the extract: 2 marks for detailed/insightful comment plus quotation/reference; 1 mark for more basic comment plus quotation/reference; 0 marks for quotation alone. e.g. Malcolm the weaver attempts to exploit the Viking raid for his own selfish aims to settle old scores within the community, such as the non-payment for cloth, to gain favour with the raiders (2) From at least one other text: as above for up to 6 marks Possible answers include: • *A Time to Keep* loyalty to the community can mean suspicion of 'outsiders' such as Inge (from just over the hill) and Bill (a whaler). Bill's sense of their 'separateness' contributes to the negative relationship he has with the other men in the community • *A Time to Keep* Bill is appalled by the community taking charge of his wife's death, represented by the women's show of grief expressed in "litany of the dead person's virtues…most of them lies", and the minister's comments. He rejects their sentimental clichés about going to "a better place" • *The Bright Spade* seven men show loyalty and heroism in setting off into the storm to look for food for the community- but the sacrifice of their lives in fact helps no one • *The Wireless Set* Howie feels he is bringing progress and development to the 'backward' community by bringing home the wireless set; his attitude contrasts with that of his parents, who uphold the traditional values of the community and view the outside world with suspicion • *The Eye of the Hurricane* Barclay's initial sense of superiority and objectification of the community ("simple uncomplicated people") gives way to genuine involvement in the face of Cpt. Stevens' suffering and flawed but heroic humanity

Text 3 — *Prose — The Trick is to Keep Breathing* by Janice Galloway

Question	Expected Answer(s)	Max Mark	Additional Guidance
21.	2 marks awarded for detailed/insightful comment plus quotation/reference; 1 mark for more basic comment plus quotation/reference; 0 marks for quotation/reference alone. Possible answers are shown in the "Additional Guidance" column. (Marks may be awarded 2 + 2, 2 + 1 + 1, 1 + 1 + 1 + 1)	4	Possible answers include: • "protection against witches" suggests something evil/sinister about the place • "well outside the place...be part of" use of irony emphasises the sense of isolation/remoteness • "undesirables"/"difficult tenants"/"shunters"/"overspill" suggests the inhabitants are unwanted in the main town • Contrast between how it is meant to appear/idyllic setting eg "wild currant bushes"/"tiny, twisty roads" and what it is like in reality eg "pubs with plastic beer glasses"/"kids use the bends to play chicken" • "lying low"/"leaping out" suggests children are wild/out of control • "buses go slow"/"infrequent" emphasises remoteness/isolation • "graffiti" — vandalism indicates neglect • "It rains a lot." short sentence highlights the sense of misery emphasised by the weather
22.	2 marks awarded for detailed/insightful comment plus quotation/reference; 1 mark for more basic comment plus quotation/reference; 0 marks for quotation/reference alone. Possible answers are shown in the "Additional Guidance" column. (Marks may be awarded 2 + 2, 2 + 1 + 1, 1 + 1 + 1 + 1)	4	Possible answers include: • "never surrenders first time" personification suggests that the key refuses to be found easily • "rummage" suggests frantic search/desperation • "as though begging to be mugged" comparison suggests Joy's feelings of vulnerability • "Not mine." minor sentence emphasises her lack of belonging/ownership • "grit"/"litter" emphasises how Joy finds the place unwelcoming/unhomely • "withered leaves" suggests Joy's obsession with death/decay • "slaters run frantic"/"insects make me sick"/"disgust me" emphasises Joy's irrationality/neurotic nature • "fight my way inside" emphasises Joy's desperation to escape the outside world. • "gritty little packets"/"skeletons outside"/"too many eyes"/"unpredictable legs" suggests Joy's fear
23.	2 marks awarded for detailed/insightful comment plus quotation/reference; 1 mark for more basic comment plus quotation/reference; 0 marks for quotation/reference alone. Possible answers are shown in the "Additional Guidance" column. (Marks may be awarded 2, 1 + 1)	2	Possible answers include: • "Try to feel (the other continent)" suggests her desperation to escape • "I find the bottle...I put an envelope...sitting the bottle aside...reshape the cushions..." list of activities suggests she is trying to impose order/structure on her own situation • "But things have to be set in place." short sentence emphasises her desire for control • "Stillness helps..."/"It keeps me contained" short sentences emphasise her attempts at self-control/order

Question	Expected Answer(s)	Max Mark	Additional Guidance
24.	Candidates may choose to answer in bullet points in this final question, or write a number of linked statements. Possible answers are shown in the "Additional Guidance" column.	10	Up to 2 marks can be achieved for identifying elements of commonality as identified in the question, i.e. how Galloway explores the impact of loneliness. A further 2 marks can be achieved for reference to the extract given. 6 additional marks can be awarded for discussion of similar references to at least one other part of the text. <u>In practice this means:</u> Identification of commonality (2) e.g. devastating life changing, destructive nature of loneliness (1) can affect mental health/ability to communicate/ability to form relationships (1) From the extract: 2 marks for detailed/insightful comment plus quotation/reference; 1 mark for more basic comment plus quotation/reference; 0 marks for quotation alone. e.g. Joy attempts to cope with loneliness by focusing on distracting herself and creating a sense of order in her surroundings: "A lot depends on stillness later and I have to get a lot of moving around out of my system now." (2) From at least one other part of the text: as above for up to 6 marks Possible answers include: • Joy tries to cope with her loneliness following Michael's death by engaging in a number of casual relationships with men • Joy distracts herself from her loneliness by engaging in a variety of mundane activities e.g. sewing, reading magazines, various rituals including bathing etc. • Joy forces herself to engage in the activities suggested by her friend Marianne, including visiting Marianne's mother, Ellen, regularly • In order to hide her loneliness from others, Joy attempts to appear upbeat and in control to others for example Tony, Myra etc. • Joy attempts to alleviate her loneliness after Michael's death by trying to re-create his physical presence e.g. spraying his aftershave

Text 4 – *Prose – Sunset Song* by Lewis Grassic Gibbon

Question	Expected Answer(s)	Max Mark	Additional Guidance
25.	2 marks awarded for detailed/insightful comment plus quotation/reference; 1 mark for more basic comment plus quotation/reference; 0 marks for quotation/reference alone. Possible answers are shown in the "Additional Guidance" column. (Marks may be awarded 2 + 1, 1 + 1 + 1)	3	Possible answers include: • "strong on Rich and Poor being Equal" suggests firmly held socialist principles; a belief that all wealth should be shared out evenly • "Broke he might be but he wasn't mean" suggests that regardless of his own financial problems, Chae is a generous host • "there was broth..." suggests that he provides an abundance of food which clearly signifies his gratitude • "he could hold to the turnip-field" suggests Chae has a lively sense of humour which often reveals the ridiculous in his fellow man
26.	2 marks awarded for detailed/insightful comment plus quotation/reference; 1 mark for more basic comment plus quotation/reference; 0 marks for quotation/reference alone. Possible answers are shown in the "Additional Guidance" column. (Marks may be awarded 2 + 1, 1 + 1 + 1)	3	Possible answers include: • "his great lugs like red clouts hung out to dry" suggests comical physical appearance (his prominent ears compared to washing on a line) • "as though he hadn't seen food for a fortnight" gross exaggeration to convey his greedy consumption of the meal • "like a colie ta'en off its chain" overstated comparison to a ravenous dog just released • "a spree to the pair of them" sense that this is a bout of self-indulgence rather than part of a day's work • "*fair an expert getting*" condescending use of the word "expert" has the intention of belittling Chris • "*The kitchen's more her style than the College.*" patronising judgement reveals his own prejudice
27.	2 marks awarded for detailed/insightful comment plus quotation/reference; 1 mark for more basic comment plus quotation/reference; 0 marks for quotation/reference alone. Possible answers are shown in the "Additional Guidance" column. (Marks may be awarded 2 + 2, 2 + 1 + 1, 1 + 1 + 1 + 1)	4	Possible answers include: • "the yokels and clowns everlasting" suggests Chris resents the total disregard for learning displayed by those she perceives as country bumpkins and forever stupid • "dull-brained and crude" suggests Chris rejects those who have laughed as slow-witted and vulgar • "a coarse thing, learning" suggests many see no refining qualities in knowledge • "a lot of damn nonsense that put them above themselves" suggests many perceive education as valueless and will lead to a false sense of superiority in their offspring • "give you their lip" suggests many think that education leads to impudence • "to put him up level with the Rich" suggests Chae contradicts the views of others by declaring that education provides social equality • "the more of sense and the less of kirks and ministers" suggests Long Rob agrees with Chae and states that education improves a person's ability to think clearly and reject organised religion • "was shamed as she thought" suggests Chris revises her view of Chae and Long Rob whose kindness she recognises, despite their lack of possessions

Question	Expected Answer(s)	Max Mark	Additional Guidance
28.	Candidates may choose to answer in bullet points in this final question, or write a number of linked statements. Possible answers are shown in the "Additional Guidance" column.	10	Up to 2 marks can be achieved for identifying elements of commonality as identified in the question, i.e. Chris's conflicting emotions towards the community in Kinraddie. A further 2 marks can be achieved for reference to the extract given. 6 additional marks can be awarded for discussion of similar references to at least one other part of the text. <u>In practice this means:</u> Identification of commonality (2) e.g. Chris is appalled by the small-mindedness of the Speak (1), but she values the innate kindness of her neighbours in times of need (1) From the extract: 2 marks for detailed/insightful comment plus quotation/reference; 1 mark for more basic comment plus quotation/reference; 0 marks for quotation alone. e.g. Chris is angered by Munro's patronising comments, aimed to reduce her to his servant, but she also acknowledges the considerate nature of Chae and Long Rob (2) From at least one other part of the text: as above for up to 6 marks Possible answers include: • The two Chrisses are torn between love of school and learning ("you hated the land and the coarse speak of the folk") and her love of the land and its people • Chris is angered by the rumours about Will and Mollie Douglas, but she begins to learn about relationships after meeting Mollie on the road • Chris is aware of gossip about the Strachans, their financial problems and insurance money from the fire, but she also knows that she, her family and the community do all they can to assist at Peesie's Knapp • Chris is initially untroubled by the community's view of her seemingly heartless lack of sorrow at the death of her father, but she is comforted by their neighbourly concern at the graveside • Chris disregards the community's sense of outrage that she should marry Ewan so soon after her father's death, but she is delighted that so many locals should celebrate her wedding and wish both of them well

rose — The Cone-Gatherers by Robin Jenkins

Question	Expected Answer(s)	Max Mark	Additional Guidance
29.	2 marks awarded for detailed/insightful comment plus quotation/reference; 1 mark for more basic comment plus quotation/reference; 0 marks for quotation/reference alone. Possible answers are shown in the "Additional Guidance" column. (Marks may be awarded 2, 1 + 1)	2	Possible answers include: • "indigo clouds" dark colour suggests the darkening, angry sky • "mustering" suggests soldiers gathering, and reflects the literal and metaphorical storm • "rumbles (of thunder)" onomatopoeia reflects the ominous sound of thunder • "whisked away" suggests the panic of the birds before the storm • "ominous" suggests something powerful/dangerous/ frightening • "river of radiance" alliteration/metaphor emphasises the long thin streak of light, shining like water
30.	2 marks awarded for detailed/insightful comment plus quotation/reference; 1 mark for more basic comment plus quotation/reference; 0 marks for quotation/reference alone. Possible answers are shown in the "Additional Guidance" column. (Marks may be awarded 2 + 2, 2 + 1 + 1, 1 + 1 + 1 + 1)	4	Possible answers include: • "frightened and exhilarated" combination suggests tumult of emotions • "frightened" suggests scared/terrified • "exhilarated" suggests a rush of energy/his identification with natural forces • "chattered...sense" suggests he is so overcome with excitement that it affects him physically • "dribble out" suggests he is so overwhelmed he loses control of his actions • "he raised his hand" suggests a need to join with the elements/wants physical contact with them • "meaningless chatters" suggests incoherence due to excitement • "screamed" suggests extreme/heightened reaction
31.	2 marks awarded for detailed/insightful comment plus quotation/reference; 1 mark for more basic comment plus quotation/reference; 0 marks for quotation/reference alone. Possible answers are shown in the "Additional Guidance" column. (Marks may be awarded 2 + 2, 2 + 1 + 1, 1 + 1 + 1 + 1)	4	Possible answers include: • "We'd better get down" indicates that Neil takes responsibility for their safety/makes important decisions • "But up here...dangerous" indicates that Neil is aware of Calum's lack of understanding/takes on role of parent • "I don't like..."/"Did you see..."/"Was it from..." simplicity of language shows Calum's childlike dependence on Neil • Repeated use of Neil's name suggests Calum seeks reassurance/comfort from his big brother • "Was it from heaven...?" suggests Calum's naivety and his reliance on Neil's wisdom • Repeated questions ("In the shed...horse?/"What shed... horse?") indicates Neil's frustration with Calum's childlike ways

Question	Expected Answer(s)	Max Mark	Additional Guidance
32.	Candidates may choose to answer in bullet points in this final question, or write a number of linked statements. Possible answers are shown in the "Additional Guidance" column.	10	Up to 2 marks can be achieved for identifying elements of commonality as identified in the question, i.e. how the writer uses symbolism to develop the central concerns of the text. A further 2 marks can be achieved for reference to the extract given. 6 additional marks can be awarded for discussion of similar references to at least one other part of the text. <u>In practice this means:</u> Identification of commonality (2) e.g. Jenkins uses characters, incidents and setting as representative of wider issues (1) such as the conflict between good and evil/devastation of war/sacrifice of innocence due to cruelty of mankind (1) From the extract: 2 marks for detailed/insightful comment plus quotation/reference; 1 mark for more basic comment plus quotation/ reference; 0 marks for quotation alone. e.g. Calum's childlike interpretation of the light on the trees as coming from heaven, despite the danger of the storm, symbolises his innocence/innate goodness (2) From the rest of the text: as above for up to 6 marks Possible answers include: • The deer drive is a small version of what is happening in the outside world and represents the violence humanity is capable of • The presence of the destroyer/planes in this natural setting represent the inescapable conflict between good vs. evil • Calum's death in the tree represents the crucifixion with his blood purifying the world corrupted by Duror • Duror is often associated with a decaying tree representing the evil spreading within him • The cones represent hope for the future/re-birth as after destruction/war new life will grow

PART C — SCOTTISH TEXT — POETRY

Text 1 — *Poetry* — *Address to the Deil* by Robert Burns

Question	Expected Answer(s)	Max Mark	Additional Guidance
33.	2 marks awarded for detailed/insightful comment plus quotation/reference; 1 mark for more basic comment plus quotation/reference; 0 marks for quotation/reference alone. Possible answers are shown in the "Additional Guidance" column. (Marks may be awarded 2 + 2, 2 + 1 + 1, 1 + 1 + 1 + 1)	4	Possible answers include: • "whatever title suit thee" rather dismissive comment creates an informal/comic tone (especially when contrasted with the introductory quotation from Milton used by Burns) • List of epithets for the Deil (in particular, "Auld Hornie" and "Clootie") convey a slightly affectionate camaraderie between the Deil and the speaker • "cavern grim and sootie" stereotypical view of the Deil's abode is somewhat mocking of the Calvinistic view of Hell • "spairges about...wretches!" ridiculous depiction of Satan torturing damned souls makes the concept of the Deil's actions seem quite comical • "cootie" use of homely term for the Deil's cauldron makes Satan seem domesticated rather than a great force for evil • "Hear me..." use of imperative makes the speaker seem more powerful than Satan, so creating a tongue-in-cheek tone • "I'm sure...gie" the speaker's unlikely camaraderie and mock understanding of the Deil's tasks/ patronising attitude to the Deil creates a humorous tone • "skelp...scaud...squeel" — alliteration highlights the ridiculousness of Satan's supposed tasks • "poor dogs like me...us squeel" the speaker's readiness to admit his sins and accept the stereotypical punishment conveys a child-like impression of small misdemeanours and punishments rather than grave sins
34.	2 marks awarded for detailed/insightful comment plus quotation/reference; 1 mark for more basic comment plus quotation/reference; 0 marks for quotation/reference alone. Possible answers are shown in the "Additional Guidance" column. (Marks may be awarded 2, 1 + 1)	2	Possible answers include: • Repetition/positioning of "great" stresses the immense power and fame of the Deil • "Far kenm'd an' noted"/"travels far" suggests that the Deil is an omnipresent being, known everywhere • "thou's neither lag...nor scaur" listing of the negative qualities which are absent from the Deil makes him seem a supremely confident being • "roarin' lion" use of the metaphor creates impression of bravery/strength/nobility • "a' holes and corners tryin'" suggests once again the Deil's omnipresence/ability to invade all places • "on the strong wind'd tempest flyin'" suggests that the Deil has the power to control/overcome the strongest forces of nature • Parallel structure of "Whyles, on...Whyles, in..." highlights the ability of the Deil to move effortlessly between the greatest and smallest places • "Unseen thou lurks" connotations of menace and threat suggest the Deil is a powerful predator

Question	Expected Answer(s)	Max Mark	Additional Guidance
35.	2 marks awarded for detailed/insightful comment plus quotation/reference; 1 mark for more basic comment plus quotation/reference; 0 marks for quotation/reference alone. Possible answers are shown in the "Additional Guidance" column. (Marks may be awarded 2 + 2, 2 + 1 + 1, 1 + 1 + 1 + 1)	4	Possible answers include: • "I've heard my rev'rend graunie say" the speaker's introduction to this anecdotal section of the poem suggest an old wife's tale, not to be taken seriously • Burns' use of a clichéd description ("lanely glens… auld ruin'd castles…the moon…eldritch croon… dreary, windy, winter night") emphasises that these anecdotes are the stuff of folklore/unbelievable tales • "graunie…douse, honest woman" the tongue-in-cheek description of the speaker's grannie suggests he is aware of the silly nature of these stories but is determined to defend them thus making them seem even less reliable • "bummin'" use of comic vocabulary undermines the seriousness of grannie's tale • Series of anecdotes becomes progressively less believable, with the speaker suggesting a natural reason for the supposed presence of the Deil (an owl's screech, the wind in the trees, the rushes waving, a startled drake) yet still continuing with his assertions of the Deil's presence • "quaick, quaick" use of onomatopoeia adds a comic note when the speaker continues to insist that he has heard/seen the Deil

Question	Expected Answer(s)	Max Mark	Additional Guidance
36.	Candidates may choose to answer in bullet points in this final question, or write a number of linked statements. Possible answers are shown in the "Additional Guidance" column.	10	Up to 2 marks can be achieved for identifying elements of commonality as identified in the question, i.e. Burns' use of humour to explore serious issues. A further 2 marks can be achieved for the reference to the extract given. 6 additional marks can be awarded for discussion of similar references to at least one other poem by Burns. <u>In practice this means:</u> Identification of commonality (2), e.g. Burns' satirical/comical observations of characters/religious beliefs/social classes (1) lend power to his, often scathing, condemnation of injustices/Calvinist doctrines/hypocritical moralising (1) From the extract: 2 marks for detailed/insightful comment plus quotation/reference; 1 mark for more basic comment plus quotation/ reference; 0 marks for reference alone. e.g. "Spairges about the brunstane cootie/To scaud poor wretches!" - the exaggerated depiction of Satan personally undertaking the stereotypical tortures of Hell is effective in ridiculing the Calvinistic views of eternal damnation and the punishment of sins. (2) From at least one other poem: as above for up to 6 marks Possible references include: • *A Man's A Man for A' That* Burns' humorous depictions of the aristocracy are juxtaposed with his admiration for the common man, thereby strengthening his appeal for social equality • *A Poet's Welcome* Burns' satirical comments concerning the gossiping critics of his daughter's social position show the lack of compassion and humanity within the Kirk • *Holy Willie's Prayer* the hypocrisy and bigotry revealed by Willie in his "prayer" allow Burns to satirise the Calvinist doctrine of predestination • *Tam O' Shanter* the humour created by the speaker's po-faced moralising on Tam's foolish behaviour at various points in the poem allows Burns to criticise those who take pleasure in judging others too readily • *Tam O' Shanter* comical anti-climax of final line, reference to horse losing tail serves as a reminder of human frailties

Text 2 — *Poetry* — *Valentine* by Carol Ann Duffy

Question	Expected Answer(s)	Max Mark	Additional Guidance
37.	2 marks awarded for detailed/insightful comment plus quotation/reference; 1 mark for more basic comment plus quotation/reference; 0 marks for quotation/reference alone. Possible answers are shown in the "Additional Guidance" column. (Marks may be awarded 2 + 2, 2 + 1 + 1, 1 + 1 + 1 + 1)	4	Possible answers include: Challenges • Isolation/bluntness of the opening line emphasises the strength of the speaker's rejection of traditional gifts • Positioning of "Not" at the start of the line intensifies the speaker's rejection of traditional symbols of love • Given the mundane connotations of "an onion" the incongruity of it as a symbol of love • Subversion of "moon" as a traditional romantic image as it is mundanely described as "wrapped in brown paper" Reinforces • "moon" traditionally associated with romantic evenings • "promises" suggests devotion/commitment/fidelity • "light" suggests something pure and life-enhancing • "undressing" suggests something seductive and sensual
38.	2 marks awarded for detailed/insightful comment plus quotation/reference; 1 mark for more basic comment plus quotation/reference; 0 marks for quotation/reference alone. Possible answers are shown in the "Additional Guidance" column. (Marks may be awarded 2 + 2, 2 + 1 + 1, 1 + 1 + 1 + 1)	4	Possible answers include: • Development of the extended image in "blind you with tears/Like a lover" highlights the pain and suffering that love brings • Imagery of "wobbling photo of grief" suggests the pain/distress caused by a failed/complex relationship • Single line stanza abrupt dismissal of more stereotypical love tokens/straightforward no nonsense approach • Alliteration of "Not a cute card or a kissogram" suggests contempt for predictable/insincere/unthinking view of love • Image of "fierce kiss" to suggest the lingering taste of the onion suggests the difficulty of escaping the relationship/an underlying threat or danger in the relationship • Word choice of "possessive" suggests the constricting/controlling nature of the relationship • Juxtaposition of "possessive" and "faithful" undermines the notion of commitment in a relationship • Bluntness/positioning of "for as long as we are" at end of verse suggests impermanence of love
39.	2 marks awarded for detailed/insightful comment plus quotation/reference; 1 mark for more basic comment plus quotation/reference; 0 marks for quotation/reference alone. Possible answers are shown in the "Additional Guidance" column. (Marks may be awarded 2, 1 + 1)	2	Possible answers include: • "Take it." Moving to an acceptance of a 'real' rather than a superficial view of love • "platinum loops...wedding-ring" the onion (mentioned earlier) becomes associated with the restrictive aspects of marriage/love • "Lethal" suggests movement towards a dark conclusion/dark view of love • "cling to your fingers" echoes earlier ideas of the negative long term effects of a broken relationship/possessiveness within a relationship • "knife" leaves the reader with final thought of love's potential to wound

Question	Expected Answer(s)	Max Mark	Additional Guidance
40.	Candidates may choose to answer in bullet points in this final question, or write a number of linked statements. Possible answers are shown in the "Additional Guidance" column.	10	Up to 2 marks can be achieved for identifying elements of commonality as identified in the question, i.e. how emotional conflict within an individual is explored. A further 2 marks can be achieved for reference to the text given. 6 additional marks can be awarded for discussion of similar references to at least one other poem by Duffy. <u>In practice this means:</u> Identification of commonality (2) e.g. the complexities of human experience can create emotional conflict in an individual's life (1), which can change significantly the individual's personality/outlook on life (1) From the poem: 2 marks for detailed/insightful comment plus quotation/reference; 1 mark for more basic comment plus quotation/reference; 0 marks for quotation/reference alone. e.g. the speaker is attracted to other, more positive aspects of love such as intimacy and tenderness but adopts a more realistic/cynical attitude towards love "Not a red rose...onion" (2) From at least one other text: as above for up to 6 marks Possible comments include: • *Anne Hathaway* the speaker is left bereft by the death of her husband, but by remembering the passionate nature of her relationship, she has become more resigned to her loss • *Havisham* the unresolved tension between love and hate that the speaker's rejection provokes, leads to an on-going deterioration in her mental state • *War Photographer* the emotional impact of the horrors the photographer has witnessed in his assignments abroad conflicts with the pride he feels in doing a professional job • *Originally* the unresolved emotional conflict of maintaining identity: where is home and all the emotional baggage the question entails • *Mrs Midas* the unresolved conflicting emotions she feels for her husband: the contempt she feels for his desires which brought about their separation conflicts with the physical intimacy she now misses.

Text 3 — *Poetry — For my Grandmother Knitting* by Liz Lochhead

Question	Expected Answer(s)	Max Mark	Additional Guidance
41.	For full marks both the past and the present must be dealt with, but not necessarily in equal measure. 2 marks awarded for detailed/insightful comment plus quotation/reference; 1 mark for more basic comment plus quotation/reference; 0 marks for quotation/reference alone. Possible answers are shown in the "Additional Guidance" column. (Marks may be awarded 2 + 2, 2 + 1 + 1, 1 + 1 + 1 + 1)	4	Possible answers include: Past • "sure and skilful hands of the fisher-girl" word choice emphasises sense of control and confidence, despite her youth • "master of your moments" — alliteration/slogan effect conveys sense that she was in charge/on top of the task • "deft and swift" monosyllables and consonance emphasise her skill and speed when gutting the fish • "slit the still-ticking quick silver fish" fast-paced rhythm and repetition of short "I" vowel sound conveys the efficiency and ease with which she tackled the task • "Hard work...of necessity" positioning and choice of words emphasises how much her efforts were needed Present • "There is no need they say" — opening, blunt statement and dismissive tone convey her lack of perceived usefulness • "the needles still move/their rhythms" sense of her passivity/lack of agency emphasised by description of the needles as the active ones, rather than the grandmother • "You are old now": blunt statement positioned at start of Stanza 2, emphasises the definite nature of her plight • "grasp...not so good" — sense of her diminishing alertness/control in the literal and metaphorical use of "grasp"
42.	1 mark for comment plus quotation/reference (x2); 0 marks for quotation/reference alone. Possible answers are shown in the "Additional Guidance" column.	2	Possible answers include: • "hands of the bride" connotations of special/romantic time when hand receives ring/holds hands • "hand-span waist" suggests that she was cherished by her husband/physically dainty and exquisite • "hands...scrubbed his back" suggests devotion/physical closeness with her husband as they worked together in difficult circumstances • "hands...six" suggests the multiple challenges of her life • "scraped...necessary" list of verbs suggests her energy and ability to cope in down-to-earth way
43.	2 marks awarded for detailed/insightful comment plus quotation/reference; 1 mark for more basic comment plus quotation/reference; 0 marks for quotation/reference alone. Possible answers are shown in the "Additional Guidance" column. (Marks may be awarded 2 + 1, 1 + 1 + 1)	4	Possible answers include: • "the kids they say grandma...already" reported speech without punctuation suggests an often-repeated 'lecture' conveying sense of isolation/lack of compassion/lack of communication • Repetition of "too much/too many" emphasises their perception of her uselessness/sense that they repeatedly remind her that her contribution is not needed • "At your window you wave...Sunday" poignant picture of the grandmother waving goodbye conveys sense of her loneliness • "painful hands...shrunken wrists" physical incongruity of hands on tiny wrists suggests how frail and clumsy she now is • "Swollen-jointed...Old" list of adjectives in minor sentences building to the climax of "Old" emphasises the pitiful nature of her physical condition • "as if...how to stop" climactic final line suggests her lack of control over her life

Question	Expected Answer(s)	Max Mark	Additional Guidance
44.	Candidates may choose to answer in bullet points in this final question, or write a number of linked statements. Possible answers are shown in the "Additional Guidance" column.	10	Up to 2 marks can be achieved by identifying elements of commonality as identified in the question, i.e. Lochhead's exploration of the theme of personal and/ or social change. A further 2 marks can be achieved for reference to the poem given. 6 additional marks can be awarded for discussion of similar references to at least one other poem by Lochhead. In practice this means: Identification of commonality (2) e.g. Lochhead uses characters to represent aspects of life past/present, encouraging us to respond to their experience (1) showing that change can be either positive or negative — destroying valuable aspects of past or looking forward to a more positive future (1) From this poem: 2 marks for detailed/insightful comment plus quotation/reference; 1 mark for more basic comment plus quotation/ reference; 0 marks for quotation/reference alone. e.g. the grandmother represents an older Scotland where traditional ways of life e.g. fishing or mining provided security and continuity, which is lacking in the modern world (2) From at least one other text: as above for up to 6 marks Possible comments include: • *Some Old Photographs* sense that Scotland of the past had social cohesion and predictability, e.g. 'all the dads in hats', though this certainty is undermined in "what was/never really" • *View of Scotland/Love Poem* the traditional Hogmanay, with its rituals which everyone followed, has been replaced by a more spontaneous celebration of life — "There is no time like the/ present for a kiss" • *Last Supper* change reflected in membership of the 'revenge group' and/or dramatic reaction to partner's betrayal • *My Rival's House* the mother is hostile to change in the relationship with her son and fights against the necessity of his growing up and forming a new relationship • *The Bargain* the speaker's relationship, which thrived in the past but now faces an uncertain future, reflected by their inconclusive visit to the stalls

Text 4 — *Poetry* — *Basking Shark* by Norman MacCaig

Question	Expected Answer(s)	Max Mark	Additional Guidance
45.	2 marks awarded for detailed/insightful comment plus quotation/reference; 1 mark for more basic comment plus quotation/reference; 0 marks for quotation/reference alone. Possible answers are shown in the "Additional Guidance" column. (Marks may be awarded 2, 1 + 1)	2	Possible answers include: • "stub" onomatopoeia suggests sudden/unexpected contact • "where none should be" conveys the idea of things being out of the ordinary/out of place • "To have it (rise)" emphasises disbelief at the action • "rise" apparent action by 'rock' suggests surprise/incredulity • parenthetical aside implying the speaker does not want to repeat the experience "(too often)" • "slounge" onomatopoeic qualities suggest slow, relaxed movement of shark in its own element where he is the intruder
46.	2 marks awarded for detailed/insightful comment plus quotation/reference; 1 mark for more basic comment plus quotation/reference; 0 marks for quotation/reference alone. Possible answers are shown in the "Additional Guidance" column. (Marks may be awarded 2 + 2, 2 + 1 + 1, 1 + 1 + 1 + 1)	4	Possible answers include: • "But not (too often) — though enough." evaluative comment suggests that the speaker continues to dwell upon the experience • "I count as gain" suggests that despite initial unease, he has come to recognise the value of the experience • "displaced" word choice suggests the shift in his thinking • "shoggled" suggests shaken out of a comfortable mind-set • "decadent townee" self-derogatory comment suggests his sudden recognition of his superficiality/alienation from nature • "shook" suggests that the speaker was literally and metaphorically disturbed by the experience • "wrong branch...family tree" suggests that he is now less sure of his place in the evolutionary framework
47.	2 marks awarded for detailed/insightful comment plus quotation/reference; 1 mark for more basic comment plus quotation/reference; 0 marks for quotation/reference alone. Possible answers are shown in the "Additional Guidance" column. (Marks may be awarded 2 + 2, 2 + 1 + 1, 1 + 1 + 1 + 1)	4	Possible answers include: • Metaphor of "Swish up...clearer" suggests the initial confusion as a result of the encounter has led to greater clarity • "I saw me...emerging" suggests rebirth of his sense of himself/humanity • "in one fling" parenthesis emphasises the sudden epiphany • "emerging from the slime of everything" suggests a realisation of humanity's primeval origins • "So who's the monster?" question emphasises that the speaker has been forced to rethink humanity's superiority to apparently primitive beings • "made me grow pale" suggests physical shock at realisation of humanity's insignificance/depravity • "sail after sail" repetition suggests realisation of grandeur/majesty/timelessness of the shark

Question	Expected Answer(s)	Max Mark	Additional Guidance
48.	Candidates may choose to answer in bullet points in this final question, or write a number of linked statements. Possible answers are shown in the "Additional Guidance" column.	10	Up to 2 marks can be achieved for identifying elements of commonality as identified in the question, i.e. how MacCaig uses symbolism to develop central ideas in his poetry. A further 2 marks can be achieved for reference to the text given. 6 additional marks can be awarded for discussion of similar references to at least one other poem MacCaig. <u>In practice this means:</u> Identification of commonality (2) e.g. MacCaig uses people/objects/places as symbols to explore important human issues/relationships (1) and in doing so makes us re-evaluate/consider our own views (1) From the poem: 2 marks for detailed/insightful comment plus quotation/reference; 1 mark for more basic comment plus quotation/reference; 0 marks for quotation alone. e.g. the shark represents the apparently primitive aspect of nature, however MacCaig's reflections challenge our perception of our superiority (2) From at least one other text: as above for up to 6 marks Possible answers include: • *Visiting Hour* "withered hand trembles on its stalk" symbolises the fragility of human life and makes us consider our own mortality • *Assisi* the contrast between the inner spiritual beauty and the outer physical appearance of the beggar makes us reflect on appearance against reality • *Aunt Julia* she represents a lost heritage which makes us consider the importance of valuing and preserving the past • *Memorial* "the carousel of language" represents the vitality of relationships and communication he can't recapture provoking thoughts on finality/loss • *Sounds of the Day* "the bangle of ice...numb" represents the pain and deadening effect of loss which makes us consider love as a destructive force

Text 5 — *Poetry — Heroes* by Sorley MacLean

Question	Expected Answer(s)	Max Mark	Additional Guidance
49.	2 marks awarded for detailed/insightful comment plus quotation/reference; 1 mark for more basic comment plus quotation/reference; 0 marks for quotation/reference alone. Possible answers are shown in the "Additional Guidance" column. (Marks may be awarded 2, 1 + 1)	2	• Repeated use of "not" and "nor" emphasises the point that the soldier is not one of the Gaelic/Scottish heroes listed/mentioned • "Englishman" general term sounds insignificant when set against Scottish/Gaelic heroes mentioned/listed • "poor little chap" diminutive word choice/description makes the soldier seem unheroic • "chubby cheeks" suggests soldier is young/baby-like and therefore unheroic • "knees grinding" suggests fear/clumsiness and is therefore unheroic • "pimply unattractive face" youthful, immature, unappealing, unheroic appearance
50.	2 marks awarded for detailed/insightful comment plus quotation/reference; 1 mark for more basic comment plus quotation/reference; 0 marks for quotation/reference alone. Possible answers are shown in the "Additional Guidance" column. (Marks may be awarded 2 + 2, 2 + 1 + 1, 1 + 1 + 1 + 1)	4	Possible answers include: • "notched iron splinters" extremely violent weaponry suggested by using the word "splinters" which are generally associated with wood and superficial injuries, here linked with iron and something more deadly is implied. Harsh consonant sounds underline this. • "the smoke and flame" description of hell-like environment • "the shaking and terror of the battlefield" 'shaking' here is ambiguous, could be the ground literally shaking with the force of explosions, or could refer to extreme fear felt by the soldiers • "bullet shower" bullets are 'raining down,' rapid, intense frequency • "hero briskly"/"wasn't much time he got" (soldier) has to respond to events without time to think/has to respond with unnatural speed/sense of life cut short • "bucking with tearing crashing screech" harsh violent word choice, participles suggest violent events happening simultaneously • "biff" ironically colloquial rendering of blow to his body • "put him to the ground" in battle soldier is victim of forces outwith his control • "mouth down in sand and gravel" the use of the word "mouth" here, rather than the more usual "face", suggests more brutality, perhaps conveying almost the "taste" of the battlefield and the indignity of his fall

Question	Expected Answer(s)	Max Mark	Additional Guidance
51.	2 marks awarded for detailed/insightful comment plus quotation/reference; 1 mark for more basic comment plus quotation/reference; 0 marks for quotation/reference alone. Possible answers are shown in the "Additional Guidance" column. (Marks may be awarded 2 + 2, 2 + 1 + 1, 1 + 1 + 1 + 1)	4	Possible answers include: • The "no"…"or"…"or" construct/structure highlights the lack of recognition afforded to the soldier and his memory and therefore creates pity • "not many of his troop alive" prevalence/victory of death among soldier's companions creates pity • "their word would not be strong" soldiers' voices seen as weak/would be ignored in terms of their accounts of the battle • image of "the mouth of the field of slaughter" pity created through awareness of the soldiers' susceptibility to the (metaphorically) greedy appetite that war has for death • "great warrior" pity created by the ironic tone created in this expression, and also genuine sense of sympathy conveyed for the soldier's fate • "poor manikin" pity created by the use of diminutive term, and this is emphasised by addition of the word 'poor' • "he took a little weeping to my eyes" reference to the traditional Gaelic expression creates genuine sense of pity for the soldier
52.	Candidates may choose to answer in bullet points in this final question, or write a number of linked statements. Possible answers are shown in the "Additional Guidance" column.	10	Up to 2 marks can be achieved by identifying elements of commonality as identified in the question, ie how the theme of destruction is explored. A further 2 marks can be achieved for reference to the text given. 6 additional marks can be awarded for discussion of similar references to at least one other poem by MacLean. <u>In practice this means:</u> Identification of commonality (2) e.g. MacLean explores the destruction of community, relationships and individuals (1) challenging the readers to consider the negative impact of war, change in community, careless treatment of others in relationships (1) From the poem: 2 marks for detailed/insightful comment plus quotation/reference; 1 mark for more basic comment plus quotation/reference; 0 marks for quotation/reference alone. e.g. the ironic description of the "soldier"/"warrior" highlights his ordinary nature and encourages the reader to reflect on the impact of war on us all (2) From at least one other poem: as above for up to 6 marks Possible answers include: • *An Autumn Day* seemingly random death of six companions highlights the futility, chaos, destruction of war • *Hallaig* the destruction of Highland communities caused by the Clearances, and the sense of loss engendered by this • *Screapadal* destruction caused by the forced Clearances, and by the modern world's intrusive impact on traditional ways of life • *I Gave You Immortality* potentially destructive power of love and the pain it can cause • *Shores* the destructive force and power of the sea and time

Text 6 – *Poetry* – *Nil Nil* by Don Paterson

Question	Expected Answer(s)	Max Mark	Additional Guidance
53.	2 marks awarded for detailed/insightful comment plus quotation/reference; 1 mark for more basic comment plus quotation/reference; 0 marks for quotation/reference alone. Possible answers are shown in the "Additional Guidance" column. (Marks may be awarded 2, 1 + 1)	2	Possible answers include: • "zenith" suggests that this moment is the pinnacle of the club's history • "majestic" suggests stately and magnificent, McGrandle is a grandiose figure • "golden (hair)" suggests something of great value • "sprinting the length" suggests an athletic prowess worthy of celebration • "balletic (toe-poke)" suggests great grace/poise/artfulness • "nearly bursting the roof of the net" hyperbolic statement emphasises the speaker's appreciation and effusiveness about this moment in the history of the club
54.	2 marks awarded for detailed/insightful comment plus quotation/reference; 1 mark for more basic comment plus quotation/reference; 0 marks for quotation/reference alone. Possible answers are shown in the "Additional Guidance" column. (Marks may be awarded 2 + 2, 2 + 1 + 1, 1 + 1 + 1 + 1)	4	Possible answers include: • "from here/it's all down" the phrase 'all down' suggests that there is no respite/decline is inevitable and complete • "pitch-sharing, pay-cuts, pawned silver" the list of worsening downturns emphasises the progression of the decline • "absolute sitters ballooned over open goals"/"dismal nutmegs" suggests decline in quality of the players • "(scores so) obscene" suggests defeats were becoming more humiliating/unacceptable • "nothing inhibits the fifty-year slide" suggests inevitability of long term decline • "then nobody" climax emphasises total absence of support • "stud-harrowed pitches" suggests neglect/disrepair/lack of care
55.	For full marks both the community and the pilot need to be dealt with but not necessarily in equal measure. 2 marks awarded for detailed/insightful comment plus quotation/reference; 1 mark for more basic comment plus quotation/reference; 0 marks for quotation/reference alone. Possible answers are shown in the "Additional Guidance" column. (Marks may be awarded 2 + 2, 2 + 1 + 1, 1 + 1 + 1 + 1)	4	Possible answers include: Community • "stopped swings" suggests all vibrancy has gone from the community/lack of youth • "dead shanty-town" suggests desolation/temporary nature of things • "cul-de-sac" suggests total dead end/lack of direction/aimless Pilot • "all that remains" suggests that every other physical part of the pilot is gone from existence and the stone is all that is left • "lone fighter-pilot" suggests isolation and vulnerability which contributes to the tragedy • "burn ... melt ... igniting" the combination of these words – all indicating heat and possible explosion – suggests danger/death • "no one around to admire ..." suggests lonely nature of death

Question	Expected Answer(s)	Max Mark	Additional Guidance
56.	Candidates may choose to answer in bullet points in this final question, or write a number of linked statements. Possible answers are shown in the "Additional Guidance" column.	10	Up to 2 marks can be achieved by identifying elements of commonality as identified in the question, i.e. how poet explores the impact of loss. A further 2 marks can be achieved for reference to the extract given. 6 additional marks can be awarded for discussion of similar references to at least one other poem by Paterson. In practice this means: Identification of commonality (2) e.g. Loss can be profound and life changing (1) and is a fundamental part of human experience, e.g. love, innocence, community, identity (1) From this extract: 2 marks for detailed/insightful comment plus quotation/reference; 1 mark for more basic comment plus quotation/reference; 0 marks for quotation/reference alone. e.g. "black shell" describes the Skelly Dry Cleaners as a husk devoid of life which emphasises this once flourishing business has now failed, adding to the hopelessness of the community (2) From at least one other poem: as above for up to 6 marks Possible comments include: • *The Ferryman's Arms* inevitability of death causes speaker to lose sense of identity ("my losing opponent … left him there") leading to feelings of hopelessness/lack of control • *11:00 Baldovan* loss of innocence leads to uncertainty/insecurity about our place in the future ("I cannot know the little good it will do me") • *Waking with Russell* the speaker has lost his old self through the birth of his son and has now gained a brighter, richer future • *The Thread* the difficult circumstances around the son's birth led to a fear of loss and recognition that life is fragile • *Two Trees* separation of the trees represents a loss of security, however their continued growth/survival suggests the resilience of the human spirit

SECTION 2 – CRITICAL ESSAY

Please see the assessment criteria for the Critical Essay on page 170.

HIGHER ENGLISH
2018

PAPER 1 — READING FOR UNDERSTANDING, ANALYSIS AND EVALUATION

Marking Instructions for each question

Passage 1

Question		Expected Answer(s)	Max Mark	Additional Guidance
1.	(a)	Candidates should identify two of the writer's feelings in the first paragraph. Candidates must use their own words. No marks for straight lifts from the passage. Award marks 1 + 1	2	Possible answers include: • she felt troubled, as though watching an illegal/senseless act • she felt responsible/guilty for a terrible act • she felt morally uncertain; questioned whether or not she was justified in doing this
	(b)	Candidates should analyse how the language emphasises the importance of trees. Award marks according to the quality of comment on appropriate language feature(s). Award **2 marks** for reference plus detailed/insightful comment. Award **1 mark** for reference plus more basic comment. Award **0 marks** for reference alone. Award marks 2 + 2 **or** 2 + 1 + 1 **or** 1 + 1 + 1 + 1	4	Possible answers include: *Word choice* • "ever more (precious)" suggests trees' increasing value • "precious" suggests trees are valuable, to be cherished • "a rebuke to built-in obsolescence": trees effectively criticise/stand in opposition to a world where products are designed to have only a limited life • "remnants" suggests precious remains from the past • "mammoth (limb)" suggests something on a massively impressive scale • "reassuring" suggests they offer comfort • "they will endure" suggests permanence, continuity, resilience • "the ancients" suggests trees have been considered valuable throughout the ages • "gods" suggests their almost religious significance • "ring by ring" suggests trees' natural, organic, unhurried growth • "worship" suggests our attitude should be respectful, reverent, devotional • "worse... worship": candidates might argue that the use of alliteration adds to the impact of the concluding statement • use in general of "religious" language ("God's arm", "cathedrals", "gods", "worship") heightens trees' spiritual significance • "our living past": trees connect us to our heritage *Imagery* • "a steady point in a churning world": trees offer steadfast permanence in a fast-changing, impermanent, turbulent world • (personification of) "reaches out", "mammoth limb" suggests a majestic living creature • "like God's arm...Rome": simile suggests majesty, beauty, spiritual significance, awesome impact • "calming like cathedrals": simile suggests their scale, majesty, spiritual quality, that they should be treated with reverence, that they are good for our inner well-being *Punctuation/sentence structure* • structure of opening sentence "I'm...world": the two phrases at the end of the sentence (heightened by the parallel structure) serve as a powerful development of the "precious" idea

Question		Expected Answer(s)	Max Mark	Additional Guidance
1.	(b)	*(continued)*		• balanced nature of final sentence: the artful juxtaposition of the near-reverent tone of the first part of the sentence, followed by the more matter-of-fact, modern tone of the second half brings the paragraph to a quietly effective conclusion
2.		Candidates should demonstrate understanding of how the protesters differ from what might have been expected. Candidates must use their own words. No marks for straight lifts from the passage. Award marks 1 + 1	2	Possible answers include: • we might have expected the protesters to be (over) zealous environmental activists/(ultra)dedicated conservationists (explanation of "eco-warriors")/ people who have rejected the conventional values of society (explanation of "hippies") • instead they are just normal people/a typical cross-section of the community/people of all ages and from all walks of life
3.		Candidates should analyse how the writer's use of language conveys her feelings of unhappiness. Award marks according to the quality of comment. For full marks there must be comment on at least two features. Award **2 marks** for reference plus detailed/insightful comment. Award **1 mark** for reference plus more basic comment. Award **0 marks** for reference alone.	3	Possible answers include: *Sentence structure* • series of three short, simple, matter-of-fact sentences at start of paragraph suggest the inevitable fate that awaits the trees and the irresistible march of the developers • positioning of "By March" at start of sentence suggests fixed, immovable timeline to destruction • structure of fourth sentence ("Local…benefits."): initial praise for efforts of local community is offset immediately by pessimistic recognition of government power; the sentence then reaches a climax with her attack on government policy • use of parenthesis "as new roads do" to emphasise the inevitable futility of government transport policy *Word choice:* • "last stand" (could be dealt with as imagery) suggests a defensive position facing inevitable defeat against insuperable odds • "only" suggests defeat itself is inevitable • "determined" suggests inflexible, unyielding nature of government policy • "market" suggests her scepticism about government policy: they are "selling" it as progress but "market" suggests this is more image than reality; suggests government is being unscrupulous, deceitful, conniving • "short-term" suggests transient, limited nature (of benefits) • "dubious" suggests deep uncertainty, unreliability (of benefits) • "fill up" suggests saturation, full to overflowing • "spanking new": hyperbole of her apparent enthusiasm could be argued to betoken her fundamental antipathy • "boarded-up" suggests the development will be to the continued detriment of an already rundown Hastings; suggests that Hastings itself needs attention *Contrast* • "spanking new" versus "boarded-up" emphasises the pointlessness of building new premises when existing ones lie empty and abandoned *Tone* • some candidates may recognise and discuss the changing tone of this paragraph, in particular the somewhat defeated, hopeless tone of the first three sentences which changes to an angry, scathing, sceptical tone in the rest of the paragraph.

Question		Expected Answer(s)	Max Mark	Additional Guidance
4.	(a)	Candidates should identify two claims the government makes about the protesters. For full marks candidates must demonstrate understanding of two claims. Award marks 1 + 1	2	Possible answers include: The government claims the protesters: • are not interested in protecting the environment • are only concerned about looking after their own (advantaged) interests • have no interest in the fate of people less well-off/less fortunate than themselves
	(b)	Candidates should analyse how at least two features of language convey the strength of the writer's belief in tree conservation. Award marks according to the quality of understanding shown of key ideas and the quality of comment on appropriate language features. Award **2 marks** for reference plus detailed/insightful comment. Award **1 mark** for reference plus more basic comment. Award **0 marks** for reference alone. Award marks 2 + 2 **or** 2 + 1 + 1 **or** 1 + 1 + 1 + 1		Possible answers include: *Word choice* • "special kind" suggests people who don't care about trees are particularly awful • "arrogance" suggests the insufferable conceit of those who don't care about trees • "bigger than history" suggests arrogance on a grand scale • (repeated) use of violent language when describing trees – felling (ie "cutting down" suggests something akin to an act of murder; "slicing into" suggests a savage, violent attack; "brutal" suggests a ruthless, crude, cruel, vicious attack; "grotesque" suggests a strange, distorted, unnatural, outrageous act; "chopping down" suggests a categorical, definitive act). • "fine" suggests the majesty, worthiness of the tree • "aching (poignancy)" suggests how deeply hurt she is when trees are cut down • writer's use of "shock tactics" in making a developed, quite visceral comparison between killing living creatures and cutting down trees: some candidates may recognise that the writer shows the strength of her feeling by developing an argument that many readers will find shocking or extreme *Imagery* • by comparing (in a very visual way) the fate of trees to the fate of whales and elephants ("mightiest mammal") the writer is associating trees with elevated concepts such as the awesome wonder of the natural world, beauty, majesty, conservation… • "enormous creature" suggests epic scale of what is being destroyed *Punctuation/sentence structure* • use of colon (line 31) introduces explanation of what this "special kind of arrogance" involves • punchy conclusion to paragraph ("Not so a tree") emphasises just how different the trees' situation is to even the most impressive or endangered of our natural creatures
5.	(a)	Candidates should identify any four reasons given for cutting down trees. Candidates should use their own words as far as possible. No marks for straight lifts from the passage. Award **1 mark** for each point made. Award marks 1 + 1 + 1 + 1	4	Possible answers include: • they may contribute to land sinking (which would affect buildings on that land) • they are regarded as potentially damaging to vehicles • they are regarded as potentially a danger to young people • they shed (twigs and leaves) and that leaves things (public spaces, houses or vehicles) looking dirty and untidy

Question		Expected Answer(s)	Max Mark	Additional Guidance
5.	(a)	*(continued)*		• some trees are considered unfashionable (and people want to replace them with something more popular) • selling trees makes money, can boost a country's economy • they are converted into timber for commercial purposes
	(b)	Candidates should analyse how their chosen image emphasises the writer's opposition to cutting down trees. Award marks according to the quality of comment. Award **2 marks** for a detailed/insightful comment. Award **1 mark** for a more basic comment. Award **0 marks** for mere identification of an image. When dealing with imagery, candidates must demonstrate recognition of the literal root of the image and then explore how the writer is extending it figuratively. Award marks 2 **or** 1 + 1	2	Possible answers include: • "butchers" suggests that municipal workers are cutting back the trees to a significant degree and that the work performed is brutal and indiscriminate • "embarrassed stumps" suggests that trees look vulnerable/exposed/self-conscious after the work has been carried out on them • "autumnal hell" hyperbolic term suggests ridicule of the wild over-reaction of those who find trees a problem at particular times of the year • "like a beautiful girl being forced to sell her hair" suggests Burma gave away part of the country's natural beauty for money
6.		Candidates should evaluate the final paragraph's effectiveness as a conclusion to the passage as a whole. Award marks according to the quality of comment. Award **2 marks** for appropriate attention to the idea of a conclusion. Award **1 mark** for a more basic comment.	2	Possible answers include: • the writer concedes that inevitably trees will be cut down to make way for developments, a point she has already made in relation to the Hastings development and government policy in general • the writer returns to an argument which she has discussed throughout the passage: economic growth versus the innate value of trees. The Hastings development is an example of economic growth (very short-term in the writer's opinion), while the writer stresses at several points the value of preserving trees (for example, establishing the majesty and wonder of trees in the opening paragraphs; showing how much they mean to ordinary people protesting against the Hastings development; suggesting they are more important than creatures great and small) • the writer concludes by re-asserting how important a part of our heritage trees are: they are a link to our past ("they are our history inscribed in the natural world") and a means by which people leave their mark on society ("which rich men, planting beautiful orchards to their own glorious memory"). The link to the past idea has already been developed, for example in lines 10–11, while the idea of planting trees for posterity is explicitly discussed in lines 38–39 ("planting...loved ones"). • some candidates will recognise the elevated quality of the writing in the final paragraph (quite different in tone to some of the almost brutally graphic sections of the passage) and link it to the persuasively idealistic message the writer has been trying to convey in much of the passage

Question	Expected Answer(s)	Max Mark	Additional Guidance
7.	Candidates should identify key areas of agreement in the two passages by referring in detail to both passages. There may be some overlap among the areas of agreement. Award marks according to the extent to which a candidate has covered two points or one. Candidates may include quotations in their evidence from the passage, but should support these with explanations. The grid below shows key areas of agreement. Other answers are possible.	5	Candidates can use bullet points in this final question, or write a number of linked statements. Award a mark which reflects the quality of response in two areas: • identification of the key areas of agreement in attitude/ideas • level of detail given in support Award **5 marks** for identification of three key areas of agreement with detailed/insightful use of supporting evidence. Award **4 marks** for identification of three key areas of agreement with appropriate use of supporting evidence. Award **3 marks** for identification of three key areas of agreement. Award **2 marks** for identification of two key areas of agreement. Award **1 mark** for identification of one key area of agreement. Award **0 marks** for failure to identify any key area of agreement and/or misunderstanding of task. NB: A candidate who identifies only two key areas of agreement may be awarded up to a maximum of four marks, as follows • two marks for identification of two key areas of agreement **plus:** **either** • a further mark for appropriate use of supporting evidence to a total of three marks **or** • a further two marks for detailed/insightful use of supporting evidence to a total of four marks A candidate who identifies only one key area of agreement may be awarded up to a maximum of two marks, as follows • one mark for identification of one key area of agreement a further mark for use of supporting evidence to a total of two marks

	Area of agreement	Passage 1	Passage 2
1.	awe/wonder/majesty	spiritual, almost religious significance; comparison to whales, elephants	magnificence of the kauri
2.	heritage/permanence	link to previous centuries; certain feature in an uncertain world; will outlive us all	have outlasted the moa; now treated with reverence in New Zealand
3.	trees as teachers	we should question our assumption of superiority	we can learn from trees
4.	ordinary people see trees' importance	Hastings protesters; gift to posterity	New Zealand conservationists; Kenyan women (impact on quality of life)
5.	government and businesses' misguided economic priorities	government short-termism (Britain, Burma, Iceland, etc); trees considered expendable in the interests of "progress"	opposition to tree-based farming; profit-driven outlook of big businesses
6.	lack of respect	councils, officialdom, some homeowners	historical clearing; governments; companies; western desire to control nature
7.	brutality	trees are cut down or cut back quite brutally	hacking and racking continues

PAPER 2 — CRITICAL READING

SECTION 1 — Scottish Text

- Candidates should gain credit for their understanding, analysis and evaluation of the extract and either the whole play or novel, or other poems and short stories by the writer.

- In the final 10-mark question the candidate should answer the question in either a series of linked statements, or in bullet points.

Detailed Marking Instructions for each question

PART A — SCOTTISH TEXT — DRAMA

Text 1 — Drama —*The Slab Boys* by John Byrne

Question	Expected Answer(s)	Max Mark	Additional Guidance
1.	1 mark awarded for comment on Jack's attitude to the work of the slab room plus quotation/reference 1 mark awarded for comment on either Phil or Spanky's attitudes to the work of the slab room plus quotation/reference Marks awarded 1+1	2	Possible answers include: Jack • 'What the lads do, basically, is dole out …'/'dump it onto'/'Then it's just a matter of' description of slab room work in matter-of-fact list of activities suggests that the work done is unskilled, routine, unimaginative • Any one example from above list (e.g., 'dole out', 'dump it') suggests his dismissive attitude to the 'unskilled' work done in slab room • 'Bit of a diff from the studio, eh?' suggests a derogatory attitude to slab room, by comparing it unfavourably to the studio where 'real art' goes on Slab Boys • 'bile green/acne yellow' suggests sickness/revulsion for the work done in the slab room OR suggests they do not take their work seriously
2.	For full marks, answers must refer to both Jack and the slab boys, but not necessarily in equal measure 2 marks awarded for detailed/insightful comment plus quotation/reference. 1 mark for more basic comment plus quotation/reference 0 marks for quotation/reference alone. (Marks may be awarded 2+2, 2+1+1 or 1+1+1+1)	4	Possible answers include: Slab Boys • 'Why don't you vamoose, Jacky Boy?' (Spanky) despite Jack's seniority, Spanky tells him to leave; tone is contemptuous and belittling • 'Plooky Chops … them boils of yours is highly smittal' (Phil) cruel comment makes light of his skin problem and seeks to humiliate Jack by joking about it • 'Keep away from me! Hector, fling us over the Dettol!' (Phil) exaggerated mock-fear of the supposed contagion of his skin condition, requiring disinfectant as a weapon to protect himself, develops idea of humiliating Jack • Sequence of comments 'It would take … with pliers' builds up the sense of absurdity about the extreme treatment needed to cure Jack's condition, further humiliating him

Question	Expected Answer(s)	Max Mark	Additional Guidance
2.	*(continued)*		Jack • 'I'm warning you, McCann' ineffectual attempt to assert his authority over Phil indicates Jack's hostility • 'Jealousy ... on a desk' Jack assumes that Phil's hostility is due to envy and sneers at his lack of success, in comparison with his own progress • 'Don't worry, you haven't been condemned to spend the rest of the day here' by reassuring Alan that he has not been 'condemned' to spend long with the slab boys, he conveys his contempt for them and what they have to offer
3.	2 marks awarded for detailed/insightful comment plus quotation/reference. 1 mark for more basic comment plus quotation/reference. 0 marks for quotation/reference alone. (Marks may be awarded 2+2, 2+1+1 or 1+1+1+1)	4	Possible answers include: • Phil and Spanky's creation of the 'folk tale'/'plague tale' narrative, complete with villagers and red paint warnings, used to continue the mockery of Jack • Phil's deliberate refusal to call Alan by his actual name, e.g., 'Eamonn ... young Dowdalls' aims to undermine his importance and the significance of his visit • Phil's 'lesson' to Alan about slab room work: exaggerated simplicity to the point of ridiculousness 'this here is what we call a sink ... s-i-n-k' to mock Alan and ridicule the idea of having to explain to him the simple work they do • Phil and Spanky's double act of quick-fire comments/using pseudo-formal address, e.g., 'Mr Mac' asserts their control over the situation • Phil and Spanky's use of Hector as a 'visual aid' in teaching Alan about the slab room work, both humiliates Hector and continues the mockery of Alan/slab boy work e.g., 'Note the keen eye ... the firm set of the jaw' (as if he is a fine physical specimen)/'They're forced up under cucumber frames' (as if Hector is a particularly exquisite plant/flower)

Text 2 — *Drama — The Cheviot, the Stag and the Black, Black Oil* by John McGrath

Question	Expected Answer(s)	Max Mark	Additional Guidance
4.	Candidates can answer in bullet points in this final question, or write a number of linked statements.	10	Up to 2 marks can be achieved for identifying elements of commonality as identified in the question, i.e. how Byrne explores attitudes to authority. A further 2 marks can be achieved for reference to the extract given. 6 additional marks can be awarded for discussion of similar references to at least one other part of the text. In practice this means: Identification of commonality (2) e.g. Figures of authority are regarded with disrespect, and sometimes openly with contempt, by Phil and Spanky (1) Promoted figures such as Curry/Jack sometimes use their authority inappropriately (1) From the extract: 2 marks for detailed/insightful comment plus quotation/reference; 1 mark for more basic comment plus quotation/reference; 0 marks for quotation alone. e.g. Phil and Spanky humiliate Jack about his skin and mock his introduction of Alan to the slab room's 'intricacies' while Jack, unable to inspire genuine respect, is reduced to making ineffectual threats (2) From at least one other part of the text: as above for up to 6 marks Possible answers include: • Curry uses his authority to belittle Phil's hopes of entry to art college: he is annoyed with Phil for applying without permission, rather than being impressed by his artistic skill • Phil's refusal to accept the authority of those in charge shown by his fury at the suggestion that he should seek permission to apply to art college

Question	Expected Answer(s)	Max Mark	Additional Guidance
4.	*(continued)*		• Mr. Barton's position of authority is used by Curry as an unseen presence with which to threaten/reprimand the slab boys e.g. 'Mr Barton's just blown his top out there.' • Hector immediately begins to assert his authority over the slab boys when he is promoted to a desk ('I'll be expecting some smart grinding from this department in the future') despite his previous low status in the slab room • Curry's appearances in the slab room are for the purpose of reprimanding the lads e.g., 'Look at this paper … 'S like bloody roughcast' his authority tends to express itself through negative and/or aggressive comments.
5.	For full marks candidates should deal with both Loch and the Speakers but not necessarily in equal measure. 2 marks may be awarded for detailed/insightful comment plus quotation/reference. 1 mark for more basic comment plus quotation/reference. 0 marks for quotation/reference alone. (Marks may be awarded 2 + 2, 2 + 1 + 1 or 1 + 1 + 1 + 1)	4	Possible answers include: Loch • 'The Marquis is not unaware of his responsibility' formal/grandiose tone suggests the appropriate gravity of the Marquis' attitude • 'responsibility' suggests that Marquis takes his role of wealthy man very seriously • 'lasting future interest and honour of his family' suggests that his aims are noble and grand • Parenthesis of 'as well as their immediate income' suggests that the actual money he can make is an afterthought, rather than his main motivation Speakers • 'immediate income was over £120,000' bald statement of figure emphasises the extent of his wealth and lack of need for more money • 'in those days … quite a lot of money' ironic understatement suggests that he was immensely wealthy and did not need to clear the Highland lands • Repetition of 'inherited' emphasises just how much he gained from his family, without having to work for any of it • 'that had coal-mines on it' mentioned at the end of the sentence as a comical afterthought, suggests the immense potential for wealth • 'inherited the Bridgewater Canal' blunt statement emphasises the incongruity of one person owning a canal a vital part of the country's infrastructure • 'he acquired three quarters of a million acres of Sutherland' huge numbers emphasises the extent of his land ownership, suggesting the unfairness of a system where one man can possess so much

Question	Expected Answer(s)	Max Mark	Additional Guidance
6.	2 marks may be awarded for detailed/insightful comment plus quotation/reference. 1 mark for comment plus quotation/reference (x2). 0 marks for quotation/reference alone. (Marks awarded 2 or 1 + 1)	2	Possible answers include: • 'parcel of beggars' categorises all the people of Sutherland using the stereotype of 'beggars' because they are poor • 'cunning and lazy' stereotypes them as vicious and shows no sympathy or understanding of their plight • 'slavery to their own indolence' suggests that they, rather than the social system of the day, are to blame for their poverty • contrast between glowing picture of 'general interests … happiness of the people' and 'the present state of Highlanders' suggests that everything about their culture is at odds with the prospect of prosperity • 'To be happy … productive' emphatic statement indicates his simplistic view of their lives • 'worship industry or starve' simple statement of these two alternatives indicates no sense of the suffering which the people will face • 'The present enchantment … broken' sums up their way of life as something to be destroyed, with no appreciation of its value to them
7.	For full marks candidates should deal with both the characters' apparently positive aims and their real motivation but not necessarily in equal measure. 2 marks may be awarded for detailed/insightful comment plus quotation/reference. 1 mark for more basis comment plus quotation/reference. 0 marks for quotation/reference alone. (Marks may be awarded 2 + 2, 2 + 1 + 1 or 1 + 1 + 1 + 1)	4	Possible answers include: Apparently positive aims • 'The coast of Sutherland abounds … fish' positive tone creates sense of the 'promised land' waiting for the people • 'Not only … herring too' suggests plenty and variety of food • 'Culgower … Kockglass' list of apparently favourable locations suggests the extensive positive possibilities for future life • 'perfect natural harbour' suggests the beauty and harmony of the location, implying that life will be easy there • 'they are just in the state of society for a savage country … Canada' presents forced emigration as an opportunity • 'wealth … palpable' list of positive effects of clearing the Highlands emphasises the range of benefits for all Real motivation • 'Believe it or not … used these words' undermines the nobility of the aims previously stated by Loch, suggesting a much more cynical aim • 'And there is said to be coal at Brora' stated as an apparent afterthought, suggests that the Highland people moved there could be exploited as miners • 'draining to your coast-line' suggests that the people are a swamp-like nuisance to be removed for the benefit of the land • 'mildewed districts cleared' suggests that the people are a disease/affliction on the land • 'swarm of dependants' dehumanises the people by suggesting they and their children are an infestation to be cleared out • The 'bargaining' exchange between Loch and Sellar, in which the rents/transport of people are included as one commodity to be negotiated emphasises their lack of humanity in considering the people's fate

Question	Expected Answer(s)	Max Mark	Additional Guidance
8.	Candidates may choose to answer in bullet points in this final question, or write a number of linked statements.	10	Up to 2 marks can be achieved for identifying elements of commonality as identified in the question i.e. how McGrath uses unusual dramatic techniques to highlight central concerns.
			A further 2 marks can be achieved for reference to the extract given.
			6 additional marks can be awarded for discussion of similar references to at least one other part of the text by the author.
			In practice this means:
			Identification of commonality (2) e.g. by having characters step outside their roles and speak directly to the audience, McGrath undermines what the characters have said (1) and encourages the audience to consider the key issues of the play in a direct and immediate way (1)
			From the extract:
			2 marks for detailed/insightful comment plus quotation/reference;
			1 mark for more basic comment plus quotation/reference;
			0 marks for quotation/reference alone.
			2 marks only for discussion of extract.
			e.g. freezing the action during the discussion by Loch and Sellar enables the Speakers to highlight the hypocrisy of those two characters by presenting the audience with a factual account of the situation (2)
			From at least one other part of the text as above for up to 6 marks.
			Possible answers include:
			• The MC speaks directly to the audience in the opening, encouraging them to sing along, sets the tone of informality which encourages them to feel part of the performance and closer to the issues highlighted
			• Sellar's speech to the audience, 'I am not a cruel man … businessman' followed by winking encourages the audience to feel complicit in his lies, undermining any further comments he makes
			• Use of Readers to read out the list of atrocities carried out against the Highlanders follows the 'normal' acting out of one such incident and conveys the extent of the horror
			• The Company become sheep, bleating and crawling towards Harriet Beecher-Stowe, emphasising the mindlessness and herd mentality of those who believe her and others like her
			• Climactic ending when the Cast, in turn, speak to the audience 'out of character', comparing the past with the present/future, leaving the audience with a final sense of the play's key themes

Text 3 — *Drama* — *Men Should Weep* by Ena Lamont Stewart

Question	Expected Answer(s)	Max Mark	Additional Guidance
9.	2 marks awarded for detailed/insightful comment plus quotation/reference. 1 mark for more basic comment plus quotation/reference. 0 marks for quotation/reference alone. (Marks may be awarded 2+2, 2+1+1, 1+1+1+1)	4	Possible answers include: • 'Aw shut up!'/'Ye stupid fool!' suggests her aggressive dismissal of Alec • 'An I'm warnin you!' throwing Alec's words back at him with increased menace suggests her total lack of respect • 'You're no the only pebble on ma beach …' image suggests Alec's insignificance in Isa's life • 'it's time ye wis making a bit o dough again' suggests she only views Alec as a source of income • 'Aye. *Mebbe*' stress on '*Mebbe*' her sarcasm/realism in the face of Alec's desperate optimism suggests her dismissive attitude/dominance • 'Aye, an I mind the last hauf dizzen times …' cutting across Alec's reminiscence suggests she has no time for his fond memories of better times • 'Whit kind o fur? Rabbit?' sarcasm suggests sense of inadequacy as a provider • 'That's a you're guid for. Rinnin.' suggests her contempt for Alec's cowardly weakness
10.	For full marks candidates must deal with both dialogue and stage directions but not necessarily in equal measure. 2 marks awarded for detailed/insightful comment plus quotation/reference. 1 mark for more basic comment plus quotation/reference. 0 marks for quotation/reference alone. (Marks may be awarded 2+2, 2+1+1, 1+1+1+1)	4	Possible answers include: Dialogue • '…I'll kill ye! I wull! I'll kill ye!' repeated exclamations/threats suggest Alec's aggression and his need to control Isa/the fact that he is at the end of his tether • 'Did I hurt ye? I didnae mean tae hurt ye …' following 'I'll kill ye!' suggests how quickly Alec's feelings swing from murderous threats to anxiety as soon as Isa is angry with him • 'Isa, I'm sorry.' Alec's pitiful apology suggests his desperate need to pacify Isa • 'I canna see naethin but him an you tae.g. ether …' suggests Alec's overwhelming sense of inferiority/insecurity • 'I'll get ye onythin ye want …' – Alec's desperate promise reveals his anxiety about losing Isa • 'I proamise, Isa! I proamise! … if ye'll stay wi me …' Alec's pitiful pleading suggests his desperate need for her • 'I love ye, Isa; honest, I dae.' his earnest declaration suggests his desperation in the face of her cold-heartedness Stage directions • '*He gets hold of her by the throat*' violent actions against Isa indicate his frustration/desperate need to control her • '*He panics and drops her*' deep fear that he has gone too far and actually hurt her

Question	Expected Answer(s)	Max Mark	Additional Guidance
11.	2 marks awarded for detailed/insightful comment plus quotation/reference. 1 mark for more basic comment plus quotation/reference. 0 marks for quotation/reference alone. (Marks may be awarded 2, 1+1)	2	Possible answers include: • '*Love*! Hee-haw!' suggests Isa believes that love as a romantic feeling does not exist • 'There's nae sich a thing.' emphatic statement denying the possibility of love • 'There's wantin tae get intae bed wi someone ye fancy ...' suggests she believes that in place of love, there is sex • 'or wantin someone'll let ye lie in yer bed an no have tae work;' suggests she believes that in place of love there is the more practical requirement to be provided for financially • 'No roon aboot here, onyway.' suggests she believes that romantic love isn't possible for people living in such straitened circumstances
12.	Candidates may choose to answer in bullet points in this final question, or write a number of linked statements.	10	Up to 2 marks can be achieved by identifying elements of commonality as identified in the question, i.e. how the theme of love is explored. A further 2 marks can be achieved for reference to the extract given. 6 additional marks can be awarded for discussion of similar references to at least one other part of the text by the writer. <u>In practice this means:</u> Identification of commonality (2) e.g. love can take many forms including that between husband/wife, parent/child, sibling etc, (1) and this can be destructive or life enriching (1) From this extract: 2 marks for detailed/insightful comment plus quotation/reference; 1 mark for more basic comment plus quotation/reference; 0 marks for quotation/reference alone. e.g., Isa's cold-hearted, mercenary attitude towards love means that she expects her husband to provide for her. She therefore rejects any warmth or affection from Alec when he fails to meet her demands (2) From elsewhere in the text: as above for up to 6 marks. Possible answers include: • Maggie believes that love (and marriage) is fulfilling, and makes a woman happy. She says to Lily, '... it's a pity ye had yon disappointment; ye might hev been real happy wi the right man and a couple weans.' • Lily is cynical about love. She does not believe that love is necessary; she is suspicious of men and prefers her independence 'Men! I'm wantin nae man's airms roon me.'

Question	Expected Answer(s)	Max Mark	Additional Guidance
12.	*(continued)*		• John shows his devotion for Maggie when, for once, he is able to treat her by buying her a new hat when he has a job • Jenny's attitude towards love is more practical. She acknowledges that being treated with respect is important and values the security that comes with a successful relationship: 'But I'm happy, an I'm makin him happy. We've a nice wee flat in a clean district, wi trees an wee gardens.' • Love for children is unconditional: Maggie says, 'Once they've been laid in yer airms, they're in yer heart tae the end o yer days, no matter whit way they turn oot.'

PART B — SCOTTISH TEXT — PROSE

Text 1 — *Prose — The Painter* by Iain Crichton Smith

Question	Expected Answer(s)	Max Mark	Additional Guidance
13.	For full marks differing attitudes must be dealt with but not necessarily in equal measure. 2 marks awarded for detailed/insightful comment plus quotation/reference. 1 mark for more basic comment plus quotation/reference. 0 marks for quotation/reference alone. (Marks may be awarded 2 or 1 + 1)	4	Possible answers: • 'certain responsibility' suggests desire to protect/care for him • 'maintained that … so clever' suggests their certainty that he is too talented for his own good • 'always pointed … pride' suggests they value his work • 'one of our greatest assets' suggests positive sense of ownership • 'wonderful artist' suggests admiration for/recognition of his skill • 'made us uncomfortable' suggests they are unsettled by his artistic vision • 'less glamorous'/'narrow and crooked'/'spindly and thin'/'confused and weird' suggests their resentment of his portrayal of the community • 'strange boy' suggests their (judgemental) view of him as different • 'slapdash manner' suggests their criticism of his bohemian disregard for convention
14.	2 marks awarded for detailed/insightful comment plus quotation/reference. 1 mark for more basic comment plus quotation/reference. 0 marks for quotation/reference alone. (Marks may be awarded 2 or 1 + 1)	2	Possible answers: • 'not a wholly harmonious place' suggests conflict in the community • 'share of barbarism' suggests uncivilised • 'violence' suggests aggression • 'quarrelled about land' suggests petty territorial disputes • 'much less often about women' suggests low status of women • 'prolonged controversy' suggests unforgiving/holding grudges • 'As is often the case … hair' suggests stereotypical views

Question	Expected Answer(s)	Max Mark	Additional Guidance
15.	For full marks both positive and negative features should be dealt with but not necessarily in equal measure. 2 marks awarded for detailed/insightful comment plus quotation/reference. 1 mark for more basic comment plus quotation/reference. 0 marks for quotation/reference alone. (Marks may be awarded 2 or 1 + 1)	4	Possible answers: Positive • 'he spent most ... shed' suggests industrious • 'when sober ... very kind man' suggests potential for warmth • 'fond of his children ... strong they were' suggests his pride in his family • 'in those moments ... his life' suggests his feeling of temporary happiness • 'sunny-tempered ... village' suggests good humoured/affability • 'singing songs happily ... suggests a capacity for intense emotions/joy Negative • 'he regularly beat up' suggests he was abusive/cruel • 'when it suited him ... temper' suggests unpredictable mood swings' • 'he would grow violent' suggests became aggressive • 'morose' suggests self-pitying • 'snarl' suggests savagery • 'especially the weakest and most inoffensive people' suggests bullying behaviour
16.	Candidates may choose to answer in bullet points in this final question, or write a number of linked statements.	10	Up to 2 marks can be achieved for identifying elements of commonality as identified in the question i.e. the theme of isolation. A further 2 marks can be achieved for reference to the extract given. 6 additional marks can be awarded for discussion of similar references to at least one other text. In practice this means: Identification of commonality (2) e.g. Crichton Smith creates characters/communities isolated because of their inability or unwillingness to fit in (1) leading to profound and/or life-limiting situations (1) From the extract: 2 marks for detailed/insightful comment plus quotation/reference 1 marks for more basic comment plus quotation/reference 0 marks for quotation alone e.g. 'he insisted on painting things as they were' suggests that William's uncompromising artistic vision sets him apart from the community (2)

Question	Expected Answer(s)	Max Mark	Additional Guidance
16.	*(continued)*		From at least one other text: as above for up to 6 marks Possible answers include: • *Mother and Son* John/his mother isolated as a result of their claustrophobic relationship and domestic circumstances which limit their choices and leads to a spiral of mutual destruction • *Red Door* After a lifetime of loneliness and isolation, Murdo is given the opportunity to break free from the restrictive environment • *The Telegram* The geographical remoteness of the community leads to emotional isolation which results in a failure to grasp the scale of/reasons behind the war • *In Church* The 'priest's' inability to cope with the war leads to his self-isolation and resultant loss of sanity/humanity • *The Crater* Robert is isolated from the other soldiers by the responsibilities of his role as an officer, which he finds overwhelming

Text 2 – *Prose* – *The Bright Spade* by George Mackay Brown

Question	Expected Answer(s)	Max Mark	Additional Guidance
17.	2 marks awarded for detailed/insightful comment plus quotation/reference. 1 mark for more basic comment plus quotation/reference. 0 marks for quotation/reference alone. (Marks may be awarded 2+2, 2+1+1 or 1+1+1+1)	4	Possible answers include: • 'That winter … island' suggests the island has suffered significant loss • 'wind squatted in the east … with her breath' metaphor/personification suggests the wind is a malevolent presence blasting the island with deadly power and destroying all life and colour by blowing on it • 'clung to life like the last tattered leaf on a branch' simile suggests the frailty of James of Moss and the desperation of his struggle to live as well as the inevitability of his death • 'lay stiff and pale as a candle' simile suggests the lifelessness and sadness/hopelessness of her death: her life snuffed out like a flame • Repetition of 'thin': 'thin harvest … ale was sour and thin' emphasises the lack of nourishment and richness in what nature produces on the island • Word choice of 'sour and thin' suggests the lack of flavour and pleasure to be had on the island

Question	Expected Answer(s)	Max Mark	Additional Guidance
18.	2 marks awarded for detailed/insightful comment plus quotation/reference. 1 mark for more basic comment plus quotation/reference. 0 marks for quotation/reference alone. (Marks may be awarded 2+2, 2+1+1 or 1+1+1+1)	4	Possible answers include: • 'This will need a deep grave' suggests that the laird's son is well-fed and privileged but this has not protected him from death, which has come to all/sense of many more relatives to follow, therefore a reminder of mortality • 'he threw up many fine white bones, the laird's ancestors, with his spade' suggests the delicate aristocratic nature of the laird's family which nonetheless receives the same rough treatment from death as do the poor • contrast between 'half a guinea' and 'nothing at all … coarse tobacco snuff' emphasises that death claims both rich and poor/death is the great 'leveller' • 'nobody expected most of the old people and sickly people to see the spring' word choice of 'nobody' and 'most of' emphasises the certainty of the extent of the deaths • '… snow and small fires the infant breathed her last' softness of 's' alliteration and vocabulary 'breathed her last' emphasises the sadness of the baby's death • 'the day after the funeral'/'never lived with Amos again' speedy departure of baby's mother/finality of 'never … again' emphasises the significance of one, 'little' human death – the baby was holding them together • 'one large grave for the foreigners' suggests the anonymity of death, when there are no loved ones to mourn
19.	1 mark awarded for each comment on two aspects of Jacob's personality, supported by reference to the extract. 0 marks for quotation/reference alone. (Marks awarded 1+1)	2	Possible answers include: • Self-indulgent when opportunity arises: 'had hardly sobered up' quickly drank all the whisky given by the widow of Moss • Decent/unselfish: prepared to bury the very poor people e.g., Samuel Ling, Jean of Ness for virtually no payment at all • Matter of fact: 'sneezed heroically for a month' suggests that the snuff was not to his taste, but he accepted it as payment because it was all there was • Demanding/stands up for himself: 'Who will pay my fee?' when asked to dig large grave for the unknown foreigners

Question	Expected Answer(s)	Max Mark	Additional Guidance
20.	Candidates can answer in bullet points in this final question, or write a number of linked statements.	10	Up to 2 marks can be achieved for identifying elements of commonality as identified in the question, i.e. Mackay Brown's use of characters as metaphorical and/or symbolic figures.
			A further 2 marks can be achieved for reference to the extract given.
			6 additional marks can be awarded for discussion of similar references from at least one other short story.
			<u>In practice this means:</u>
			Identification of commonality (2)
			e.g. Mackay Brown uses characters to comment on significant aspects of humanity such as death, the journey through life, belonging (1)
			The universal nature of these characters means that all readers can relate to them (1)
			From the extract:
			2 marks for detailed/insightful comment plus quotation/reference;
			1 mark for more basic comment plus quotation/reference;
			0 marks for quotation alone.
			e.g. Jacob represents death, who comes to rich and poor, loved and unknown alike, wielding his bright spade like a scythe, cutting down all before him (2)
			From at least one other text:
			as above for up to 6 marks
			Possible answers include:
			• *The Whaler's Return* Flaws represents flawed humanity, journeying across the island, facing challenges and trials which test his resolve/character (such as the incident with the tinkers) until he reaches the safety of home, represented by the worthy, though ugly, Peterina
			• *A Time to Keep* Bill is the 'everyman' character who struggles to be an individual and to have a passionate and genuine relationship in the face of community pressure and the trials of an uncaring natural world
			• *The Wireless Set* Howie represents the desire for change and progress: young, naive and confident, he brings the destructive outside world into the community in the form of the wireless set of which he is so proud, leading ultimately (through the war) to his own death
			• *The Wireless Set* the missionary represents the insensitive role of the 'outside' church, failing to understand the pain of Howie's parents or the values of their community and dismissing their reaction to their son's death as callous
			• *The Eye of the Hurricane* Cpt Stevens represents flawed and, at times, self-destructive, humanity, which nonetheless has a certain heroism, evidenced by the devotion of his old shipmates and their stories of his courage and determination at sea

Text 3 – *Prose* – *The Trick Is To Keep Breathing* by Janice Galloway

Question	Expected Answer(s)	Max Mark	Additional Guidance
21.	2 marks may be awarded for detailed/insightful comment plus quotation/reference. 1 mark for more basic comment plus quotation/reference. 0 marks for quotation reference alone. (Marks may be awarded 2+1, 1+1+1)	3	Possible answers include: • 'It never looks as good as I'd like' sentence following list of housework creates an anti-climax highlighting her efforts are perpetually fruitless/expectations are unrealistic • 'running … for the biscuits' suggests her desperation to appear as though she's coping • 'I get different ones … she will enjoy' suggests Joy is keen to please/seem hospitable • 'I can't choose in a hurry' blunt statement conveys her placing too high an importance on a trivial task/conceals her inner turmoil • 'I wait for too long … confused … wrong money' fixation on minor details conveys her frustration/negative perception • 'clutching'/'nearly drop the milk'/'flustered' suggests the futility of her intense desire to create a good impression • 'These visits are good … sends this woman out of love. He insisted.' Emphatic short sentence highlights Joy's reluctance to accept the help, signalling the likelihood that the visit will be unsuccessful
22.	2 marks may be awarded for detailed/insightful comment plus quotation/reference. 1 mark for more basic comment plus quotation/reference. 0 marks for quotation reference alone. (Marks may be awarded 2+1, 1+1+1)	3	Possible answers include: • 'I said … strangers' suggests self-doubt/fear of not coping • 'she would find me out and let me talk. *Make me* talk' sequence of verbs suggests Joy's perception of the visit as combative • 'without knocking and frightens me' suggests her lack of control and perceived invasion of her personal space • 'Tray … spoon' layout of list/list emphasises her deliberate attempt to think through what she is doing/calm herself down/appear organised • 'the biscuits the biscuits' repetition/layout of lines emphasises her panic/excessive desire to create a good impression • 'I burst … I polish … I make …' list of verbs emphasises her frantic attempts to take control • 'It sloshes' suggests physical manifestation of her nervousness/lack of control • 'still wearing my slippers dammit' Joy's thoughts reveal her disappointment in herself for not appearing perfect

Question	Expected Answer(s)	Max Mark	Additional Guidance
23.	2 marks may be awarded for detailed/insightful comment plus quotation/reference. 1 mark for more basic comment plus quotation/reference. 0 marks for quotation reference alone. (Marks may be awarded 2+2, 2+1+1, 1+1+1+1)	4	Possible answers include: • 'She does it every time.' emphatic sentence suggests that the visit follows the same pattern every time • 'thinking her way into the part' suggests they are following what seems like a rehearsed script/lack of naturalness • 'I throw a little difficulty every so often' suggests Joy's deliberate attempts to appear convincingly natural • incongruity of insertion of drama into prose text suggests their interaction resembles a rehearsed script • 'So, how are you … how's life …' suggests the same formulaic questions are repeated every visit • 'improvise' suggests that even apparently more spontaneous comments are in the context of the constraints • 'knowing I don't want her … can't talk to her' suggests both are aware of the lack of any real meaning in their interaction

Text 4 — *Prose* — *Sunset Song* by Lewis Grassic Gibbon

Question	Expected Answer(s)	Max Mark	Additional Guidance
24.	Candidates may choose to answer in bullet points in this final question, or write a number of linked statements.	10	Up to 2 marks can be achieved for identifying elements of commonality as identified in the question, i.e. Joy's difficulties with social interaction. A further 2 marks can be achieved for reference to the extract given. 6 additional marks can be awarded for discussion of similar references from at least one other part of the text. In practice this means: Identification of commonality (2) e.g. Joy finds it difficult to speak honestly to family, friends and colleagues (1) due to her reluctance to reveal her vulnerability/to acknowledge to herself that she is not coping. (1) From the extract: 2 marks for detailed/insightful comment plus quotation/reference; 1 mark for more basic comment plus quotation/reference; 0 marks for quotation alone. e.g. Joy struggles to express her true feelings to the Health Visitor, who is there to support her, because of her conflicted state of mind 'I don't want her to be here/that I want her to be here but I can't talk to her.' (2) From at least one other part of the text: as above for up to 6 marks Possible answers include: • Joy struggles to express her true feelings with the various doctors that she sees as she feels that they do not help or understand her

Question	Expected Answer(s)	Max Mark	Additional Guidance
24.	*(continued)*		• Joy finds it difficult to cope with Ellen's attempts to look after her and feed her because of her need to hide her anorexia • Joy conceals her feelings when replying to Marianne's suggestion about positive ways forward as she doesn't want to disappoint her; for example, her 'right choice' in seeking medical help • Joy engages in a number of problematic and meaningless relationships with men in an attempt to overcome her overwhelming grief at the loss of Michael • Uneasy relationship with her sister Myra stems from early experience of bullying, for example 'Hands like shovels. Myra left marks.'
25.	2 marks awarded for detailed/insightful comment plus quotation/reference. 1 mark for more basic comment plus quotation/reference. 0 marks for quotation reference alone. (Marks may be awarded 2+1 or 1+1+1)	3	Possible answers include: • 'carelessly' suggests lack of focus • 'breath of them rising up like a steam' suggests insubstantial quality • 'seemed fine … Spring' suggests sense of their greatness • 'their feet … behind' suggests their mythical qualities • 'looked at them over-long' suggests transfixed state • 'glimmered' suggests fleeting • 'ceased to be there' suggests sense of altered reality • 'mirages' suggests sense of unreal vision • 'dreamt by a land' suggests that they are a creation of the land • 'shook her head … daft' suggests coming out of dreamlike state
26.	2 marks awarded for detailed/insightful comment plus quotation/reference. 1 mark for more basic comment plus quotation/reference. 0 marks for quotation reference alone. (Marks may be awarded 2+1 or 1+1+1)	3	Possible answers include: • 'farming folk did well' suggests farming was highly profitable • 'drove of Irish steers' suggests plenty • 'lush green grass' suggests the land was fertile and productive • 'grew fat and round' suggests the cattle would thrive/farmers would make good money at market • 'in the shortest while' suggests a quick financial return • 'so many beasts' suggests abundance of livestock

Question	Expected Answer(s)	Max Mark	Additional Guidance
27.	2 marks awarded for detailed/insightful comment plus quotation/reference. 1 mark for more basic comment plus quotation/reference. (Marks may be awarded 2+2 or 2+1+1 or 1+1+1+1)	4	Possible answers include: • 'Chris gave a loud gasp' suggests her shock at the change in his physical appearance • 'so altered' suggests he has been profoundly changed • 'thin' suggest physical privations experienced • 'his fine eyes queered and strained' suggests he has experienced trauma • 'Even his laugh seemed different' suggests that everything about him has been altered, even the most natural responses • *'I'm not a ghost yet!'* suggests his acknowledgement of change/death he has witnessed • 'the lice ... awful ... some devil fair sucking and sucking the life from his skin' suggests the constant physical suffering from the conditions of war • 'his old laugh queerly crippled' suggests that beneath surface appearances, Chae has been disabled/weakened by his experiences of war • 'gey green and *feuch!*' emphatic description of decay, followed by the exclamation of disgust indicates the horror of what Chae has seen
28.	Candidates can answer in bullet points in this final question, or write a number of linked statements.	10	Up to 2 marks can be achieved for identifying elements of commonality as identified in the question — i.e. how Grassic Gibbon uses symbolism to explore the central concerns of the text. A further 2 marks can be achieved for reference to the extract given. 6 additional marks can be awarded for discussion of similar references to at least one other part of the text. In practice this means: Identification of commonality e.g. Grassic Gibbon uses characters, incidents and setting as representative of wider issues (1) such as loss of a way of life, impact of war, aspects of Scotland. (1) From the extract: 2 marks for detailed/insightful comment plus quotation/reference 1 mark for more basic comment plus quotation/reference 0 marks for quotation/reference alone e.g., Chris' vision of Rob and Ewan seeming to emerge from the land symbolises the old Scottish agricultural way of life which is ending. (2) From at least one other part of the text: as above for up to 6 marks Possible answers include: Scottish Chris represents the land and English Chris represents pursuit of education/modernity Standing stones represent continuity in human history/what has gone before

Question	Expected Answer(s)	Max Mark	Additional Guidance
27.	*(continued)*	4	The cutting down of trees represents the death of a generation of young men in the war/ change of use of the land
			John Guthrie represents the patriarchal society/grim Calvinism of the past
			Celebration of wedding represents the richness of Scottish culture and community spirit

Text 5 — *Prose* — *The Cone-Gatherers* by Robin Jenkins

Question	Expected Answer(s)	Max Mark	Additional Guidance
29.	2 marks awarded for detailed/insightful comment plus quotation/reference. 1 mark for more basic comment plus quotation/reference. 0 marks for quotation/reference alone. (Marks may be awarded 2 or 1+1)	2	Possible answers include: • 'his friends the finches' Calum is identified with nature, and is among those he loves/ trusts • 'safe from the hawk' the security of the finches, hidden from predators, makes Calum feel comfortable/reassured • 'ground of snares and stumbles was far below' suggests distance between him and danger/clumsiness on the ground, emphasising that he is in his element • 'seals were playing' suggests innocent/ carefree enjoyment of life • 'cushat doves were crooning' suggests comforting, harmonious sound • 'his brother ... singing' suggests pleasure in that Neil is at ease • 'present joy' suggests immediacy of his feeling of pleasure • 'nor did he see ... toppled down' suggests lack of awareness of future destruction
30.	The impact on both Calum and Neil should be dealt with, although not necessarily in equal measure. 2 marks awarded for detailed/insightful comment plus quotation/reference. 1 mark for more basic comment plus quotation/reference. 0 marks for quotation/reference alone. (Marks may be awarded 2+2, 2+1+1, 1+1+1+1)	4	Possible answers include: Calum: • 'in agitation' suggests his anxiety at the approach of Duror • 'could not concentrate' suggests he is worried/distracted by Duror's presence • 'like an animal in danger' (simile) suggests he reacts like a frightened creature when trapped/cornered • 'began to whimper' animal cry suggests vulnerability • 'panicky' suggests Calum's desperation as Duror approaches • 'let some cones dribble' suggests he has lost control and confidence and is making mistakes by dropping the cones Neil: • 'he would still pass by' suggests that he is thinking through Duror's probable movements • 'murmured to Calum' suggests a quiet calmness in Neil's voice as he tries to reassure Calum that there is no threat • 'felt sympathy' suggests Neil's awareness of humanity's isolation • 'typical of nature' suggests Neil's resentment that nature is against them as there is no camouflage from the leaves • 'objected to this spying' suggests Neil's heightened awareness that they are being watched

Question	Expected Answer(s)	Max Mark	Additional Guidance
31.	2 marks awarded for detailed/insightful comment plus quotation/reference. 1 mark for more basic comment plus quotation/reference. 0 marks for quotation/reference alone. (Marks may be awarded 2+2, 2+1+1, 1+1+1+1)	4	Possible answers include: • 'What's the matter with you?' question suggests Neil's irritability/impatience with Callum • 'He's just doing his work, like you and me.' explanation suggests Neil's pragmatism, his sense of needing to cope • 'He became angry' suggests annoyance with himself due to his lack of control of the situation • question 'What are you moaning for?' suggests that Neil's protectiveness expresses itself in an aggressive way • 'passion of resentment' suggests his sense of a clear injustice • tone of the final sentence indicates his cynicism in that Lady Runcie-Campbell/Duror value the trees more than the workers
32.	Candidates may answer in bullet points in this final question, or write a number of linked statements.	10	Up to 2 marks can be achieved for identifying elements of commonality as identified in the question, i.e. how Jenkins develops the theme of power. A further 2 marks can be achieved for reference to the extract given. 6 additional marks can be awarded for discussion of similar references to at least one other part of the text by the writer. In practice this means: Identification of commonality (2) e.g. Characters from the upper-class, such as Lady Runcie-Campbell, are seen to be powerful in the novel. Her actions have an impact on the main characters of the novel. (1) As gamekeeper, Duror wields power on the estate and is able to exploit this to intimidate Calum. (1) From the extract: 2 marks for detailed/insightful comment plus quotation/reference; 1 mark for more basic comment plus quotation/reference; 0 marks for quotation alone.

Question	Expected Answer(s)	Max Mark	Additional Guidance
32.	*(continued)*		e.g. Duror's powerful presence in the woods is enough to unsettle both Calum and Neil: Calum panics and begins to drop his collected cones, whereas Neil's bitterness and resentment build as he tries to calm his brother. (2)
			From at least one other part of the text:
			as above for up to 6 marks
			Possible answers include:
			• Duror exerts power over Calum by exploiting his love of nature: he cruelly involves him in the deer drive knowing that it would pain him to see an injured animal
			• Duror has power over his wife and can choose when he spends time with her, much to the anger and resentment of his mother-in-law
			• Duror has power over Lady Runcie-Campbell in the absence of her husband when he influences her/advises her not to let the cone-gatherers stay in the beach hut as he does not want his wood 'defiled'
			• Roderick challenges his mother's power when he disagrees with her over her failure to give the cone-gatherers a lift or to let them shelter from the storm in the beach hut
			• Neil attempts to exert some degree of power over Lady Runcie-Campbell by refusing to help Roderick when he is stuck in the tree

PART C — SCOTTISH TEXT — POETRY

Text 1 — *Poetry — A Man's A Man For A' That* by Robert Burns

Question	Expected Answer(s)	Max Mark	Additional Guidance
33.	2 marks awarded for detailed/insightful comment plus quotation/reference.	4	Possible answers include:
	1 mark for more basic comment plus quotation/reference.		• 'honest poverty' suggests being born into poverty can go together with integrity
	0 marks for quotation/reference alone.		• 'coward – slave' suggests being ashamed of being poor is shameful in itself/shows a lack of courage, spirit, manliness
	(Marks may be awarded 2+2, 2+1+1 or 1+1+1+1.)		• 'hangs his head' suggests servility/shame in response to poverty which speaker goes on vehemently to reject
			• 'toils obscure' suggests poverty and hard work go together; the hard work of the poor is unacknowledged
			• question creates a sense of disbelief that anyone would be ashamed of honest poverty
			• 'guinea stamp … gowd' suggests true worth is the real substance of the man whereas wealth is a superficiality

Question	Expected Answer(s)	Max Mark	Additional Guidance
34.	2 marks awarded for detailed/insightful comment plus quotation/reference. 1 mark for more basic comment plus quotation/reference. 0 marks for quotation/reference alone. (Marks may be awarded 2+2, 2+1+1 or 1+1+1+1.)	4	Possible answers include: • 'hamely fare' suggests something wholesome, unpretentious as opposed to 'wine' suggests luxurious and non-essential • 'hoddin grey' suggests sense of homeliness or ordinariness as compared to 'silks' something luxurious, for show, for creating an impression • 'fools'/'knaves' derogatory terms to underline his contempt • 'tinsel show' suggests the flashy, fancy but ultimately entirely superficial nature of luxury • contrast in idea of 'honest' 'e'er sae poor' man being a 'king o' men' – a contradiction in worldly terms • 'struts/stares' suggests one posing around, but to no effect • 'riband, star & a' that' suggests dependence on others/superficial insignia for his status • 'belted knight/marquis/duke' all mere titles/all can be created by man • 'rank'/'their dignities' man-made distinctions that have no value in themselves/are all about status/can be bought'
35.	2 marks awarded for detailed/insightful comment plus quotation/reference. 1 mark for more basic comment plus quotation/reference. 0 marks for quotation/reference alone. (Marks may be awarded 2 or 1+1)	2	Possible answers include: • 'let us pray' suggests we should unite in our desire for a fairer world • 'As come it will' suggests certainty that the day must come when the best human qualities are valued more than rank or privilege • 'o'er a' the earth' suggests such ideas will be welcomed globally/transcend national boundaries • 'Shall brothers be for a' that!' suggests universal brotherhood/humanity is coming/will change the world • Repetition/climax of 'for a' that' reinforces inevitability of change

Question	Expected Answer(s)	Max Mark	Additional Guidance
36.	Candidates can answer in bullet points in this final question, or write a number of linked statements.	10	Up to 2 marks can be achieved for identifying elements of commonality as identified in the question, i.e. Burns' use of contrast to explore central concerns.
			A further 2 marks can be achieved for reference to the extract given.
			6 additional marks can be awarded for discussion of similar references to at least one other poem by the poet.
			In practice this means:
			Identification of commonality (2)
			e.g. Burns uses contrast to ridicule people/ideas (1) to undermine their status/position within society (1)
			From this poem:
			2 marks for detailed/insightful comment plus quotation/reference
			1 mark for more basic comment plus quotation/reference
			0 marks for quotation/reference alone
			e.g the contrast between the self-importance of 'thon birkie, ca'd a lord' and the inte.g. rity of 'The man of independent mind' highlights the central concern of the value of ordinary men. (2)
			From at least one other poem:
			as above for up to 6 marks.
			Possible answers include: • *Address to the Deil* contrasts the stereotypical depiction of the devil with a far homelier persona to highlight the ridiculous nature of contemporary theological teachings • *Holy Willie's Prayer* the persona's view of himself as an epitome of righteousness contrasts with his actions which are lustful and spiteful highlighting the central concern of hypocrisy • *A Poet's Welcome to his Love–Begotten Daughter* contrast between his love for his daughter and the narrow-minded and judgemental moral attitudes of the time highlighting the pettiness of the prevailing social attitudes • *Tam O'Shanter* moralising narrative voice contrasts with energetic description of Tam's actions highlights the life-affirming tone of the poem • *To a Mouse* mouse's suffering being confined to the present is contrasted with the speaker's awareness of future uncertainty to highlight the fragility of life

Text 2 — *Poetry* — *Originally* by Carol Ann Duffy

Question	Expected Answer(s)	Max Mark	Additional Guidance
37.	2 marks awarded for detailed/insightful comment plus quotation/reference. 1 mark for more basic comment plus quotation/reference. 0 marks for quotation/reference alone. (Marks may be awarded 2 or 1 + 1)	2	Possible answers include: • 'fell through the fields' suggests the loss of control/uncertainty the speaker felt about the move • 'cried … bawling' suggests intensity of upset/intensity of physical reaction • '*Home, Home*' repetition suggests depth of longing • 'vacant rooms' suggests the emotional emptiness the speaker now feels • 'blind toy' suggests the speaker's incomprehension of the events taking place/identification with child's helplessness • 'holding its paw' suggests the speaker's need for reassurance and comfort in the face of the events taking place
38.	2 marks awarded for detailed/insightful comment plus quotation/reference. 1 mark for more basic comment plus quotation/reference. 0 marks for quotation/reference alone. (Marks may be awarded 2 + 2, 2 + 1 + 1 or 1 + 1 + 1 + 1)	4	Possible answers include: • abruptness/word choice 'your accent wrong' emphasises her sense of exclusion • parenthesis of 'which seem familiar' suggests an unpleasant sense of disorientation brought about by her surroundings • 'unimagined' suggests a sense of trepidation/confusion/fear • word choice/alliteration of 'big boys' suggests her sense of vulnerability when encountering local youths • word choice of 'eating worms' suggests her horror at the outlandish behaviour of the local youths • word choice of 'shouting' suggests she feels intimidated by the way the local youths spoke • word choice of 'You don't understand' suggests her sense of exclusion from the society of her peers • 'stirred like a loose tooth' suggests her nagging insecurity about the move
39.	2 marks awarded for detailed/insightful comment plus quotation/reference. 1 mark for more basic comment plus quotation/reference. 0 marks for quotation/reference alone. (Marks may be awarded 2 + 2, 2 + 1 + 1 or 1 + 1 + 1 + 1)	4	Possible answers include • 'skelf of shame' suggests that she is only mildly bothered by her brother's actions in this new environment • 'my tongue … snake' suggests her old accent is fading, another stage in her process of assimilation • positioning of 'But' suggests a change of status, from being excluded to being accepted • sequence 'you forget … or change' suggests the gradual process of assimilation she has gone through/an uncertainty as to how exactly the process took place • positioning at end of poem/abruptness of 'And I hesitate.' suggests a slight uncertainty about what culture she identifies with, or where she belongs

Question	Expected Answer(s)	Max Mark	Additional Guidance
40.	Candidates can answer in bullet points in this final question, or write a number of linked statements.	10	Up to 2 marks can be achieved by identifying elements of commonality as identified in the question i.e. how the poet explores concerns about identity
			A further 2 marks can be achieved for reference to the text given.
			6 additional marks can be awarded for discussion of similar references to at least one other poem by the poet.
			In practice this means:
			Identification of commonality (2) e.g. Duffy presents us with characters who have to face situations which prompt them to consider who they are (1); some are able to adapt their view of themselves whilst others are incapable of doing this, to their cost (1)
			From the poem:
			2 marks for detailed/insightful comment plus quotation/reference;1 mark for more basic comment plus quotation/reference;
			0 marks for quotation/reference alone.
			e.g. the speaker's sense of alienation from her new surroundings gradually subsides as she starts to become assimilated; the cost of this assimilation however, is an uncertainty about her cultural identity (2)
			From at least one other poem:
			as above for up to 6 marks
			Possible comments include:
			• *Anne Hathaway* a feature of the speaker's sense of who she is – the lover and wife – is threatened by the death of her husband; however, through her memories she can still retain a part of her previous identity
			• *Havisham* the deterioration in her state of mind due to the conflicting emotions she feels for her ex-lover leads to losing a stable sense of who she is
			• *War Photographer* his difficulty in reconciling his public identity as a professional photographer – getting on with the job – and his human response to the horror and suffering he has encountered
			• *Valentine* the speaker is unwilling to be defined by society's conventional view of romantic love which prompts her attempt to break free of e.g., romantic stereotypes and be more 'truthful', more authentic
			• *Mrs Midas* given the consequences of her husband's 'wish', she struggles with the loss of certain aspects of her previous identity – wife, lover, potential mother – due to her prioritising her own self preservation

Text 3 — *Poetry* — *Some Old Photographs* by Liz Lochhead

Question	Expected Answer(s)	Max Mark	Additional Guidance
41.	2 marks awarded for detailed/insightful comment plus quotation/reference. 1 mark for more basic comment plus quotation/reference. 0 marks for quotation/reference alone. (Marks may be awarded 2+2, 2+1+1 or 1+1+1+1)	4	Possible answers include: • 'weather evocative as scent' synaesthesia creates an appealing and atmospheric picture/suggests that strong/powerful/pleasant memories are stirred by the photographs • 'romance' suggests a passion/nostalgia for the moment captured in the image • 'big skies over the low wide river' assonance echoes the slow flowing river and suggest that those looking at the photographs are momentarily captivated/held by the picture • 'fabulous' suggests the images were extraordinary/almost mythical in quality • 'film-noir stills' conveys a magical, graceful impression which contrasts with the functional subject of 'Central Station' • 'freezing fog silvering the chilled, stilled parks' alliteration/assonance/consonance creates an enchanting/sentimentalised view of the city as captured in the photographs • 'silvering' suggests that the black and white images had an ethereal/otherworldly quality • 'glamorous' creates the impression that this period was enchanting/elegant/exciting to remember • imagery of 'drops on a rainmate are sequins' links the ordinary with the exotic as caught in a photograph/moment in time • repetition of 'of' phrases conveys the idea that the observer was enjoying looking quickly/flicking through the photographs • structure of lines echoes the idea of a series of memories being jogged as the photographs are browsed
42.	2 marks awarded for detailed/insightful comment plus quotation/reference. 1 mark for more basic comment plus quotation/reference. 0 marks for quotation/reference alone. (Marks may be awarded 2+2, 2+1+1 or 1+1+1+1)	4	Possible answers include: • 'your' personal address conveys intimacy and invites the reader to share the past with the speaker • 'still-lovely mother laughs' the snapshot of an earlier time conveys the joy and energy of the subject and creates a touching/sweet/tender memory • 'whipped up ... beach' reference to seaside suggests a joyous/carefree/youthful time reflected in the photograph • 'before you were even born' links to the romantic/idealistic view that the younger years are the happiest period in one's life • 'all the Dads in hats' suggests a familiar, unified crowd who represent a settled/more gentle period of time • list of weathers conveys the routine/familiar/ordinary/nature of the fathers' working lives in the past • contrast of 'dark/white' symbolises the predictable pattern of life at that time

Question	Expected Answer(s)	Max Mark	Additional Guidance
43.	2 marks awarded for detailed/insightful comment plus quotation/reference. 1 mark for more basic comment plus quotation/reference. 0 marks for quotation/reference alone. (Marks may be awarded 2 or 1+1)	2	Possible answers include: • alliteration 'starlings swarming … perfect/permanent' signifies a change in focus from the sentimental to a more pragmatic view of the past • 'permanent cloud' suggests the photographs may conceal/obscure the reality of the past • 'what was/never really' reinforces the idea that the images belong in the past by denying their reliability • 'all the passing now' suggests that the images are merely a moment in time and should be treated as no more than this • evocation of senses 'noise/stink/smoky breath' serves as a reminder of the reality of Glasgow's industrial past
44.	Candidates may answer in bullet points in this final question, or write a number of linked statements.	10	Up to 2 marks can be achieved by identifying elements of commonality as identified in the question, i.e. , Lochhead's exploration of important aspects of life through everyday objects and/or situations. A further 2 marks can be achieved for reference to the text given. 6 additional marks can be awarded for discussion of similar references to at least one other poem by the poet. In practice this means: Identification of commonality (2) e.g. Lochhead chooses a variety of everyday/commonplace situations/objects as representations such as meetings, buildings, household furnishings (1) to illustrate her reflections on the complexities of human interaction. (1) From the poem: 2 marks for detailed/insightful comment plus quotation/reference; 1 mark for more basic comment plus quotation/reference; 0 marks for quotation/reference alone. e.g. The photographs present an idealised picture of the past which illuminates her views on the transient/fleeting nature of time.(2) From at least one other poem: as above for up to 6 marks Possible comments include: • *View of Scotland/Love Poem* 'dusted mantelshelves' represents the true value she places on the hospitable/generous nature of others much more so than material wealth • *For my Grandmother Knitting* the knitting needles represent the care and effort she placed in ensuring that her children/grandchildren were cherished and loved which seems not to be valued anymore

Question	Expected Answer(s)	Max Mark	Additional Guidance
44.	*(continued)*		• *The Bargain* what seems like an ordinary shopping trip is actually used as an opportunity to reflect on the past in order to make sense of the present • *My Rival's House* the visit to her boyfriend's mother highlights the destructive impact of emotional manipulation • *Last Supper* the simple preparations for a meal provide the opportunity to reflect on the intense nature of betrayal

Text 4 — *Poetry — Sounds of the Day* by Norman MacCaig

Question	Expected Answer(s)	Max Mark	Additional Guidance
45.	2 marks awarded for detailed/insightful comment plus quotation/reference. 1 mark for more basic comment plus quotation/reference. 0 marks for quotation/reference alone. (Marks may be awarded 2+2, 2+1+1, 1+1+1+1)	4	Possible answers include: • repetition of 'When a … it was' build up of 'puzzles' and answers creates a sense of the unknown • inversion delays the explanation for the sounds thus creating anticipation • 'clatter' (onomatopoeia) discordant sound suggesting unease • 'creaked' suggests disturbance/eerie mood • 'lapwing … premises' suggests a change in circumstances • 'snuffling puff' (onomatopoeia/assonance) suggests quiet sound before build-up of tension • 'black drums rolled' suggests ominous hint of event to follow • 'water falling sixty feet into itself' suggests disturbing/destructive force
46.	2 marks awarded for detailed/insightful comment plus quotation/reference. 1 mark for more basic comment plus quotation/reference. 0 marks for quotation/reference alone. (Marks may be awarded: 2 or 1+1)	2	Possible answers include: • 'When the door scraped shut' sound of closing door is a metaphor for the end of the relationship • onomatopoeia of 'scraped shut' creates harsh sound which contrasts with silence to follow/ the natural sounds earlier in the poem • the sentence structure/inversion of the previous stanza is reversed with object mentioned before sound 'door … scraped shut,' • the hyperbole of 'it was the end/of all the sounds there are.' emphasises the significance of the moment

Question	Expected Answer(s)	Max Mark	Additional Guidance
47.	2 marks awarded for detailed/insightful comment plus quotation/reference. 1 mark for more basic comment plus quotation/reference. 0 marks for quotation/reference alone. (Marks may be awarded 2+2, 2+1+1, 1+1+1+1)	4	Possible answers include: Tone • direct/monosyllabic language 'You left me' creates bitter tone • hyperbole of 'quietest fire in the world' creates tone of despair • 'the whole hand goes numb' creates tone of hopelessness/finality Imagery • 'quietest fire in the world' suggests the contrast between the previous love/passion of the relationship and the absolute devastation/loss of the separation • 'plunge' suggests total immersion in relationship/resulting in grief/shock • 'bangle of ice' suggests the restriction/coldness of losing love • 'the whole hand goes numb' suggests inescapable/overwhelming/debilitating effect of loss of love
48.	Candidates may choose to answer in bullet points in this final question, or write a number of linked statements.	10	Up to 2 marks can be achieved for identifying elements of commonality as identified in the question i.e. how relationships are used to develop key themes. A further 2 marks can be achieved for reference to the text given. 6 additional marks can be awarded for discussion of similar references to at least one other poem by MacCaig. In practice this means: Identification of commonality (2) e.g. MaCaig presents relationships in which there is a crisis/difficulty of some kind (1) to explore the impact of loss/suffering/death/isolation etc. (1) From the poem: 2 marks for detailed/insightful comment plus quotation/reference; 1 mark for more basic comment plus quotation/reference; 0 marks for quotation/reference alone. e.g. the end of the relationship has affected the speaker so badly that he is no longer aware of/he is unable to appreciate the sounds of nature all around him 'It was the end of all sounds' emphasising the profound impact of loss (2) From at least one other text: as above for up to 6 marks

Question	Expected Answer(s)	Max Mark	Additional Guidance
48.	*(continued)*		Possible answers include: • *Aunt Julia* the speaker regrets the opportunities for communication missed as a result of her death and sees this as part of Scotland's heritage being lost • *Memorial* the speaker is haunted by the death of a loved one to such an extent that he can no longer enjoy visiting places where they had once been together and this conveys the universal and life-changing nature of loss • *Visiting Hour* the speaker's relationship with a dying relative and his inability to come to terms with the inevitability of their death • *Basking Shark* the speaker's chance encounter with the shark makes him reconsider humanity's destructive relationship with nature 'So who's the monster?' • *Assisi* the speaker reflects on society's relationship with vulnerable people represented by the beggar 'It was they who had passed the ruined temple' suggesting themes of lack of compassion, self-interest

Text 6 — *Poetry* — *The Ferryman's Arms* by Don Paterson

Question	Expected Answer(s)	Max Mark	Additional Guidance
49.	Both sides of the contrast must be dealt with for full marks but not necessarily in equal measure. 2 marks awarded for detailed/insightful comment plus quotation/reference. 1 mark for more basic comment plus quotation/reference. 0 marks for quotation/reference alone. (Marks may be awarded 2+2, 2+1+1 or 1+1+1+1.)	4	Possible answers include: Atmosphere at beginning of the specified lines – the atmosphere of wonder/calm/security suggested by: • 'Screapadal in the morning/facing Applecross and the sun' or 'Screapadal that is so beautiful' Direct, descriptive simplicity of the language suggests calm/serenity/wonder • 'No words can be put …' and/or 'no picture, music or poem made for it' suggest the inexpressible wonder of Screapadal • 'Screapadal the sheep-pen and the cattle-fold' suggests that Screapadal is a world in itself, peaceful, self-contained • reference to 'Sanctuary' suggests a place of peace, shelter/respite, security, holy place Atmosphere towards the end of the specified lines –The atmosphere of threat/destruction/forced hardship suggested by: • 'half-dead'/'dead' repetition of references to death is unsettling, suggests threat • 'Rainy' reference to an individual who is associated with the forced movement of people out of Screapadal • 'put off the land' suggests forced removal of people, inhuman treatment • 'castle' and/or the associated word 'violence' suggests a place of threat/defence/aggression

Question	Expected Answer(s)	Max Mark	Additional Guidance
50.	2 marks awarded for detailed/insightful comment plus quotation/reference. 1 mark for more basic comment plus quotation/reference. 0 marks for quotation/reference alone. (Marks may be awarded 2 or 1+1)	2	Possible answers include: • Reference to 'green, red-rocked, yellow, light-grey, whiteness' many (and varied) adjectives of colour suggests that the place is bright/vibrant, etc. • Repetition of 'green' and 'light-grey' suggest that these colours stand out, and that the place is bright/vibrant • 'towers, columns and steeples,' comparing them to these man-made structures suggests the vastness/perpendicular height of the rocks • 'speckled light-grey' and/or 'whiteness in the sun' suggests that the place is lit/made bright/almost favoured by the sun
51.	2 marks awarded for detailed/insightful comment plus quotation/reference. 1 mark for more basic comment plus quotation/reference. 0 marks for quotation/reference alone. (Marks may be awarded 2+2, 2+1+1 or 1+1+1+1)	4	Possible answers include: • 'the Church of Falsehood' creates sympathy for the people in the suggestion (historical reference) that they might have been deceived by the Church at the time of the Clearances • 'high water'/'spring tide' suggests danger of flooding, and therefore creates sympathy for the people in that they were 'swept off' the land by the Clearances • 'lies' suggests deliberate deception • 'betrayed' creates sympathy in that the people were let down (historically) • 'the great pietist (Rainy)' bitter irony of the word 'pietist' (the opposite being suggested) creates sympathy for the people • 'without ... no ... only' accumulation of absences highlights the loss of a way of life
52.	Candidates may choose to answer in bullet points in this final question, or write a number of linked statements.	10	Up to 2 marks can be achieved for identifying elements of commonality as identified in the question, i.e. in how MacLean explores change in relation to people and/or places. A further 2 marks can be achieved for reference to the text given. 6 additional marks can be awarded for the discussion of similar references to at least one other poem by the poet. <u>In practice this means:</u> Identification of commonality (2) e.g. MacLean explores change in relation to individuals through the impact of traumatic circumstances/experiences (1) and change to communities due to wider world events/the passage of time (1) From the poem: 2 marks for detailed/insightful comment plus quotation/reference; 1 mark for more basic comment plus quotation/reference; 0 marks for quotation/reference alone. e.g. Reference to 'the great pietist Rainy' – ironic comment on his betrayal of local people in clearing the communities from Screapadal, which has left it desolate and uninhabited (2) From at least one other text: as above for up to 6 marks

Question	Expected Answer(s)	Max Mark	Additional Guidance
52.	*(continued)*		Possible comments include: • *Hallaig* a way of life/community changed/ destroyed by the actions of man (specifically the impact of the Clearances) • *An Autumn Day* change brought by war (chaos, death) • *Heroes* individuals changed/altered by war • *I Gave You Immortality* changes caused by love and by the impact of time passing • *Shores* the speaker expresses a wish or desire for things not to change, however has to acknowledge that the only thing which lasts is the landscape
53.	2 marks awarded for detailed/insightful comment plus quotation/reference. 1 mark for more basic comment plus quotation/ reference. 0 marks for quotation/reference alone. (Marks may be awarded 2+2, 2+1+1, 1+1+1+1)	4	Possible answers include: • 'I was magnetized' suggests lack of control/ influence of fate • 'remote' conveys the sense that there is something distant and isolated • 'drawn (like a moth)' suggesting persona is pulled involuntarily away • 'darkened (back room)' connotations of the unseen and unknown/mystery • 'hummed to itself' suggests the pool table is a living/threatening presence • 'whole place deserted' suggests abandonment/isolation • 'I stood with my back turned' suggests vulnerability/lack of control • 'abrupt intestinal rumble' suggests discomfort/monstrous qualities • 'batted awake' suggests that inanimate object has life of its own • 'dusty green cowl' allusion to grim reaper
54.	2 marks awarded for detailed/insightful comment plus quotation/reference. 1 mark for more basic comment plus quotation/ reference. 0 marks for quotation/reference alone. (Marks may be awarded 2 or 1+1)	2	Possible answers include: • 'screw back the globe' suggests a sense of absolute power/ability to control the world/ turn back time • 'As physics ... negotiable' suggests the ability to exist outside the normal laws of the universe/control your own destiny • 'miracles' suggests winning outcome against all the odds • 'I went on to make' suggests active intervention of the speaker in own fate • 'immaculate clearance' suggests sense of perfection/pride in taking control • 'wee dab of side' suggests light-hearted confidence
55.	2 marks awarded for detailed/insightful comment plus quotation/reference. 1 mark for more basic comment plus quotation/ reference. 0 marks for quotation/reference alone. (Marks may be awarded 2+2, 2+1+1, 1+1+1+1)	4	Possible answers include: • 'boat' allusion to ferry across the River Styx suggests transit from life to death • 'without breaking the skin of the water' the silent gliding of the ferry suggests death is unpredictable/can arrive unannounced • 'stretching' suggests endlessness of eternity • 'as black as my stout' emphasis on intensity of darkness suggests death is a mysterious presence

Question	Expected Answer(s)	Max Mark	Additional Guidance
55.	*(continued)*		• 'read and re-read the shoreline' repeated attempts to decipher his bearings suggests confusion/lack of control of direction in life • 'my losing opponent' reference to another part of himself suggests the divisions which exist within us • 'stuck in his tent of light' a moment frozen in time suggests that we can't eradicate our past/death
56.	Candidates may choose to answer in bullet points in this final question, or write a number of linked statements.	10	Up to 2 marks can be achieved by identifying elements of commonality as identified in the question, i.e. how Paterson explores the challenges of human experience. A further 2 marks can be achieved for reference to the text given. 6 additional marks can be awarded for discussion of similar references to at least one other poem by the poet. In practice this means: Identification of commonality (2) e.g., Paterson presents challenging experiences such as birth, growing up, relationships, death (1) to show how these shape our perception of the world and ourselves (1) From the poem: 2 marks for detailed/insightful comment plus quotation/reference; 1 mark for more basic comment plus quotation/reference; 0 marks for quotation/reference alone e.g. While waiting for the ferry, the speaker's pool game with himself forces him to confront his own mortality/accept that death is an inevitable part of life (2) From at least one other poem: as above for up to 6 marks Possible comments include: • *Nil Nil* through the deteriorating fortunes of the football team and the community, the speaker is forced to consider the inevitability of decline and death • *11:00 Baldovan* the negative effects of the passage of time are explored through the boys' altered perceptions after the bus journey • *Waking with Russell* the challenges of becoming a father allow the poet to explore how the direction of our lives can be altered by love • *The Thread* the poet deals with the difficulties of Jamie's birth, allowing him to reflect on the fragility of life • *Two Trees* the metaphor of the separation of the trees is used to explore the challenges in relationships/significance of human aspirations

Section 2 — CRITICAL ESSAY

Please see the assessment criteria for the Critical Essay on page 170.

Acknowledgements

Permission has been sought from all relevant copyright holders and Hodder Gibson is grateful for the use of the following:

The article 'Rude, impulsive, sulky . . . still, let our 16-year-olds vote' by Catherine Bennett, taken from 'The Guardian', 14 October 2012. Copyright Guardian News & Media Ltd 2018 (2016 Reading for Understanding, Analysis and Evaluation pages 2 & 3);

The article 'Letting 16 year-olds vote in the EU referendum would be a car crash' by Julia Hartley-Brewer, taken from 'The Telegraph', 19 November 2015 © Telegraph Media Group Limited 2018 (2016 Reading for Understanding, Analysis and Evaluation pages 3 & 4);

An extract from 'The Slab Boys' © 1982 John Byrne. 'The Slab Boys' was first performed at the Traverse Theatre, Edinburgh, on 6 April 1978. All rights whatsoever in this play are strictly reserved and application for performance etc. should be made to the Author's agent: Casarotto Ramsay & Associates Limited, Waverley House, 7–12 Noel Street, London W1F 8G (rights@casarotto.co.uk). No performance may be given unless a licence has been obtained (2016 Critical Reading pages 2 & 3);

An extract from 'The Cheviot, the Stag and the Black, Black Oil,' by John McGrath. © John McGrath, 1981. Published by Bloomsbury Methuen Drama, an imprint of Bloomsbury Publishing Plc. (2016 Critical Reading pages 4 & 5);

An extract from 'Men Should Weep' © Ena Lamont Stewart, 1947. Reproduced by permission of Alan Brodie Representation Ltd (www.alanbrodie.com) (2016 Critical Reading pages 6 & 7);

An extract from 'The Crater' by Iain Crichton Smith, taken from 'The Red Door: The Complete English Stories 1949–76', published by Birlinn. Reproduced with permission of Birlinn Limited via PLSclear (2016 Critical Reading pages 8 & 9);

An extract from 'The Whaler's Return' by George Mackay Brown, taken from 'A Time To Keep', published by Polygon. Reproduced with permission of The Literary Estate of George Mackay Brown (2016 Critical Reading pages 10 & 11);

An extract from 'The Trick is to Keep Breathing' by Janice Galloway, published by Vintage, reprinted by permission of The Random House Group Limited. © Janice Galloway 1989 (2016 Critical Reading pages 12 & 13);

An extract from 'Sunset Song' by Lewis Grassic Gibbon, published by Jarrold Publishing, 1932. Public domain (2016 Critical Reading pages 14 & 15);

An extract from 'The Cone-Gatherers' by Robin Jenkins, published by Canongate Books Ltd. (2016 Critical Reading pages 16 & 17);

The poem 'A Poet's Welcome to His Love-Begotten Daughter' by Robert Burns. Public domain (2016 Critical Reading pages 18 & 19);

The poem 'Mrs Midas' from 'The Other Country' by Carol Ann Duffy. Published by Anvil Press Poetry, 1990. Copyright © Carol Ann Duffy. Reproduced by permission of the author c/o Rogers, Coleridge & White Ltd., 20 Powis Mews, London W11 1JN (2016 Critical Reading page 20);

The poem 'The Bargain' by Liz Lochhead, taken from 'A Choosing: Selected Poems', published by Polygon. Reproduced with permission of Birlinn Limited via PLSclear (2016 Critical Reading page 22);

The poem 'Memorial' by Norman MacCaig, taken from 'The Poems of Norman MacCaig', published by Polygon. Reproduced with permission of Birlinn Limited via PLSclear (2016 Critical Reading page 24);

The poem 'Shores' by Sorley MacLean, taken from 'Caoir Gheal Leumraich/White Leaping Flame: collected poems in Gaelic with English translations', edited by Christopher Whyte and Emma Dymock 2011. Copyrighted by Sorley MacLean. Reprinted with permission of Carcanet Press, Manchester, UK (2016 Critical Reading page 26);

The poem 'The Thread' from 'Landing Light' by Don Paterson. Published by Faber, 1993. Copyright © Don Paterson. Reproduced by permission of the author c/o Rogers, Coleridge & White Ltd., 20 Powis Mews, London W11 1JN (2016 Critical Reading page 28);

An extract from the article 'Want to exercise your mind? Try playstation' by Steven Johnson © The Times/News Licensing, 13 May 2005 (2017 Reading for Understanding, Analysis and Evaluation pages 2 & 3);

An extract from the article 'The Writing Is On The Wall' by Boris Johnson, taken from 'The Telegraph', 28 December 2006 © Boris Johnson/Telegraph Media Group Limited 2006 (2017 Reading for Understanding, Analysis and Evaluation pages 3 & 4);

An extract from 'The Slab Boys' © 1982 John Byrne. 'The Slab Boys' was first performed at the Traverse Theatre, Edinburgh, on 6 April 1978. All rights whatsoever in this play are strictly reserved and application for performance etc. should be made to the Author's agent: Casarotto Ramsay & Associates Limited, Waverley House, 7–12 Noel Street, London W1F 8G (rights@casarotto.co.uk). No performance may be given unless a licence has been obtained (2017 Critical Reading pages 2 & 3);

An extract from 'The Cheviot, the Stag and the Black, Black Oil,' by John McGrath. © John McGrath, 1981. Published by Bloomsbury Methuen Drama, an imprint of Bloomsbury Publishing Plc. (2017 Critical Reading pages 6 & 7);

An extract from 'Men Should Weep' © Ena Lamont Stewart, 1947. Reproduced by permission of Alan Brodie Representation Ltd (www.alanbrodie.com) (2017 Critical Reading pages 10 & 11);

An extract from 'The Red Door' by Iain Crichton Smith, taken from 'The Red Door: The Complete English Stories 1949–76', published by Birlinn. Reproduced with permission of Birlinn Limited via PLSclear (2017 Critical Reading pages 14 & 15);